*"A good education uplifts ourselves and humanity."*

*To Layli —*
*Best wishes! Sophia*

# FINDING MY OWN WAY:
## A Journey to Wholeness Against the Odds

### By Sophia Bracy Harris

*Sophia Bra[...]*
*May 21, [...]*

D1411517

Library of Congress Control Number: 2021905128
Data available upon request.
ISBN: 978-0-578-24721-2 | ISBN: 978-0-578-24722-9

FIRST EDITION
Book designed by Mona Davis, Noir Notes Creative Services
Jacket photography by Auburn University Photographic Services

# Dedication

*This book is dedicated to the memory of my parents, Roosevelt and Mittie Marie Bracy, whose guidance and wisdom continue to provide inspiration and courage to stay the course of life's journey.*

*To my late husband, Albert L. Harris, Jr. whose love and support was the "wind beneath my wings" in pursuing the purpose that I felt God had intended for my life. Without his encouragement and sacrifice, much of what I have achieved would not have been possible.*

*Lastly, I dedicate this book to my sister Debra M. Bracy who has silently carried the painful scars of mistreatment from her bold act of courage in confronting a personal injustice.*

*Thank you, Debra.*

# ENDORSEMENTS

"Sophia Bracy Harris is a visionary reformer whose story and voice is both compelling and timely in this era of unjust inequality which threatens the lives of millions. There is much to be learned about how we find our way in this inspiring reflection on resistance and love."

**- Bryan Stevenson, Founder/Executive Director, Equal Justice Initiative and author of the New York Times best-selling book Just Mercy**

"Thirty years ago when Alan Gleitsman asked me who should receive his first-ever Gleitsman Award for People Who Make a Difference, I said: Sophia Bracy Harris. Then, people were talking about the importance of early childhood education, but only Sophia was traveling through the rural south, writing messages on shirt cardboards, holding meetings in living rooms and churches, and making this happen where it was needed most. For that and an entire lifetime of reasons, I've been hoping she would tell her story. Right now, it's needed more than ever before. Sophia is not only a rare and trusted bridge between the most needy and the most able to create change, she knows how to bring them together as allies and friends. I've always thought she should write a book, and that book should be a movie or television series. Her story personifies history in the way that it grows deepest and most lasting, like a tree, from the ground up."

**- Gloria Steinem, writer, political activist, and feminist organizer**

"Sophia Bracy Harris is one of the many unsung southern women civil rights leaders. For more than fifty years, she has led the fight for quality access to childcare for all of Alabama's families. Her story will inspire a new generation of activists to learn from her legacy and take up today's continuing struggles."

**- Leymah Gbowee, Peace Activist, 2011 Nobel Peace Prize Recipient**

"Finding My Own Way is the beautifully told story of Sophia Bracy Harris, whose resilience is matched only by her brilliance and passion to make a difference in the lives of others. I was touched by Sophia's life long before her memoir was written. In the words of the late Robert Kennedy, Sophia sees life not as it is and asks why, but rather dreams of things that never were, and asks why not. Her inspiring memoir challenges us to ask the difficult questions, to push back against systems of inequity, and our own complacency. Finding My Own Way shows how an ordinary individual can go on to achieve extraordinary things when their steps are motivated by the desire to serve others."

**- Martha Hawkins, author, speaker and owner of Martha's Place Restaurant**

"Sophia Bracy Harris' story is one of courage and defiance, soaring highs and crushing lows, and the determination to try all over and over again. A woman who fought against barriers of race, class and gender to rise to national prominence as an advocate for marginalized children and communities, yet often—as many great leaders do—privately wonder if they are 'good enough.' Her story empowers anyone with the great responsibility of leading change to confront the negative internalized messaging often passed down in childhood. It provides the tools they can use to tell themselves a different message—one that communicates that they are worthy and whole. This is a must-read book for all interested in leadership, resilience, organizing and transformative change."
- **Dorian Warren, President of Community Change, MSNBC Contributor**

"Sophia Bracy Harris' coming of age story is the perfect book for this explosive moment in America and the world. This organizer, mother, and visionary shares her deep understanding of racism, honed from her Alabama childhood, integration of Wetumpka High, the firebombing of her family home, and her lifetime of advocacy for black children. Sophia's gripping journey toward justice could be a road map for today's fierce young leaders."
- **Kit Miller, President of Orchard House Foundation**

"The gripping autobiographical narrative of Wetumpka native Sophia Bracy Harris recounts the trials and tribulations of growing up and maturing in civil rights Alabama. In excruciating detail, Finding My Own Way offers a judicious treatment of the relentless fury and impact of second-class citizenship."
- **Richard Bailey, Ph.D., Author/Historian**

"Starting fifty years ago, Sophia Bracy Harris has paved the road in Alabama— the heart of the Bible Belt— to a new society based on equity for all. Her tireless leadership changed the lives of children and their families in the state with the sixth highest poverty rate in the nation. In her new memoir, Sophia recounts how one black woman created social justice and opportunity for so many. Her story will be a source of inspiration for generations to come."
- **Michael Seltzer, Distinguished Lecturer, City University of New York**

"Sophia's story is a story for the white suburban housewife, the inner-city black kid, the undocumented farm worker and the returning war veteran. It is a story for all of us. While facing racism, oppression, hatred and poverty Sophia's story is one of inspiration, grit, love and community: an indispensable guide to connecting and inter-connecting with that universal light shining within each of us and among all of us."
-**Rebecca Adamson, Indigenous Economist, First Peoples Worldwide**

"As one of the few black students at Auburn University in the late 1960s, Sophia did as she always had: she transcended challenges through hard work, practicality, determination, and an unrelenting focus on her life's vision of helping those who needed her. Without an obvious template, Sophia followed her heart to achieve greatness through servanthood. Her story is both inspiring and instructive for those in every generation."

**- George Littleton, Communications Director, Auburn University**

Finding My Own Way is a must read for young activists, community organizers, childcare advocates, policy makers, politicians, historians, women's history advocates, and almost anyone who is a knowledge seeker.  It is especially important if you need to know how to pick up and keep on going when the going gets tough. One senses by the end of Finding My Own Way that Sophia Bracy Harris, although formally retired, has certainly not thrown in the towel; we have not heard the last from her. As the song goes, she is curious enough to believe (she'll) "…run on, see what the end's gonna be."

**- Billie Jean Young, Actress, Speaker, Author and Human Rights Activist**

# CONTENTS

# FOREWORD

By Marian Wright Edelman
Founder and President Emerita, Children's Defense Fund

I can't fully express how pleased I am that my friend Sophia Bracy Harris has written this stirring memoir. It deserves a wide readership.

When Sophia Bracy Harris was a child growing up in Wetumpka, Alabama, in a five-room cinderblock house lit by kerosene lamps and surrounded by cotton fields, she might have had a difficult time imagining where life would take her. Like generations of black children growing up in the segregated South, the outside world did not teach her to dream big.

Sophia Bracy Harris' story reflects many of the changes that came to the South and nation during her lifetime. She faced challenges early on, including serious chronic illness that kept her out of school for a full year at age 10 without access to swift diagnosis and treatment. As a teenager, Sophia and her sister were among the often unsung heroes of the school desegregation movement as they joined the small group of black students who chose to integrate Wetumpka High School, braving racist peers, teachers, and administrators every day to try to get a better education. Her memoir follows her journey as she graduated from high school and college and ultimately went on to lead FOCAL, the Federation of Child Care Centers of Alabama, working to ensure that children across Alabama felt valued and cared for, and to support the child care providers taking care of them. She and FOCAL have been long-term partners with the Children's Defense Fund in the Southern Rural Black Women's Initiative, and her work in the 1970s, 1980s, and 1990s reflects a larger cultural narrative of black women learning to understand their power, network with each other and others, and work together to ensure a better future for the next generation.

In her lifetime Sophia Bracy Harris has now seen the first African American elected president of the United States, and closer to home seen a young local leader and fellow church member become the first black mayor of Montgomery, Alabama. But as she says in this book, there is still work to be done, and she is still "practicing and growing."

One of the stories she shares is that of the white teacher who shamed her on her first day at Wetumpka High School when the teacher asked the class to write a composition on "utopia" and Sophia did not know what the word meant. Now, Sophia Bracy Harris says, "What I have learned about my Utopia in my life's journey may be uncommon, but it fits…I see clearly how I once let other people value or devalue my worth on this planet. I also see ways in which I have soared far beyond what most people would have expected to be 'my lot' in life. I want to encourage young people to seek their own personal utopia and do all they can to live the changes they want to see in the world."

Reading this important book, we see that regardless of where we were born, regardless of race, gender, physical condition or financial circumstances, we share the same Creator, and we can be the masters of our own fate. With faith and determination to examine all of our strengths and dysfunctions, we can become all of what God has created us to be. It is the message of this brave pathfinder's life and a message urgently worth reading and sharing. I am sure Sophia's story will inspire others to recognize the power of supports in the first five years of a child's life to shape the way that child sees itself in the world, whether as "givers" or "takers."

Sophia's passion, made beautifully clear in this memoir, is to ensure that no child is made to feel less than another person. ✦

# PREFACE

My story is a journey of one woman's struggle to find wholeness through breaking a cycle of inadequacy rooted in racism, poverty and gender inequality. Though the details are mine alone, feelings of being "less than" and the superior/inferior messaging that I received as a result of internalizing racist messaging are hardly unique. It is a shared experience by people of African descent and other marginalized groups in this country, and without rebuilding our collective conscience and recognizing the valuable contributions these groups have made to our country, the cycle won't easily be broken. When my ancestors came to this country, they were in chains and were punished for trying to read and write. Many of their stories are lost to history and I seek to honor them by making sure mine is preserved. I have found writing about my experiences to be healing and hope that my story encourages others toward a path of finding healing.

My entry into the cycle began at birth. As a Black girl born in the 1950s in Elmore County, Alabama my world comprised a stark dividing line between those who were deemed better, and those who were less. The line was no less real for being invisible and crossing those racial lines could easily get you killed.

Being sickly as a child created another root of inadequacy in my life because I sincerely believed my sickness had caused my family's poverty and my mother's humiliation. Though it has been more than 50 years, I can still remember the sting of the white doctor's words: ".... until her Mammy pays her bill, I am not touching her!" For years I blamed myself for this insult to my mother. It's one of the reasons I've championed affordable health care, the expansion of Medicaid and other services that provide health care to those who need it, offer dignity with care, and don't punish the poor for being sick.

As a teenager, I helped to integrate the white high school in town. Every day I, along with the other black students, endured negative messages: "You don't belong," "We don't want you here," "You can't write," "You're less worthy." White rage and defiance to school integration ultimately resulted in the firebombing of our family home. Fortunately, we escaped without any physical injuries, but it would be years before I was able to fully recover from the internal scars from the incident. The message "your life doesn't matter" was reinforced again in the days and weeks following the bombing by the inaction of the investigators who determined there was no foul play in the matter. Having experienced this, I can empathize with the frustration and pain of families who've been given similar answers in response to the shooting of unarmed black males by a system that is supposed to protect them. The Black Lives Matter refrain today isn't much different than the one we proclaimed in my day. Despite the courageous acts by white and black individuals who put their lives on the line to help the black families who integrated the schools, the cycle of feeling less than, vulnerable and —at times—fearful still permeated much of my early life no matter how much I'd achieved.

I later came to understand that the systems that perpetuate the cycle are as harmful to those imposing it as it is to those living within it. These black students and I were frequently attacked and harassed on the school bus and we knew that the white bus driver was as scared as we were, fearing that the violence would escalate. Though we believed him to be our only white friend at the school, he, like us, was trapped by custom and law in the cycle, too, rendering him powerless to change what was happening.

Many years later and after several attempts, I was able to connect with him and let him know how much his kindness meant to me and the other Black students on his bus. An elderly man at the time, he cried, saying he could not remember receiving a better gift. "My parents taught us to love all people, and you all weren't treated right." I was moved that after all those years, he'd remembered each of us by name and wanted to know where they were and how they were doing. When he died, I read his obituary and learned that he'd been a two-time Purple Heart recipient and a World War II veteran.

The determination of women like my mother and the other Black women of Elmore County, and their fight to ensure that their children had a decent upbringing and education, had watered the seeds of resistance that had already been growing in my young mind. There was simply no going back.

Of course, I couldn't have known at the time that my experiences would shape the next 43 years of my life fighting primarily for Black childcare providers and other groups as executive director of the non-profit Federation of Child Care Centers of Alabama (FOCAL). Like my mother, these dynamic women insisted on their right to choose who would teach their very young children, what they would be taught, and receive their rightful share of resources.

Fortunately for me, the support my family received and the educational and cultural experiences my siblings and I were provided after the firebombing allowed me to go beyond the world I'd known. As a young woman, community service gave me a strong sense of what my life and purpose could be.

I'd grown up siding with underdogs because I felt like I was one. When I came to lead FOCAL at 23 years of age, I found myself giving to children the affirmation and protection I'd wanted for myself as a child, even though there were times I didn't know how to give that gift to myself. Being an advocate was the only way I knew how to push back against injustice, and I followed that impulse not only in my fight against racism, poverty, and gender inequity, but my own personal battle with internal self-doubt. It's a fight that has brought me face to face with things about myself that no one can fix, change, or improve for me. I've had to find my own way to break the cycle of inadequacy and understand that what I was seeking was simply self-acceptance.

Years ago, in the grocery store, my granddaughter Timiya saw a little white girl in a ballerina dress. Seconds later, Timiya was halfway down the aisle, holding the little girl's hand and deep in conversation with her, as though they were best friends. The girl's parents looked on slightly amazed, politely trying to move forward with their shopping.

When I was Timiya's age, I could never approach a white girl like that, and there were many reasons I lacked permission to respond as Timiya did. Hopefully, my granddaughter's journey has been made a little easier because of my experiences and the sacrifices of countless others. She is reaping the benefits of the seeds our generation has sown, just as I benefited from what my parents instilled in me.

I want Timiya to know how far we have come, and how far we still have to go. I want Timiya and others growing up today to understand where my life started, and what society said about my worth and the worth of our ancestors. I want her to know her worth, and never allow anyone or anything malicious to define or limit what she can be or do, in this beautiful, flawed world of ours.

My life's work and my service to philanthropic and civil rights organizations around the country were all manifestation of the seeds that were planted in my youth. It didn't matter if the ground wasn't always nurturing. Every test and challenge, every chance to educate and influence, and every opportunity to build bridges and seek understanding, have given me the opportunity to break the cycle of inadequacy and share with others how they can do the same. ✦

## A NOTE ON QUOTATIONS

This memoir tells my life story as truthfully as I am able.
There are no invented incidents and no composite characters. Nothing has been made up, but I have taken the liberty of changing three or four names in the story. I did this only where I thought it was important to record what a person said or did but did not wish to embarrass that person in print. The reader should also know that in retelling my life of some 70 years, I have recreated many conversations from the past, and have taken the liberty of using quotation marks. I've used all possible effort to ensure the accuracy of quoted dialogue and have made up no dialogue for dramatic purposes. Still, the quoted dialogue should not be considered a verbatim account.

# 1
## A "SICKLY" CHILD

*"Kindnesses made me a caregiver which became*
*both a blessing and a yoke."*

My older brother Roosevelt died at birth, and I had to wonder as a little girl how long I might live myself. I was the second of eight surviving children born to Roosevelt and Marie Bracy. Debra, a year older than me, would fight a bear if she had to. I was the "sickly" one; that was the label I wore. When I was about 10 years old, I was sick so much that I missed a whole year of school. Before I was 12, I'd had scarlet fever, asthma and rheumatic fever, and I have childhood memories of health scares that brought me near death.

At one time, I was wasting away, and could feel my own ribcage. Missionary ladies were coming to the house, peeking at me in bed and whispering to Mom, "I'm so sorry… I'm praying for you." I was sick, I couldn't really think straight, I knew something was different, something bad was happening — but I didn't know what.

It was my big brother Harvey who broke the spell. He was in the military, stationed in Germany, and sent me a letter and a Nina Simone album. He wrote, "Mama duck, I hear some talk about you're not being around much longer. Don't do it. I'm real busy, and I don't have the time to get no black suit."

I realized at that moment: "All these people coming to the house think I'm going to die! —but Harvey doesn't, or he wouldn't be talking like this." That gave me more confidence.

Part of the fear was never knowing what was wrong with me. There was no diagnosis. Only after several years of colds and fevers, of swollen limbs, blisters on my lips, skin peeling off the insides of my hands, did my parents learn that I had rheumatic fever.

But this weakness of mine, and the sense of mortality it brought, helped me to find purpose in life, and to be serious about living a life unstained by malice or rank selfishness. I was deeply grateful for acts of kindness shown me during the illnesses of my childhood. These kindnesses made me a caregiver myself, and so those illnesses of mine were both a blessing and a yoke.

I lived in Wetumpka, a town of 3,000 people, in Elmore County, Alabama. Wetumpka sits on both sides of the Coosa River, connected by the Bibb Graves Bridge. Its name means "rumbling waters" in the Creek language. Downtown Wetumpka in my childhood was two city blocks long, buttressed by the river to the northwest. At the far east corner was the cotton gin where my Dad took his harvested cotton. Across the street was the "colored" section of town: two black funeral homes, one co-owned by my Pastor, J. L. Jones. Connected to these buildings was a barber and beauty shop.

My family's home was a five-room cinderblock house, enclosed with forsythia and red and white rose bushes. A concrete porch was the entrance into the front room which was my brothers' bedroom. The back porch housed the blocks of stove wood for cooking and logs for our brick fireplace. Family discussions took place in the dining room around that fireplace.

The large stained oak table was surrounded by chairs Dad had made himself with bottoms woven from dried sugar cane leaves. Our fireplace heated the house in winter, and cast irons pressed our Sunday wear and warmed our covers on cold winter nights. We baked sweet potatoes and parched peanuts on the fireplace hearth while Dad entertained us with jokes, sometimes at our expense. In this room, we learned to pray and recite Bible verses, received visitors, learned family history and how hard it was to be black in the United States of America.

Before we had electricity, three kerosene lamps were our light: one in the dining room, one in the kitchen, and one in Mom and Dad's room. Dad insisted that all lamps and lights be turned off at 8:30 p.m. so all business had to be finished by then.

When I was around four, my cousin Margaret turned to me and said, "Girl, let me hear you say your speech."

When we were coming up on a celebration or a special occasion at the church, we would rehearse our speeches, poems, or songs. Someone helped me up on top of the big trunk, and looking out at my audience, I gave my first speech:

"Twinkle, twinkle little star
How I wonder what you are
 Up above the world so high
Like a diamond in the sky
Twinkle, twinkle little star
How I wonder what you are…"

Mom had taught it to me, and my cousin Margaret had coached me all day, saying "Talk loud," and "Stop twisting," and "Look straight at the people and speak clearly. That's good, say it again."

Now the smiling faces and applause buoyed my spirit and left a lasting impression. I didn't know it then, but this was my debut into public speaking and a public relationship with God. The two were entwined in the culture of my community, a powerfully affirming message.

Listening to this first speech was my extended family who were all gathered in the sitting room of Uncle Charlie and Aunt Lacy's home, nestled in tall pines and oaks, a mile off the main road. This wood frame house, built by my Uncle Charlie, was three times the size of Mom and Dad's first home, which was located nearby. A fire burned in the fireplace and the room was full of people I knew and loved: Mom, Dad, Debra, Uncle Charlie, Aunt Lacy, Margaret, and another nephew raised by Uncle Charlie, Arthur Marion, his wife Catherine and their baby.

After dinner, we'd sit near the fireplace. Adults would tell stories or jokes. Kids joined in the conversation only when asked, and you'd better not laugh at any of the grown-up jokes or ask questions about anything you heard.

In 1966, the Chamber of Commerce marketed our town with the slogan "Wetumpka Has Everything." But an NAACP Legal Defense Fund brochure called Wetumpka a "citadel of prejudice." Racial segregation was the practice, and black people knew there could be dire consequences if we stepped outside the social norms — or were unlucky enough to be in the wrong place at the wrong time.

When I was six years old and Debra was seven, we attended a community school for black children. My mother's sister, Aunt Pearl, taught the first through the third grades, all in one classroom. Aunt Pearl lived about three miles from our house and although she drove the 20 miles to the school every day, we had to walk the distance to and from her house to catch a ride with her to school.

It bothered Dad that she could have easily dropped us off at home, but he would have had to give her gas money, which they didn't have. At that time our only transportation was the mule and wagon. So, Debra and I walked, sometimes dusted by cars or pick-up trucks passing by on this flat, unpaved road. Dad felt Aunt Pearl was being tight-fisted and unfair, especially after we had so often done chores for Aunt Pearl, washing dishes, dusting, and mopping floors. It was a special sore spot when these chores caused us to be late getting our own chores done at home. That caused some heated exchanges between the two sisters.

Dad didn't talk in our presence about why he worried about our walking, but one August day his fears were realized. The road we walked was surrounded by cotton fields. Around the bend, for the last mile, we could see our house in the distance. On this day, as we headed home along the dirt road, a low-flying plane crossed the road, swooped down and barely cleared the cotton rows as it roared over our heads, then sprayed. It was a crop duster. We dropped to the dirt, screaming in fear. The plane rose higher and we took off running.

We heard the plane circle and start roaring back toward us. The pilot had seen us and was amusing himself by terrifying two young black girls. It was then we saw Dad, a fast runner, racing toward us at full speed. He had spotted the plane, then us, across the fields. When he reached us, he grabbed Debra in one arm and me in the other.

It was only after we were calm and walking on our own that we saw Dad's anger. Only when we were safely back home did Dad rage and curse to Mom about the cruelty of the pilot.

I could see very clearly Dad's love for us, but I couldn't see why the pilot had been so mean to Debra and me when he didn't even know us. I knew I was a sickly child, but what I understood less clearly then was that there was also a sickness in my hometown — the sickness of racism, the disease of white supremacy. This ideology, that white people were inherently superior to all other racial groups, and especially black people, led to the mean mistreatment of Native Americans, black people, and all others who were judged to be inferior. As I grew older, I saw it applied to Jews, non-white immigrants, women, gays and those who did not embrace the white supremacy doctrine.

There was a "rolling store" that used to roll up to our property at times. The two men in that rolling store were white men. The "Watkins man" came selling medicines, and an insurance man came along monthly, and they too were white men.

My parents tried to shield us from contact with white people, but I heard scary stories told about them. Often at night, when neighbors came to the house, or at gatherings, folks got into animated discussions about conflicts they'd had with whites or had heard about. One of my mother's cousins was murdered and it was said this evil was done because the man's wife was coveted by the white farmer who owned their land. Such stories left me with a sense that I'd better be very careful around white people.

It wasn't white oppression all the time; there were long periods when I barely saw a white person. But what you felt as a black person in Alabama was that white people were always watching to see that you didn't get too high, too "uppity." You could buy things in the country store, but you'd better not ask for a lot of sales help or give any trouble or the white store owner might turn on you. You didn't even make eye contact with him. When Dad and Mom were buying seed in the store, we children would wait in the truck because they were wary of our going in the store. I knew that Dad wanted us to stay out of the way of the white folks.

One white neighbor of ours seemed to be different. Many white people spoke to Dad and Mom as though they were children, called elderly blacks "auntie" or "boy" and avoided making eye contact with us. But this man seemed different and didn't speak with a southern drawl.

One day this neighbor brought his 7-year-old son with him to our house. My brother Ed was about the age of this boy and they were playing. The white boy hit Ed. When Ed struck back, the boy ran to his dad crying. The man straightened his shoulders, looked directly at Dad, and said in a commanding tone: "Do not hit my son again." I had never heard the man use this voice before.

Dad spoke up. "If he hits, he should expect to be hit back." The neighbor rejected that. He said, "If he hits, you come tell me." He was clearly invested in the segregationist taboo against a black child ever hitting a white child, regardless of the provocation. His tone of voice, and the rigid posture of his body, said so clearly "I am white! Stay in your place!"

His facade was that of a non-racist, but inside he was just the same as all the other whites around there. Once the irate neighbor left, Dad voiced his disgust with a couple of choice words and instructed us not to play with that white boy again.

I was also aware of things going on between blacks and whites a few miles away in Montgomery. We'd heard of the Bus Boycott touched off by Rosa Parks not giving up her seat on a public bus. We had heard stories of violence against blacks by whites.

One image I couldn't shake was a photo I saw in Jet magazine when I was eight years old. A dead black man lay on an examining table, naked except for a covering over his genitals. The story explained that this man had been kidnapped, killed by whites and castrated. I later learned his name was Aaron Henry and he had lived in Birmingham. The year was 1957. I was haunted by the image and my question that no one could answer: "What did he do wrong?"

I not only felt ashamed and guilty about what my being sickly had done to my family. I also carried the belief that my illness had caused my parents' poverty and kept Debra from loving me as a sister should. Our mother took so much time with me, watched and nursed and fussed over me, and some of that time was stolen from Debra. She was thin and brave and fierce. I was heavy and clumsy, and sometimes I felt like a coward. I didn't want to have Debra's feisty temper, but I admired her courage and her boldness.

I was pretty big for my age but leery of the bullies and the fighters. Peace always made sense to me, from the time I was a very young girl. In the first, second and third grades, I was teased sometimes for being "a coward," afraid to fight. But that label didn't get much traction until one day in fourth grade, when Mary Lee came along and whipped my butt.

It was late one school day, and school buses were lined up around "the bowl," a bowl-shaped area outside for school activities. Mary Lee lived near school and could walk home; she had a small, wiry, strong frame and was known for her long fingernails and her image of 'Mess with me and I'll whip your butt.' I had always steered clear of Mary; she liked to scratch people in the face with those fingernails.

But somehow that day, I offended Mary Lee and she pushed me— hard. I pushed back. The next thing I knew both of us were tumbling down the incline into the bowl. When we stopped tumbling, she was on top of me and gave me a good licking in full view of all the kids who were sitting in buses or standing around, waiting to load up.

I did manage to prevent her from scratching up my face, but she didn't spare my bare arms and I couldn't stop her. When it was over, I looked and felt mauled. My hair was filled with grass, my clothes were dusty, and my body was bruised and tender.

But the pain I felt from the beating didn't compare to the shame and humiliation from the teasing on the bus ride home. I had allowed a "city girl" to get the best of me. Country folks might not have had all the fine things they had in Wetumpka, but we took pride in our toughness. If you came from the country, you were supposed to be able to handle yourself in a fistfight. Losing a fight so badly to Mary Lee was a blemish not only on myself and the Bracy family but on all my country neighbors. I'd embarrassed them all.

I'd also outraged Debra. She and Mary Lee were rivals, with matching "don't mess with me" attitudes and reputations. Debra, I am sure, settled the score with Mary Lee by delivering her own payback.

Four years later in the eighth grade, I sat reading one day while the rest of our class had physical education. Mary Lee shocked me by approaching and asking nicely: "What are you reading?" Embedded in her question and tone of voice was a longing for respect; Mary Lee still had her intimidating nails and thuggish air, but people called her dumb and she knew it.

It was the first time I realized: I won that fight. I had something more valuable than a gorgeous face or great physical strength. I had knowledge—and as much as I'd disliked Mary Lee, I felt sad for her that she didn't have as much knowledge. I could feel her sense of isolation and rejection by her peers. It didn't help that people thought her half-white younger sister was much more beautiful.

For the two years that we spent together at that school, Mary Lee and I became friendly. It was a lesson to me: enemies of the moment need not remain enemies always; the world turns and sometimes the unlikeliest of friendships can grow.

Then another bout of illness would come along. I hated the moment when I first realized I'd started to wheeze. I felt my chest tightening, my lungs fighting for air. But I denied what was happening, sometimes even to myself. I turned away from others in the room, taking my little gasping breaths in secret for as long as I could. I knew no one in the family wanted to hear I was sick again, and Dad would be disappointed with me. But hiding the symptoms of my cold or an asthma attack only made it more painful and dangerous when it hit me full on.

Because I was sickly, I was bossed and got a lot of "do's and don'ts" from my elders. Even when I was not ill or in pain, I was still reminded by my elders, "Don't be trying to run," or "Stop laughing; you'll be out of breath," or "Sit yourself down or you'll be up hurting tonight," or "Put something on your arms so you don't get a chill – I don't plan to be up with you all night." It hurt me to hear those words.

On the other hand, being "sickly" provided me extra attention, and boosted my sense of being "special." To white people around Wetumpka, black girls like me were largely invisible, so being "seen" by my family, being noticed and cared for was so important to my self-image. Surviving scarlet fever and rheumatic fever left me feeling obliged to make proud all those who'd invested so heavily in my staying alive.

I also heard these things said about me:

"She's a strong girl even though she's sick."
"I get home and she'll have dinner cooked. She helps me with the children."

"She's sickly but level-headed; I can count on her. "

"Yeah, she's sickly, but she doesn't ever complain; you just have to make her stay still."

"I hate she's sick because she's my best worker. I sure need her in the field."

These words made me feel loved and needed. Like most black children I knew, I got both a lot of negative messages and a lot of positive ones. I heard words that hurt me, and words that raised me up, and made me feel proud.

Instinctively attentive to my four younger siblings, I became a caregiver at an early age. My family used to say the youngest kids were Sophia's during the day and Mom's at night. I was very protective and was an authority figure for all four.

"Y'all go do your chores."

"Ed, leave Georgia Mae alone."

"Bring in the stove wood and make a fire."

When we needed drinking water: "Y'all hurry up and go to the spring before it gets dark."

"Do y'all want me to read you a story? Well, hurry and finish and I will."

When John's eyes were running with mucus or bleeding from allergies:

"John, stop picking at your eyes. Come let me put a cold rag on 'em."

"Charles, I'm gonna whip you if you don't come inside and get your bath and stop hitting Katherine."

I was learning how to be a leader, which was a very healthy thing for me. But I was also absorbing some unhealthy ideas: that I didn't deserve to rest, have fun or take care of myself, because someone else always needed me, and I had to make up for being sick. Around age eleven, I missed an entire year of school. This was the only time I can remember not being a caregiver.

Debra would be playful with the kids one minute, and then hit them the next if they didn't comply with one of her commands. That's when I would step in. "You were playing with him a moment ago; you should let him know that you're taking his action seriously before hitting him."

Then Debra would turn on me. "You can't tell me what to do; I'm in charge and I'm older than you, anyway. I'll do what I want, and if you're big enough, stop me."

We settled with a scrap unless I backed down. Sometimes after a fight it would take days, with a clever arrangement of clothes, or combing of hair, to try to conceal the scratch marks. But sooner or later, I would hear Mama say, "Sophia, where did this scratch on your neck come from?" I knew I couldn't lie. "Debra and I were fighting."

"When did this happen?"
"When you were gone to town."
"What was this about? How come you didn't say nothing to me about it?"
I didn't say much to that.

Then she'd get biblical with me. "You know God doesn't like sisters fighting with each other, don't you? And what do you think the other children goin' to take from your fighting?"

Now my stomach was churning because I knew what was coming next: "You know, I'm going to whip you for fighting and trying to hide it. You know that, don't you?" Yes, Mama, I knew. But what I never had the nerve to ask was, "How come you can have so many physical fights with my Daddy, and talk about Debra and me setting a bad example?" That question would have brought me more pain.

I hated and feared having to go to the doctor for penicillin shots. I'd see that great big needle about to go into my arm and be deathly afraid.

My parents usually got me to do what they wanted by threatening to whip me if I didn't. But getting shots from the doctor was something I dreaded far more than a whipping. My mother had to beg a ride to the doctor from my aunt, uncle or a neighbor, then see her daughter furious and terrified and then, the very next week, go through the same thing all over again.

I hated getting those shots so much that I got to thinking that everything the white doctor was doing for me was worthless. Mom would make me tea and bring me "butter stew" — butter, sugar and vinegar — for my asthma and colds. But I had no faith at all in the different color pills — orange pills, yellow pills, blue-green pills

—that Mom brought me for my rheumatic fever, especially after hearing something the doctor said about her. I pretended to swallow the pills, then took and stored them in a little brown bag underneath my bed.

One day when everyone was in the field and I was alone, I slipped outside and planted those pills in the ground under a thriving rose bush. After that, the rose bush never looked fully healthy again, at least not to me.

During my year out of school, when I felt well enough, I'd walk a mile to the bus stop, ride the school bus to town, see the doctor, then get picked up by the school bus in the afternoon.

All day I sat in the doctor's little red brick office, next to the Dairy Queen and the Piggly Wiggly grocery store, within a few blocks of the Coosa River. Some days I brought a jelly biscuit for lunch; other days I went hungry.

One day, it got near the time for my afternoon bus to come and I hadn't yet been called in to see the doctor. I summoned my courage and asked the colored nurse why. She told the doctor: "This girl wants to know why she hasn't been seen."

He asked, "What's her name?"
The nurse said: "Sophia Bracy."
The doctor's reply could be heard in both the white and colored sections:
"Tell her until her mammy pays me some money, I'm not touching her."

Oh, those words stung! In front of everybody, the doctor had deliberately degraded my mother by calling her "mammy" and saying she didn't pay her bill. On the school yard, if someone called your mother "mammy" it was fighting time. I hated the doctor for the cruelty of his words, but I blamed myself. The whole thing would never have happened if I hadn't been sickly.

Then, I had to go home and tell my mother what the doctor had said.

# 2
## A BIG FAMILY

*"I'd rather sleep on the floor at Baby Ree's house than in the bed at some of my other folks."*

Let me tell you about my younger siblings. Edwin, three years younger, had a leg injury at birth that required trips to the Cripple Children's Clinic in Montgomery. Some of the first care giving I ever did was changing Ed's diaper as he tried to jump and run away from me. Then came Georgia, a "tom girl" with a flair for decorating. John was terribly allergic, which bothered his eyes. He was the family comedian.

Charles was rambunctious, a real challenge to care for. We teased Katherine that she was the "adopted" one. Her light skin color and shy personality disguised her knack for getting what she wanted. Aretha detested being "the baby," and always let us know what she thought and what she wanted. She studied hard and was an honor roll student.

Besides the eight of us, there were three more. Harvey was born to Mom before she was married. He lived close by with Mom's sister Pearl and was the first male who was ever affectionate with me. He'd hug me, ask "How you doin'?" and really wanted to know. He let Debra and me ride his bicycle and we competed for his attention. I grew close over time with Dad's two other children, Dorothy Jean and Charles, who were raised in separate households. (Yes, I had two different brothers named Charles, and the older one had a son named Charles, Jr. That was interesting when we all spent time together.) Mom bore her first child in 1939, and her last one in 1963.

My mom was the youngest of twelve surviving children; my dad was one of nine. Dad's family was from Lowndes County, Alabama.

His mother, Virginia Brooks Bracy ("Big Mama") and most of her children had moved north to New York State, but his sister Essie, his aunt Irene, and their families were a real part of our lives. Dad's father John Williams lived in Cumberland, Kentucky where he'd worked the coal mines. We saw him rarely, but we knew we were family. I was proud of being part of such a large group of kin who were happy together and drew strength from one another.

Some of Mom's many relatives lived nearby; others visited from New York, Chicago, Virginia or Fort Lauderdale.

Around the 4th of July, relatives came driving up to our modest home in their big cars, wearing stylish, colorful outfits. We later learned that the cars were often rented just for the trip and living "up north" wasn't as grand as we thought. But at the time, sweaty in our ragged field clothes and having no car, these visiting relatives looked like royalty.

Coming to Mittie Marie and Roosevelt Bracy's home ("Baby Ree" and "Baby Lee," as Mom and Dad were affectionately known) was the favorite first stop for relatives — a guaranteed meal.

"Baby Ree, you got any of those good biscuits in the kitchen?"
"Boy, I've been tasting your pear preserves for the past week."

Mom would already be on her feet heading to the kitchen, even if she'd just walked in from the field. She'd say, "Give me a few minutes and I will have something for y'all to eat."

"Bracy, you got any of your peach brandy left, while we wait?"

Dad didn't want to bring out his homemade brandy, but the excitement in Mom's voice and the hugging, back-slapping and pulling out of small gifts by the guests added to the euphoria of the moment and Dad would join in the fun. In no time, Mom was putting hot biscuits, fried streak of lean or fat back strips on the table and her best freshly canned preserves, figs, pears or peaches, all gathered from Dad's fruit trees.

By now the conversation was into a second round — what they ran into during their trip or the latest on graduations, weddings, illnesses, trouble with the law or jobs.

Nieces, nephews and cousins were known to say, "I'd rather sleep on the floor at Baby Ree's house than in the bed at some of my other folks." Mom knew how to roll out the welcome mat.

Mittie Marie Fleming, my mom, was born to Porter and Mittie George Fleming. In her lifetime, she would wage many battles; some in the fight for social justice that was boiling over then; some over what she felt the community should be doing to lift up our children and prepare them for the future; some in head-to-head disagreements with our dad. Conflicts were inevitable since Dad worried about the here and now. Mom was the one who lived with vision and hope.

Mom was big on names and knowing people's birth dates. She named each of her children carefully and attached significance to our names. Although we were Baptist, she named my sister Katherine for a Catholic nun who'd befriended us in hard times and gave Aretha the middle name "Denise" for another nun who'd helped our family.

Mom's siblings, Pearl Sattiewhite and Charlie George, and Uncle Charlie's wife Lacy, helped shaped my life. Aunt Lacy was the closest person to a grandmother that I knew as a child. Dad's mom lived in New York and Mom's mother died when I was a toddler.

Aunt Lacy had a light complexion, long silky hair, a serene manner and magical healing hands. "Bracy, send somebody to get Sis Lacy. It's time." She was the first person mom sent for when having a baby, even before the midwife. Aunt Lacy was at our house often.

At times Mom would send me to her house where it was quiet. Our house was full of noisy busy bodies. By the time I was an adolescent, Uncle Charlie and Aunt Lacy were by themselves since their three children were on their own. Their children were actually two great nephews and a niece they had raised. They had no biological children.

Most of the time Aunt Lacy was home alone. Their three-bedroom, wood-framed house with a living area and kitchen was elevated and required about eight steps to the main entrance from the back and five steps in the front. They had running water, but only in the kitchen. Once I got in the house, Aunt Lacy wouldn't allow me back outside.

When my rheumatic fever gave me pain in the joints, when my knees would swell up to twice their normal size and I couldn't walk, Aunt Lacy was so gentle, appearing with a pail of hot water and a towel to provide heat compresses on both my knees. At night, she helped me hobble to the "night pot."

My bedroom in her home faced the morning sun. In the morning, she'd open the white sheer curtains and the sunshine beamed into the room and across the quilted bedspread. She'd apply another heat compress to my knees. The towel was warm, her hands were soothing, and her voice was kind and nurturing as she inquired about my night and asked what I wanted for breakfast.

She'd say "Sophia, let's try and get you out to the back porch for some of that morning sun." Or: "Take it slow, baby; don't try to move too fast." She told me the morning sun was healing, and I had a feeling of peace and tranquility.

Aunt Lacy was about fifteen years older than Mom. She seldom raised her voice and almost never complained. Only once do I recall feeling Aunt Lacy's anger. "Sophia, put that boy down and let him walk. He's not gonna break and he's almost as big as you!" Nursing aches for others was a part of who Aunt Lacy was, but she was fiercely protective of young girls who might injure themselves; I was told that Aunt Lacy had lifted something too heavy as a child and caused an injury that prevented her from bearing children.

Years later, studying child development at Auburn University, I learned the name for the nurturing and affirming attention given by Aunt Lacy with no expectations. It's called "unconditional love."

I had several first cousins who were as close to me as my own siblings. It takes a village to raise a child, and our village was large. Some of my younger siblings, I can close my eyes even today and almost feel them tugging at my legs, needing something that I wanted to give them.

There was one other aspect of family which I absorbed but didn't focus on as a girl. Because we were so close, and because I could tell Mom anything, there was a tendency to assume that you did not tell your business outside the family. I was comfortable sharing what was going on at home. Other siblings were more private and called me "motor mouth." Often, this kind of teasing didn't bother me; but it was painful if I realized I'd been hurtful or violated a confidence. The thing that hurt me most growing up, and what I never talked about outside the home, was Mom and Dad's fights.

# 3
## MOM

---

*"My mother had given me life and given me the idea that giving birth is a commission given to a woman by God; the finest thing a woman ever does."*

My mother's family, the Flemings, were poor, but well-educated. I grew up hearing that education is the way to a better life. Mom's sisters Aunt Sophia and Aunt Pearl were teachers and had both been to college. Most of the Flemings had high school diplomas. Of Porter and Mittie George Fleming's twelve children, nine girls and a boy lived to adulthood. My mother was the baby. It was her mother and older sisters' dream that she would attend college. Even after she dropped out of high school and had Harvey at 18, they still held out hope for her going to college.

When Dad came courting her, a tenant farmer with a third-grade education, my mother's older sisters were not very welcoming. Dad struggled to support our family. My mother was reminded by her family from time to time that she could have found a better husband. On the other hand, Aunt Sophia and her husband, Malcolm Slaughter, a retired miner and minister, did give Dad 200 acres of land to farm.

Mom always battled for what she wanted and believed, starting with her decision that marrying Roosevelt Bracy was the right thing to do.

My mother had given me life and the idea that giving birth is a commission given to a woman by God, the finest thing a woman ever does. Whatever tragedies might befall her, whatever mistakes she might have made, a woman can look back and say: "I gave birth to my babies. I carried those children in my womb, and I gave them to the world…"

Mom loved me deeply and I knew that, but she also whipped me at times, and those whippings were terrible. I was afraid of the dark, afraid of not being able to breathe, afraid of boogie men, but getting a whipping from my mother was the most awful thing of all. Dad whipped me, too, but with the whippings from my mother came extra shame and guilt. Mom didn't just whip me; she told me how disappointed she was in me and reminded me of all that she'd sacrificed to teach me right from wrong. She would be in tears herself as she beat my butt, all the time insisting: "This is hurting me more than it's hurting you." She used her tears to bring us to our knees with guilt.

I never stopped thinking: "Have I been good enough for Jesus to love me and welcome me to heaven if I died?"

Mom inspired and encouraged me, but also planted fear in me. On one occasion I felt Mom was beating the very life out of me. Once she told me not to do something, then caught me in the act. When she called to me and started in my direction, I ran the other way. Little did I know she'd sent my sister over there to catch me. Turning around, I ran into a Mack truck—my mother. She caught me, threw me to the ground, and sat on my head and she weighed not a pound under 250. Then she whipped my butt until I felt death was imminent.

There were many instances where Mom would sit, and have you talk for a moment, strike a lick or two, then talk some more and so on for ten minutes or more. I never quite knew which was worse, the fast, passion-filled whippings from Dad or the slow, reflective ones from Mom. They both left me determined to do whatever was necessary to avoid their wrath.

But before judging my mother as cruel and abusive, hear me out about her. I had colds, and when I had asthma attacks at night, she spent hours sitting by my bed, sometimes all night. She put hot menthol compresses on my chest, rubbed and soothed me with soft words, prayers, and sweet songs to calm my fears and panic of the dark and of being short of breath. That butter stew I mentioned was the only medicine I got because there was no money or transportation to get me to a doctor, and there were few options anyway to a poor colored woman at night.

Living miles from the nearest neighbor, with no car or telephone, Mom did her best to keep her children well. Playing in the rain, especially me with my weak immune system, could be cause for a whipping. Each child got their due of attention, and the sickly ones got more.

Mom exposed her children to every chance for leadership, whether in school, church or at a community function, and she strongly supported her children when they were on a program. I remember one early morning school assembly program that my sister and I were in. The day before, Mom met the bus and asked the driver if she could catch a ride to the school to attend the assembly. He said no, that was against school rules. Mom left the house walking, long before our bus came, hoping to flag a ride to the school, 10 miles from our house. It was painful to see her walking, having made it only three or four miles when the bus rolled right by her.

The program was nearly over when she finally arrived, and I'm not sure if she saw either of us perform, but it was great to see her arrive at the assembly. That's the kind of devotion she brought to supporting her children. She would walk over water and fire for us — and she never let us forget that she was doing this, so we could have a better life, one easier than hers.

Mom was, in some ways, a big kid at heart, and she enjoyed playing with her children, even when Dad cautioned her that by doing so, she would lose our respect as an authority figure. She kissed and hugged us, and I can see my brothers now wiping her kisses off their faces.

But it was in no way all sweetness and light. Mom and Dad loved hard, and they fought equally so. There were many physical altercations between them. Mom loved Jesus but would fight like hell even though Dad was physically stronger, and would get the better hand in their fights, at least until we kids were older. I hated this part of my childhood most, because I thought one would kill the other, and then have to go to jail and I would be left with the responsibility of taking care of the kids. Then I knew I'd have to drop out of school and spend the rest of my life working in the fields for somebody.

A deeper part of this dislike was that their fighting went counter to Mom's teachings which resonated deep into my soul. I became the mediator in our family at a very early age, which is quite a task for a child. It destroyed my childhood and made me an adult far too soon. Abuse of any sort at home leaves children feeling insecure and unprotected, and I felt low and inadequate.

Regardless of Mom and Dad's rocky relationship, which was fueled in part by his drinking and infidelity, she loved him and respected him as her husband, and required everyone else to do the same, especially her children.

One day I found her in tears from something Dad had said or done, and I lashed out with unflattering words about him. I was jolted into reality with a slap across my face.

She said, "Don't you ever let me hear you speaking about your daddy that way, as long as you live, you hear me?"
I said in tears, "I was just trying to help."
"I don't need your help!" she snapped. "You should respect your father so that your days may be long on this earth; that's what the Bible says."

For all the years I knew my mother, she was in a love affair with Jesus Christ. She talked about Jesus with a shine in her eyes. This relationship was her beginning and end in all of her relationships. My mother was no saint —far from it. But, oh, she had some saintly qualities. Singing was defined as giving praise to God for one's very being, followed only by praying.

We would be awakened in the early mornings, first hearing Mom praying for everything and everybody and most definitely her children—whom she called out by name in case God had forgotten. This prayer was followed by a song which alerted us to her mood; if it was an upbeat one like "I'm satisfied with Jesus, I'm satisfied with Jesus in my heart" then Mom was happy and things would go well. If it was a heaviness of heart kind of day then, as she began breakfast, an old hymn like "Father I stretch my hands to thee, no other help I know, if thou withdraw thyself from me, oh where shall I go?", could be heard from the kitchen, along with the clinking sounds of pots and pans.

Mom always wanted a piano for our house, but she never got one. That remained a dream deferred. She loved singing, had a beautiful voice and did not believe in the notion that only good-sounding voices should sing. In our house, with the exception of Dad, everybody sang for every action, whether it was mopping floors, washing clothes, dirty dishes, picking cotton—you name it, we sang it, as long as it was gospel or spiritual. Singing blues, rhythm and blues, pop or anything suggestive was off limits. My youngest sister Aretha was named for the gospel singer Aretha Franklin.

Listening to the radio was not permitted except for gospel music and then only when Mom was present. We older kids, who were in charge when our parents were away, would slip and listen to the radio. When we spotted Mom or Dad coming, we would wet cloths to cool off the radio to keep from getting in trouble. It was years later before we discovered that Mom was on to us with our little wet cloth trick.

Singing was also a gift that Mom offered many families during their hour of sorrow. She was sought out to sing at most of the funerals in our community and many other church programs. Mom felt it was her duty as a mother and Christian woman to teach us about Jesus. We had to learn Bible verses and recite a different one before eating; learn whole chapters such as Psalms 23 and 100; 1 Corinthians 13; and Matthew 5.

Missing church was not an option and that included Sunday School, Baptist Training Union, Missionary Society and prayer meeting. When folks like my aunt or other ladies of the church needed youth to participate in church activities outside of our community, it was common knowledge that Marie's children were available.

Mom's love affair with Jesus was a relief from the hardships of a poor, black woman, with sickly children and a husband with whom she was often at odds. They had different beliefs and values when it came to the best way to make their mark on the world and raise their children to do the same.

Mom believed in teaching by example; Dad was "Do as I say and not as I do." Mom saw education as the way to a better life while Dad valued working hard and learning how to plant a crop and harvest it as the means to survival. Religion was crucial to Mom; Dad was much less about going to church and more about keeping your word— "Say what you mean and mean what you say."

When Mom was burdened, she talked and shouted her pain to God, which included what we called "getting happy" — fits of jerks up and down, waving hands and sometimes even fainting. When she was happy and things were going right, she offered praises and thanksgiving that included a little shouting, too.

My mother had love and affection for almost everyone that she developed a close relationship with, but there were a few she fell in love with. From the reverence with which she spoke of her mother, Mittie George Fleming, I knew it was a love affair. She became misty-eyed, tender and oh so inspired speaking of the strength of my grandma Mittie. My photograph in the arms of Mom at her mother's funeral is the only memory I have of me as a baby.

I learned that Ma Mittie was a pillar in the church, saved extended family land several times and had a reputation of someone who was persuasive and would not take no for an answer. Clearly, many of those qualities rubbed off on Mom.

My mother had the falling in love effect with Sister Mary Catherine, for whom my sister was named. This Catholic nun, administrator of the local hospital, became my mother's friend and later employer over a 15-year span.

This woman was a source of food and support for our family during the time my father was seriously ill, and Mom was trying to farm and care for Dad while still raising six children.

A white man from the city had stumbled across us and went to a nun asking for her help, saying that he had come across the poorest family that he had ever seen in his entire 60 years. Sister Catherine, Sister Denise and others would come on a weekly basis, for a couple of years, and bring us food. But as much as Mom loved Sister Catherine, she did not agree to us to be trained in Catholicism.

Winifred Green, a field organizer for the American Friends Service Committee, came into our lives after my sister and I were among the first black students who integrated the public schools in Wetumpka. Winifred was introduced to my parents as a resource for getting my sister back in school after she had been arrested and expelled from school following a fight with a white student.

There were a number of other Friends Service Committee women for whom Mom had great affection including Constance "Connie" Curry, Eleanor Eaton, Barbara Moffitt, Addie Ringfield and Jean Fairfax. But it was Winifred who put the shine in her eye, the tenderness in her speech. Mom spoke of her as though she were a cross between a saint and a lover. Dad preferred Connie Curry: I think he sensed that Winifred had a somewhat controlling nature and Dad wasn't going to be beholden to anyone.

Winifred was responsible for getting the Department of Justice involved in my sister's case, assistance with NAACP Legal Defense Fund scholarships for several of us to attend college and, later, the formation of FOCAL. The light never dimmed when Winifred's name came up and it's safe to say that my mother was in love with her until death.

Mom wanted us to know Jesus for ourselves and she wanted us to know what she wanted for our lives. Each of us got turns sitting in Mom's lap as she caressed and loved on us, calling each who held the space "my baby." At the time, no matter how many others were in the room, you felt that you were the only "baby" she had.

She would say words like "Baby, mama's not going to be with you always. And you must prepare yourself for when you have to face this life by yourself. No matter what, if you know Jesus, you will be all right."

# 4
## DAD

---

*"If you work hard and have somewhere to grow something, you won't go hungry and you won't have to sell your soul to somebody to feed your family."*

As a little girl, I had a love-hate relationship with my father. I loved that he was a protector of his family and I loved his directness; there was no confusion about where you stood with him. But deep inside, I hated him for fighting with Mom and being so mean.

Dad was a perfectionist when it came to tending to his vegetables, picking clean cotton and not disturbing his watermelon patches. Hoeing a row and damaging a plant could be cause for a whipping; not picking the expected amount of cotton was another. Allowing a cow to get into the vegetable fields was a definite whipping.

That resentment I felt about the way he treated us was deeply mixed with the admiration I felt for him, and this was confusing to me as a young child.

Dad wasn't particular about names, and he let Mom name the children. He didn't pay as much attention to our birthdays, either. Dad was an intelligent, colorful person but with no longing to be seen as educated. He was a farmer and proud of it.

Both my parents were believers in owning a piece of land. We knew we all descended from slaves who'd never been allowed to own the land they worked. Owning land gave you pride and independence. As we complained about working in the fields, Dad would remind us that, "If you work hard and have somewhere to grow something, you won't go hungry and you won't have to sell your soul to somebody to feed your family."

We were awakened most mornings at 4:00 a.m. and given just a few minutes to pull on our clothes and head to the fields. By the time the sun came up, we'd been working for nearly an hour. We children were Dad's tools, the members of his orchestra, and always with one goal in mind: a good crop!

We stopped working only long enough to eat the biscuits and fat back which Mom would have prepared and brought to the field in a dish pan. I can still see Dad standing up from his sitting position on the bucket that held the "soda" (sodium nitrate fertilizer) perching himself on his hoe handle with one hand and pushing back his sweaty cap with the other to allow whatever breeze was present to cool his perspiring head. Before finishing his last bite he'd say: "Y'all hurry up, the sun's gon' be mean in a little while. Git your water now cause we ain't gon' be stopping—this work got to be done." Dad was in full control.

Because Mom and Dad raised me as a farm girl, I was acutely aware of the seasons and, from an early age, each one had its own distinctive meaning for me. Spring was hope bursting forth from the harshness of winter—a celebration of surviving the brutal cold. It was as if each spring brought hope to Dad that he had another chance to "make it," to pull out of his hard times. He looked at Spring as another man might look at a lottery ticket—this just may be the year. A good crop meant having enough to get by without going deeper into debt to get through winter or having to borrow money to buy fertilizer and seeds before planting.

Summertime was when hope gave way to pure labor and brute determination to make every effort to succeed—sheer mind over might, mind being Dad and might being the sun. The heat of the summer sun was harsh.

But there was also a sweetness to June, July, August and September. We had all the fruits and vegetables we could want. We feasted on cantaloupes, blackberries, peaches and plums, figs and watermelon, and, as we moved into the fall, scuppernong grapes, apples and pears.

Around late August came the harvest. Cotton was a main staple for our family income and Dad's children were his hands. "Y'all, we got about two weeks before the rain is supposed to set in. We got to git that cotton picked by then."

Each time I heard those words, muscles tightened in my lower back. I loved living on the farm, but detested picking cotton. The hot sun fried my brain like an egg. I got so thirsty my own saliva tasted sweet. Gnats, mosquitoes and yellow jackets swarmed around my face, no matter how much I slapped at them. As the sack got heavier — 50, 75, 100 pounds, its strap cut into my shoulder.

We bent, squatted, and stooped, pulling cotton from the razor-sharp bolls, putting it into the sack with enough rhythm and speed to hit the magic number of pounds Dad required each day. We all had raw hands and scratched legs. The tallest cotton plants provided shade from the blazing sun, but snakes might be lurking there, especially after a rainy season when weeds and grass were thick in the cotton rows.

The coming of fall always seemed to be punctuated by the death of an elder, a cornerstone in our community. There was a sadness about the fall. After the unyielding, unbearable heat of summer came that distinct hint of coolness in the air, and with it a kind of impatience. The leaves faded from lush shades of green to a dusty orange, and then to a dying brown. I could feel the barren time coming when the leaves had fallen, and the trees were bare. The birds had stopped singing.

Each year my father seemed to be reassessing, "Do I really want to go through another winter?" Winters in our home could be cold and harsh, and it was often difficult for us even to keep warm.

Dad planted every fruit tree he could find, plus we were blessed with eight pecan trees, a strong stand of sugar cane, and at least four peanut shocks — vertical poles where peanut vines were placed in layers to protect the nuts from the damp. Sweet potatoes we dug up and banked through the winter in a three-foot deep, half-under ground shed.

Retrieving sweet potatoes from the bank was never pleasant; rats and other undesirables took cover there as well.

I used to sit under Dad's homemade scuppernong arbor which was about ten feet long, built up on six poles, about five feet off the ground. Mom made delectable scuppernong jelly. When I had 20 minutes free, I would go to the arbor, straddle one of the larger vines and eat to my heart's delight.

General Andrew Jackson had defeated the Creeks in the decisive Battle of Horseshoe Bend in the nearby Tallapoosa River, and in 1814 forced Chief Red Eagle to sign the Treaty of Fort Jackson, ceding to the United States 23 million acres of Creek lands. So, the Creeks had been defeated militarily but their spirit was still very much a part of the land. While planting in newly plowed ground, or chopping cotton, my siblings and I often ran across their arrowheads. Studying Alabama Civics in the 7th grade, I realized we were occupying land taken from a proud people who were here long before us.

My mother's maternal grandmother Frances was a Native American. We had a large, framed photo of Frances on the wall above our fireplace. I used to look at her, a large woman with a round, light brown face, long brown hair, a cream-colored blouse and a dark skirt. I wished I knew more about her.

Dad would often joke, "Some of y'all would give away everything you own for a bag of candy." He prided himself on being hard to fool. He could quickly size up a person and determine whether that person would be useful to our family, dangerous to our family or just someone to be dismissed from his thoughts entirely.

He spoke with a thick Lowndes County accent. The first time I took my driver's test, the examiner failed me because I had no idea what an "emergency brake" might be or where it was in the car. Daddy was incredulous when he heard I'd failed since he'd often used "the Mershon brake" when I was in the car with him. Well, of course I knew "the mershon brake." I'd just never realized until that day that it was his deep Black Belt pronunciation of what others called "the emergency brake."

He sometimes acted as if his wife and children were his possessions, and he was tight with his possessions and with his money. Because of his illiteracy, he didn't have a bank account; he instead chose to bury a few hundred dollars here and there on his property in Mason jars.

He'd grown up without a father and was thrust into the role of provider much too early in life. He seemed to feel that playing with his kids would compromise his authority, that being affectionate with Debra or me would be perceived as weak and might cross the taboo line of incest.

Everyone in our family had a role and a responsibility—and Dad made sure that the children, the farm animals, even our dog and cat knew exactly what he expected of them. Our dog knew that Dad expected him to chase game to a tree for us and stand guard under the tree. Also, the dog knew to alert us whenever anyone approached the house, whether a family member or an intruder. Our cats knew their job was to catch rats and mice; if they didn't do it, he would banish them out of doors. Chickens had to lay eggs. Pigs made pork. Cows made milk and butter and were held in high esteem in the family. When Ole Betsy the cow died, after being ill for a few days, both Mom and Dad wept with deep feeling. She was family.

When any of us stepped over the line and refused to play the role Dad had laid out for us, he had his ways of bringing us back in line. Our mules, Ada and Shine, were crucial to us; they pulled the wagon that hauled our equipment, water, and wood, and plowed the soil for planting our vegetables and cash crops. But one day Ada and Shine decided to jump a fence and help themselves to some fresh peas, corn and other tender vegetables.

When Dad came storming into the house, Mom knew what was next. She pleaded: "Bracy, Bracy, don't do something you'll regret!" but he grabbed his 12-gauge shotgun, rushed back outside and started blasting away at the butts of those misbehaving mules. We were terrified that he'd kill one or both of them. But with their behinds full of buckshot, the mules jumped back over the fence and into the pasture area where they belonged.

As a farmer, Dad knew his vocation. If he'd been educated, he could have been a scientist. He knew what grew well in many different soils and what moon to plant them by. He knew the names of trees, knew that yellow root and also the leaves of the mullein plant could be boiled and used to treat sore throat, cold, coughing and asthma. He taught his children what poison ivy and poison oak looked like and warned us not to eat the wild huckleberries that grew in the woods. Dad had a love for the land and everything on it.

I tried to please dad by working hard and loved to hear him say "Sophia's my best worker." He offered all his children the chance to plant our own little gardens on the farm, but I was the only child who did so. I loved the land the way Dad did, the trees and nature in all their glory. During my time out of school, when my younger siblings were taking a nap, I would grab a quilt and a book, walk out under a tree and read.

Dad was as different from Mom as night is from day, and that made for surprises, uncertainties, elements of comedy as well as tension in our daily life. In some ways, I'm still that country girl that he raised. If a black cat crosses the road, I'll turn around.

Mom didn't smoke or drink. Dad got drunk almost every weekend, and he smoked, too. He bought Prince Albert tobacco and rolled his own cigarettes.

Both of them liked to dance.

Mom would provoke him, jab at him a little, call him a sinner. That was a weapon where I came from and a real put-down.

"Bracy, you need to go to church," she'd tell him.
"I don't need to go to any church," he'd retort.
Mom would say: "You need to go to church for your children."
"I don't need to go to church for anyone but me!"

Then he would often say: "They want the same thing at church that I want: money. If you want to go there and give them our money, that's okay. But I'm not going."

After he got sick, Dad went to church for a while. He stopped when he couldn't stand it any longer. It didn't feel real, and it didn't feel right. Dad was always against anything that felt dishonest. He felt the Christian church in Alabama, both black and white, were putting on a front, and he refused to be part of it.

He was going to drink on weekends and have a good time and he knew the church frowned on that. But there was another aspect to Dad's aversion to church. He couldn't read the prayer books, and I think he felt humiliated by that.

My parents loved each other, but there were a lot of toxins between them. She was big on education and he was big on hard work. She had dreams of a better life; his dream was to make a good crop and pay the rent. She was big on church and the afterlife; he was big on having fun in this life and we'll worry about the other one later.

He made moonshine liquor, not for the money it made him, which was very little, but because he enjoyed the thrill of doing something illegal, living on the edge — and irritating Mom in the process.

She was an idealist, and he was a realist.

There wasn't enough money coming in the door; neither of my parents had been educated in how to handle money; they didn't agree on what to spend their money on; and they didn't communicate well. Those four interrelated problems combined to start some explosive arguments in our home.

Yet they loved each other. Mom was attracted to Dad, impressed by how hard he worked, and how devoted he was to his siblings and to his mother, whom we called Big Mama. Big Mama never forgave Mom for taking Dad away from her.

Mom was devoted to bettering the community and the race and doing this by finding allies among the white folk; Dad wanted his family protected and completely independent of white folk. He saw no allies in that community, only trouble.

One Sunday morning, we were all at the breakfast table when we heard the jarring sound of a honking car or truck horn. Dad got up from the table and went out the front door to investigate. By the time the rest of us got to the door, we saw the white farmer who was our neighbor shaking his finger in Dad's face and telling him angrily to make sure our cows stopped grazing in the white man's pasture.

Dad denied that our cows had done any such thing and told the white man to get off our property.

Mom saw this and went right to the bedroom, got a shotgun and came back to the door. She ordered the rest of us to stay in the house, and then she leaned herself again the door frame, with the gun at her side, but out of sight. Both men had their voices raised and my siblings and I kept expecting this white man to reach in his back window rack where he kept his gun and shoot Dad for speaking to him in a disrespectful tone. But peering out from behind Mom, we also knew that white man would never be able to shoot Dad, because Mom would shoot him first. Finally, the white neighbor backed away and left our front yard.

We still couldn't feel relief; we expected him to come back later or do something terrible to us in the dark. He did come back, but it was nearly six years later.

Dad would stand up one day against our nasty white farmer neighbor, but on another day he'd be "skinning and grinning" with the white man who owned the country store when he needed to buy something "on time," paying the store owner back in installments, when the vegetables sold or the cotton was ginned. The store owner expected a pose of deference, with Dad grinning and scratching his head, and he gave the store owner that, in order to get what he needed that day.

I hated seeing him skinning and grinning. He was strong and invincible! Why was he acting so subservient? Lord, I knew so little about how hard it was to be a black man in that time and place, to run a farm and raise a large family. It was impossible for dark-skinned people to keep our dignity in that degrading system of laws and customs. Dad did the best he could, and better than most who'd gotten such a modest start in life.

Dad took each of his kids out and taught us how to use a gun and hunt game for food. He was particular; one round of ammunition equals one piece of meat, usually a rabbit or squirrel. Shooting into a nest could land you in trouble with Dad. His guns were a 12-gauge shotgun and a rifle. I was proud to have the distinction of being the child Dad said was the best shot with the rifle.

Dad plowed the mules and planted crops, from sun up to sundown. While Mom put so much stock on our black heritage, Dad was just happy to have lots of hands to help out in the planting and harvesting of the farm, gathering firewood for heating and cooking, watering the animals and the myriad of other chores on a farm. His biggest worry was the weather: either too much rain or a drought could cost him his cotton crop.

He didn't touch alcohol all week, just worked like a fool. Then on Friday evening, he'd put on his nice khaki pants, the starched crease standing tall, his best shoes, and he'd leave home walking. Now he wasn't Roosevelt Bracy the farmer anymore. He was Gator, a clean dresser and a good dancer, with a fine baritone voice and a sly grin. A lady's man. He was going off to see his friends, who were very important to him. We wouldn't see him until Sunday near dark, when a slow-moving car driven by one of his buddies brought him home sloppy drunk.

When I was ten, Dad came home from one such weekend very ill. He'd been poisoned by moonshine liquor. For three months, he was in the John Andrews Hospital in Tuskegee, 35 miles away. Mom had to take over farming the crops, caring for all of us and trying to catch rides to visit him at the hospital.

Dad had never been ill before and when he came home, unable to be the man of his household, he had an emotional breakdown. For three or four months he was committed to Bryce Psychiatric Hospital in Tuscaloosa, two hours from Montgomery. Finally, a patient wrote my mother and told her if she wanted her husband to live, she'd better get him out of that hospital. With the help of Dr. Zdanis, a Yankee doctor who was Dad's vegetable customer, Mom got him released.

After the alcohol poisoning and the psychiatric breakdown, Dad didn't drink or smoke anymore. He was baptized and became a regular churchgoer for several years, even became a deacon in the church. He was also bored stiff by all of this abstinence from alcohol.

He missed his drinking buddies, and took up selling a little moonshine on the side for my cousin. That was enough to keep some of his old friends coming around.

My father was simple and complicated; hard and soft; dead serious and full of fun; anti-religious and deeply spiritual; paranoid and trusting. It depended on what day it was.

# 5
## GOD AND THE CHURCH

---

*"I didn't want Jesus to be sad or disappointed in me; and I thought if I was bad, He might stop loving and protecting me."*

From a very young age, I understood that God created the world and everything in it. I knew that each and every one of us should strive to be what God intended for us to be.

But no one can know precisely what God intends for anyone else. Therefore, I believe there can be no validity to any earthly hierarchies of status based on size or shape of the body, on hair or skin color, on religion or the place where your ancestors lived. The claims of one human group to be genetically superior to another are strange and dangerous delusions.

I believe that any group of people who try systematically to hold down another group of people is sinning not just against that group but against God, who wants all of us to be as great as we can be.

I will pass along here a sermon which has been preached in many a black church over the years but can never be told enough. I heard the theologian Dr. Samuel Dewitt Proctor preach this sermon. It's about an eagle on a chicken farm. Remember, the eagle is the king of birds, with great, powerful wings. Eagles can fly at 60 miles an hour, and swoop down on their prey even faster. Regal and majestic, the eagle is often described in Scripture.

> *"Now it came to pass that a poultry farmer was hiking in the hills near his home and farm, when he spotted an odd-shaped egg. He knew it was no chicken egg, but he brought it home to hatch in a nest of chicken eggs. The egg broke; the bird hatched, and it was a peculiar-looking bird, out of place among the chickens. But the chicken farmer raised it as a chicken, surrounded it with chickens and fed it with chicken feed, and the peculiar bird tried to act like a chicken.*

*One day, a visitor at the farm noticed the peculiar bird. He asked the farmer: "Why do you have an eagle here with your chickens?"*

*The farmer replied: "He may look like an eagle, but he eats like a chicken, walks like a chicken — and a chicken is all he'll ever be."*

*The visitor had to disagree: "You can't tamper with the soul of one of God's creations. You're confining this regal bird in a barnyard, but God intends him to fly in lofty places and has planted in him the seeds of greatness." Saying this, the visitor lifted the eagle off the ground and told him: "God did not create you as a chicken. Lift your mighty wings, and fly."*

*But as the eagle began to ascend, the farmer threw chicken feed on the ground, and the eagle dropped to the ground, ate the feed and showed no more interest in flying. The farmer grinned and said: "I told you he was nothing but a chicken."*

*The visitor next brought the eagle to the top of the farmer's barn, and gave him a view of the countryside, a hint of everything that lay beyond. The eagle took off to fly — but the farmer played the same shabby trick, throwing chicken feed on the ground. Again, the eagle landed on the ground and made no more effort to fly. The farmer gloated: "I told you: he's nothing but a chicken."*

*But the visitor refused to give up and, with the farmer's permission, took the eagle out just before dawn broke. Together, they climbed a mountain and as the sun was just beginning to break the darkness on the eastern horizon, the visitor pointed the eagle to the rising sun and said again: "You were not created to be a chicken, but an eagle. Stretch forth your wings and fly."*

*The rays of the rising sun struck a gleam in the eagle's eye. The bird's slack body began to tremble and pulsate with energy. Then with a great leap, on outstretched wings, the eagle flew away toward the dawn, never looking down or looking back, only toward the greatness that God intended."*

Six days a week, daily life in Alabama was controlled more than it should have been by white people with their strange doctrine of white supremacy. Black people could not strive toward the full potential that God intended for us.

But Sunday was the Lord's day.

My mother put into practice Proverbs 22:6: "Start children off in the way they should go and even when they are old, they will not turn from it."

My Aunt Pearl headed up the children's program at our church. Short and round, she had bulging eyes and a bass voice from an undiagnosed thyroid condition. She was strict, almost harsh with her students, but she taught us appropriate speech and behavior. She and Mom were cut from the same cloth when it came to learning something. You memorized it! No looking down at a paper, no forgetting. That was not acceptable. Every misbehaving child was Aunt Pearl's to correct. My appreciation for Aunt Pearl grew as I got older.

Pearl found poems, songs and different parts for each child. At Christmas and Easter, during Black History Week, on Mother's Day and Father's Day, Pearl gave children poems or skits to perform.

I started transferring Biblical images to help relieve my doubts and fears. I heard these words in my Sunday school class: "Yes, Jesus loves me, yes Jesus loves me, yes Jesus loves me, for the Bible tells me so." That began to calm my fears. In Sunday school, I learned that Jesus loved and protected the little children, and that Jesus was everywhere. These words made me feel safe, loved and protected, like a blanket I could snuggle down under and hide from what scared me. My Sunday school teachers talked about being good and told us that Jesus was sad when children misbehaved. I didn't want Jesus to be sad or disappointed in me; and I thought if I was bad, he might stop loving and protecting me.

As I grew older, and fears peppered my days, I came to understand and hold onto faith. Many times during church as an adult, and even now, I feel that same balm— peace, and the sense that all is well with my soul.

Mom busied herself on Saturday directing the cleaning of our house, scrubbing floors, washing, hanging out and folding clothes which required three or four trips to the spring beneath the hill, at least a mile round trip, with a couple of gallons of water in each hand. We prayed for rain to fill the barrels posted at all four corners of the house under the roof gutters. Barrel water was used for washing and bathing.

By mid-morning, two wash pots would have fires made underneath with boiling water: one ready for a load of white clothes and the other for coloreds.

Saturday night was getting ready for church time; shoes polished and baths in the tin tubs used earlier for washing and rinsing clothes. We bathed the younger children, then took our own baths. Either Debra or I would get the fire going in our wood stove for supper; usually cornbread and buttermilk and a vegetable left over from summer's canning.

Mom's mood was heavy. She would hum a hymn she planned to lead in the church service, as she ironed stark white usher shirts for Debra, Ed and me. "Ed, bring me the iron" she called from her makeshift ironing board, a foot wide piece of plywood, covered with a sheet resting on the backs of two chairs. It was the second of two cast irons being heated on the fireplace hearth.

I cooked supper, Debra gave John and Georgia their baths and Ed polished his shoes and those of his younger siblings. Debra and I wore our little black patent leather shoes. They just needed a little Royal Crown hair oil.

In the Bracy house, church attendance was required. That included any guests we might have staying over on Saturday night. So Sundays meant an early start with lots of bodies trying to get to the wash basin, get their hair combed, and get the little kids dressed.

Afterwards, we had to dress and eat breakfast in time to catch a ride with Uncle Charlie in his pickup truck or else get packed in Uncle Lee's green-and-white 1956 Chevrolet, like sardines in a can. If we missed both those rides, our walk was several miles through woods, across a stream, up a steep hill and then another long mile on a dusty road.

Mom would commit her children to anyone who needed child delegates to conventions, associations, institutes or any other church function. Debra and I always had to be ready to perform a duet or to recite Bible scripture. With our Aunt Pearl and Uncle Charlie in leadership roles in our church, believe me, opportunities to perform often arose. Sometimes it was boring, but it was a way to stay out of the cotton fields, so we didn't complain.

I saw the Bible as a rooted, grounded, sacred book — but also as a radical document, telling the story of underdogs like Daniel in the lion's den, and of those in resistance to the status quo, including Jesus.

Despite the church work performed by countless unsung women, in the 1960s women were not deemed fit to serve as pastors or deacons in our houses of worship. Protest against that would not begin in earnest for several more decades. Though the Bible made clear that slavery was wrong, it also spoke about the duty of servants to obey their master. The Bible told us that we are all made in God's image — yet it seemed to condone the awful inequalities we see all around us. Exodus tells us that we may take 'an eye for an eye, and a tooth for a tooth,' yet the Book of Matthew urges us to 'turn the other cheek.' The Book of John teaches that we may not hate, "for God is love" — but the fifth Psalm tells us, "Thou hatest all workers of iniquity." These contradictions tugged at my heart.

# 6

# HOPE— AND HOPE DASHED

*"On November 22, 1963, President Kennedy had been shot and had died, and I felt that our fledging hopes for a better life were dashed."*

In November of 1960, John F. Kennedy, the Democratic Party candidate, narrowly defeated the Republican Richard Nixon and was elected President. Kennedy had reached out to Coretta Scott King during the campaign when Kennedy was told that Martin Luther King, Jr. had been arrested and was in some danger.

John Kennedy's presidency brought hope that change was on the way for black people. He made his brother Robert head of the U.S. Justice Department and Robert Kennedy pressed for full voting rights for black people in the South. We had pictures of John Kennedy and Martin Luther King Jr. framed in the front room of our home. Mom spoke of both of these men as though they were relatives. We believed both of them were putting their lives on the line to help black people get our full rights as citizens.

Because Dr. King had been a pastor in Montgomery, we felt that he was one of us. The pastor of our church, the Reverend J.L. Jones, knew Dr. King well and spoke with reverence about his civil rights work and non-violent beliefs. Reverend Jones held services twice a month, every second and fourth Sunday. At each service, he urged us to join King's activities. We worried about his well-being as if he were a member of the family.

Reverend Jones was a tall, dark-skinned, educated man about 40 years old. He was a serious type and had a stellar reputation in his business and personal life. He was moderator of the District Association of Baptist churches and co-owner of one of the two black funeral homes in Wetumpka. Reverend Jones was in the know and brought with him the ear of about two dozen churches.

In his Sunday sermons he spoke about things changing in our society. Through the messages of Reverend Jones and my Uncle Charlie, who was president of the local NAACP, my family kept abreast of what was happening in the Civil Rights Movement.

My family didn't have television, so most of what we heard was on the radio or when we visited Uncle Charlie and Aunt Lacy, or secondhand information mom picked up from the Elmore County Civic and Improvement League, which met monthly to discuss voter registration, land disputes between black families, education issues in the black schools and police abuse of black people. After school integration, these meetings became weekly. My mother attended the League meetings whenever she could, often catching a ride with my Uncle Charlie.

By 1963, I was quite aware of the Civil Rights Movement. My world was rocking on its foundations, and I was trying to put all of this information in my mind together, to make sense of it all. I saw Dr. King as a deeply religious man, yet he broke the law and led others to do the same. They were confronting an unjust system and landing in jail.

All of the people I'd grown up with owned guns and believed when attacked, you have the right to defend yourself with force. I struggled with King's message of loving thy enemy. How could you love someone who spit at you, hurled nasty words and hard objects at you? Trying to understand Dr. King's approach — turn the other cheek and refrain from violence — I could not shake the deaths that haunted me.

In June of 1963, Medgar Evers, head of the NAACP in Mississippi, was murdered in his own driveway, in front of his wife and children. What had Medgar Evers done wrong?

In August 1963, when Dr. King delivered his "I Have A Dream" speech at the March on Washington, I heard it on the radio. Later that evening, seeing the large crowd of 250,000 on my uncle's television brought me nearly to tears, moved by the thought, "This is a Negro speaking to all these people. Many of them are white and came with him because they chose to."

In September of that year, the Klan had planted dynamite sticks under the 16th Street Baptist Church in Birmingham and when the dynamite exploded, four little black girls were murdered — in church.

Then on November 22, 1963, in biology class, our teacher, Mr. Fred Briars announced that President Kennedy had been shot and had died. Mr. Briars wept, we wept, and I felt that our fledging hopes for a better life were dashed.  After all, the President of the United States, a popular, wealthy, well-meaning white man, had been gunned down in broad daylight, quite possibly because of his stand for racial justice. I thought: "It's just a matter of time before they kill Martin Luther King."
I had plenty of reasons to feel that my own life was in danger.

# 7
## SMALL ACTS OF GOOD WILL

*"He placed the marble on the top of one of the fence posts at the corner of these two worlds, one black and one white, which came together on that day."*

There are so many stories of bad things that white people in Alabama did to black people — mean things, sometimes brutal things. Yet there were always nice white people as well, provided the act didn't go out of the status quo.

Away In A Manger, and O, Come All Ye Faithful, and Silent Night; O, Little Town of Bethlehem, and O, Holy Night… All of these songs remind me of the Christmases of my youth. They filled the air waves of school and church rehearsals, all in preparation for our joyous celebration of the birth of Jesus on December 25th. The anticipation of this day had a magic in the air; the mood was light, and people smiled and offered wishes of Christmas merrymaking and good will for the coming year. There was something special about the smell of Christmas—cedar trees, apples, oranges, potato pies, and chocolate cake icing—adding to our expectancy and wonderment.

In junior high, as a member of the school choir at Doby, I was asked to sing O, Holy Night at the Christmas assembly. I was excited but apprehensive; this was the season of colds and I always feared I'd get sick and have a voice too scratchy to sing my part. O, Holy Night was not an easy song to sing, and required uncluttered lungs.

Something about this season, with all of its joy, reminds me of those who are no longer physically present in my life. A poignant memory is of Christmas Eve at our house.

Mom had put her cooking on hold to usher us through a last recital of the play at the church. All the props were gathered, sheets for angel wraps, ragged overalls for shepherds' dress. Dad's homemade axe handle was the staff, pillowcases were the head dresses, and other items were the wise men's gifts. We piled in the old pickup truck and off we went. After the program, while adults were making baskets for the homebound, sick and needy, which was almost everyone in our church including our family, the older teenagers huddled around the gas heater to keep warm, and those of us who were younger tried to listen in on the Santa Claus gossip, while trying not to seem too interested.

Sure enough, I came down with a cold two weeks before my O, Holy Night performance, after only one rehearsal. It was during the time my father had his nervous breakdown, and our family was in desperate need.

In the valley was a Christian camp for whites. The Bracy family was one of the School Choir's missionary projects. For two Christmases, members of that Christian camp piled in an old pickup truck and came to our home bearing gifts, helped us decorate our Christmas tree, and even had Santa with them.

The leader of the group, Brother Robert Morris, asked what we wanted most for Christmas. I answered, to be able to sing O, Holy Night at the school assembly. I shared that I had missed school because of the cold, and I didn't know the song well enough to sing it.

Brother Morris asked, "Do you want to learn it?" I replied yes.

When I went back to school the day of the program, the choir director said she was so sorry but I couldn't perform the song because I'd missed rehearsals. She looked puzzled when I pleaded with her to allow me to sing because I had learned the song.

Brother Morris had made two trips from Montgomery to my home in Wetumpka and taught me a song that is still my favorite Christmas carol.

Another time, a thin elderly white lady named Mrs. Allen saved the life of my younger sister Georgia. Mrs. Allen lived not far from our house in the valley to the north side of the Slaughter's place. Just five feet tall and slightly bent, she was a relative of our most difficult white neighbor. She had a grandmotherly way about her, and allowed her granddaughter, who was Georgia's age, to come up and play with us girls, but not with the boys.

Georgia and my brothers were playing with marbles and Georgia put a marble in her mouth to keep her brothers from taking it. But she accidentally started to swallow it, and when it lodged in her windpipe, she began to choke.

Mom started screaming for help — but we were at least 10 miles from a doctor, with no vehicle and no phone. If you don't breathe, you can get brain damage within five minutes and be dead a few minutes later. Dad grabbed up Georgia and ran with her toward the main road, a mile from our house. Mom screamed: "Go down the hill to see if Mrs. Allen is at home!" The hope was if someone was home, they might drive Georgia to a doctor.

Mrs. Allen had already heard the screams and was coming up the trail of this steep, bushy hill toward our house when she met my sister. Mrs. Allen commanded: "Go tell your daddy to turn that gal upside down and shake her!"

She didn't stop there but turned around and headed in the direction of a short cut to the road where Dad was running, yelling at the top of her voice: "Turn her upside down and shake her!" Right at the point where the dirt roads intersected into a fork, up the hill from the valley where Mrs. Allen and another white family lived, and around the bend from where we lived, was a pastured field for grazing cattle. Two wooden posts provided the structure for the wire-fenced gate to the pasture.

Dad shook Georgia upside down and out came the marble. He placed the marble on the top of one of the fence posts at the corner of these two worlds, one black and one white, which came together on that day. For years I passed this marble on the post as I made my way to catch the bus, or walk to church, and each time I recalled the act of kindness that had saved my sister's life.

# 8
# DOBY HIGH

*"Take every chance to better yourself for the progress and uplifting of our race."*

School was something precious and Mom made sure we knew this. She would talk about the changes that had to take place for black folks and how important it was for us to be ready for those changes.

"Education is the key for the black man," she would say. "I want you to apply yourself and study hard. I want you to go places that I can only dream about. That's why I'm working so hard and fighting for you all to go to school."

She would look past us as though she was looking into the future and we would peer around her outstretched hand to see where she was looking. Again and again, she told us: "You are my future, our future; it's in your hands. Don't let me down, don't let the people down who've had a stake in raising you and are counting on you. Keep your mind focused and let that other stuff that can block you— let that stuff wait, you'll have plenty of time to do grown up things. Don't make the mistake that I made, and not stay in school — go as far as you can go. I'm counting on you." Then she would ask, "Do you hear me?"

It was a practice that I continued with my children, because it had a powerful effect on me, especially as I became a teenager. When I found myself in a passionate moment with my boyfriend, Mom's words and the image of her face and the other women in my growing up would always clear my head. Mom's words were my birth control.

The schools for black kids and the schools for white kids were supposed to be "separate but equal" but we all knew that wasn't the case. Many white people seemed threatened by any black person who rose up through hard work and attained a professional degree of any kind. White people seemed to want to keep all the status for themselves: the better homes, the better churches, the better schools. When I entered seventh grade, I attended W.B. Doby High, the facility built to replace the old school for blacks, Elmore County Training School. Doby classrooms were an improvement over the old training facility; there were new desks and tile floors. But our buses were often still broken and the lab room had very little equipment. Doby's teachers and students were always having to raise money to keep our programs going.

I enjoyed Doby High, which was named for a local black educator. I was comfortable there. We had talent shows at Doby. We had a Black History assembly. Our choir sang gospel and freedom songs. We competed in oratorical contests.

The teachers at Doby were my allies. Ms. Amanda Grayson, my Alabama Civics teacher, encouraged me to take an interest in politics and public speaking, and got me started reading the *Wetumpka Herald* and the *Montgomery Advertiser*, on the rare occasions when I saw those papers.

Though I was shy, Ms. Grayson chose me to recite a poem on the role of slaves in building America. "Enunciate your words and pause for emphasis," she told me. "No one should have to strain to hear you." Another teacher, Mrs. Crenshaw, counseled me: "From seventh grade on, everything counts." She pushed me hard on the debate team and convinced me to join the student council. Teachers spoke reverently of Spelman College, a first-rate black college for women, in Atlanta. We had real camaraderie at Doby.

I took my studies seriously and we loved our school, but we constantly heard teachers say, "We don't have the science equipment you need to study these subjects." At Doby, it seemed someone was always selling something to raise funds for basics at the school. The teachers told us we would have to work doubly hard to succeed in college because Doby didn't have what other schools had to prepare their students.

"You're going to have to struggle, because we don't have the resources here. We can give you the best we know to give, but you're going to have to compete in the world out there, and it's going to be up to you to work harder."

It nagged at me that some of Doby's best graduates, valedictorians and salutatorians, had struggled when they got to Tuskegee Institute. Some had even had to transfer to a less stringent college. Why was this? Was there something wrong with Doby, or something wrong with Tuskegee? Or — scariest of all to think about — was there something wrong with us? Though my parents had worked heroically to find positive messages for us, I was vulnerable to feeling lesser than.

I remember the bus rides home from Doby, the kids playing and joking on each other, the smell of sweat hovering. Some days a breeze brought a hint of honeysuckle in the window of this rattling old school bus loaded with 35-45 colored students from first through 12th grades. Some were my kin, church members and neighbors. Couples sat near the back of the bus exchanging gazes and quick smooches. Mr. Evander Anthony, the driver, owned a barber shop in Wetumpka. Sometimes, he had to caution a child to stay seated.

Sitting on the inside seat next to the window, I could shut out most of the happenings. My thoughts were far away on images of a story I'd read, but not far enough to escape the dark thoughts lurking. Looking at the dust-covered kudzu vines, the plum trees and other greenery that lined the unpaved gravel roads, hunger pains and dry thirst played a game in my gut.

I tried to fan away the dust stirred by passing cars and trucks, knowing if I sneezed too much I'd have to struggle to breathe. I prayed silently that my parents would be alive when I got home.

Mom urged all of her children "Take every chance to better yourself." She had dreams for us: getting a good education, then becoming leaders "for the progress of humanity and uplifting of our race." I heard in mom's words her own deferred dreams. She was adamant that we be kind and mannerly to our elders.

She preached daily about giving back to others as we had been blessed.

If I challenged her: How have we been blessed? Mom pointed out we were alive, had a roof over our heads and two parents in the home, and that was quite a blessing. On late Spring evenings of 1965, I was doing some deep thinking. I was curious and excited when the teachers at Doby High passed out Freedom of Choice forms at the end of the school term.

The U.S. Supreme Court had ruled, a whole decade earlier, that racially segregated public schools were unconstitutional. White Southerners have never liked being told what to do by the federal government and they took their time desegregating. But now, prodded by the Justice Department under President Lyndon Johnson, desegregation of the public schools had finally come to Wetumpka.

Our teachers told us to take these Freedom of Choice forms home and discuss with our parents whether to remain at Doby or to enroll at all-white Wetumpka High. Debra and I thought hard about this. Desegregating white high schools had never been a major goal of our family. Education, holding down a good job, and making our family proud of us… these were the ambitions we were raised with.

But now we told Mom we wanted to go to Wetumpka High. She asked us why. I let Debra make the case: "We're tired of getting hand-me-down books with love notes and hearts drawn all over them." She added: "I want to go Tuskegee and not flunk out."

Mom didn't take much convincing, but she did say: "Do you have any idea what y'all will come up against? You can expect some rough times so you'd better be sure this is what you want. And we'll have to see what your daddy has to say."

When we heard that, our hopes fell. Dad believed that the best way to handle white folks was to stay out of their way and avoid getting tangled in any kind of dispute with them. We figured he'd never let us go to Wetumpka High, and Mom wouldn't push him on the issue.

But, to our surprise, Dad told mom, "If you go along with it, I won't stop you, but we better know what you gittin' us into." Our desire to attend Wetumpka High didn't even stir the usual dispute between Mom and Dad over how many classes we'd have to miss to help in the fields. So whether or not to face the whites at Wetumpka High and get a better education was really mine and Debra's decision to make.

I knew in my gut that integrating Wetumpka High would be difficult. Even sheltered as I was by my parents' love, I'd seen and heard enough of the callousness and hatred of white people to have a sense of what I was facing. I knew what racial "separation" meant to white folks.

There was also a junior at Doby named Frank Mitchell to consider. Back at Doby High school, during this, my freshman year, I was being pursued by Frank, whose advances I had gently shunned. We talked often at school, during PE, in which neither of us participated. He would seek me out, tell me about the book he was reading, ask about what I was reading. He asked if he could come see me at my house, but I declined with a little lie, telling him my daddy wasn't allowing me to date.

Frank was tall and well built, though a little close to lanky, an excellent writer, very personable —but he took abuse from other students because his skin color lacked pigmentation. He was albino, with woolly blond hair. Kids at Doby said he looked like part of an uncooked chicken. They called him "Gizzard."

At first, I was too proud to be the girlfriend of such a homely young man, but I admired him.

Leaving Doby would mean I wouldn't see Frank every day.

But I thought of my mother's words: "Take every chance to better yourself. Uplift the race." How could I turn my back on this chance to uplift the race? I asked my parents to sign the forms that enrolled me at Wetumpka High.

# 9
## A SEA OF ANGRY FACES

*"You do not know what a composition is – and you do not know the meaning of utopia…and you think you are fit to come to school here."*

In the sultry late-August heat of 1965, as the first day of school loomed closer, I began to hear the buzzing about those of us who were going to the white schools, Hohenberg Elementary or Wetumpka High. We were leaving all our teachers and our friends. I could feel my stomach tightening. Will I understand what the teachers are saying? Do I have the right clothes? Who will I talk to? Will I have any friends? Will I be able to sing in the school choir?"

And the hardest question of all: Will they hurt me or my family for enrolling at their school? Towns like Wetumpka, though not far from Montgomery and its civil rights activities, were quiet on racial matters through 1965. But these sleepy towns were quite capable of state-sanctioned violence in order to enforce segregation and the status quo on race. Debra and I, along with the other black children integrating Hohenberg Elementary and Wetumpka High, were challenging that status quo, and we had ample reason to be afraid.

Mrs. Ethel Tillman, our neighbor, took her daughter Annie Pearl, my mom, Debra and me to the school early that first morning. We traveled the dusty dirt road five miles to reach the paved highway that took us into the town of Wetumpka and across the river bridge to the school. Mom and Mrs. Ethel made small talk about what vegetables they had canned and the recent church revival. We three sat silent on the back seat, absorbed in our own thoughts.

Nothing could have prepared us for our reception at the school. When I saw the crowd of white people, I was shocked. I had been sheltered so far in life from this sort of racial rage, and despite the heat, I felt goosebumps.

Wetumpka High was a red brick building. The concrete walkway leading to the school was lined on both sides with a sea of angry white faces. Ironically, in the families of nearly all of these white people, black women served as nursemaids and housekeepers. Many of these white kids played happily with black children, but they were furious at the idea of our "polluting" their school.

There was no way but through, and as we made our way through the crowd, they erupted into jeers, name calling, pointing and hissing. Some sported Confederate flags. Among the tormentors, I saw men, women, and children, small to tall, lanky to big-bellied, of every age group. I tried not to make eye contact but couldn't ignore the slurs hurdled at me.

"We don't want you at our school, nigger." "Go back where you came from, nigger." "Beware, coon passing."
"Niggers you don't belong here; go back to your nigger school."
"Leave outta here or you'll be sorry."

I could barely breathe. I had no way of knowing that in the days to come, the insults, spit balls, paper wads and sling shots would only escalate.

Once inside the school building, I felt numb. But I tried to focus on what would come next. A tall man with a clipboard approached. He looked to be the one in charge —that is, if you could look "in charge" and scared at the same time. He led us into the office labeled "Principal."

Looking at his clipboard, he asked our names one by one. Once the last black student and her mother arrived, we were taken to the study hall located in the school auditorium. The large room had white walls with gold drapes pulled closed across a stage and a black valence to match the "Mighty Indians" mascot on the podium. The immovable wooden seats seemed to swallow the handful of black students and our moms.

The counselor spoke briefly with each of us students about our class schedules and subjects. The principal went over the school rules: no fighting, no cheating and no leaving the school grounds without approval from the office. A few emergency contacts and telephone numbers were taken from each adult. Mom gave the number of her brother, Uncle Charlie, because we had no phone.

One mother asked about the bus schedule and which bus her child would ride home. When my mother inquired, "What is being done to keep the children safe?" the principal brusquely replied, "We are not in the business of law enforcement." With that, our parents were told to leave and we were sent to our classes.

My mom and the handful of other moms, who had walked with us into the school, had no authority, no recourse, and no way to protect their children. They walked in silence armed only with "prayer and hope," as my mother shared later that night.

"Class, take out your pencil and paper. Your task is to write a composition on utopia."

It was mid-morning on that first day at Wetumpka High. As I listened to the assignment, my mind was racing. What is she talking about? Did she say she was Mrs. Smith or Mrs. Johnson? I was distracted by the smell of the cedar varnish from the hardwood plank floor and by the barred institutional-looking windows that denied my impulse: Run, Sophia! Run, get away! You don't belong here.

By now, the English teacher, a slightly heavy-set woman whose pleasant face and accent was not too deeply influenced by southern dialect, had started moving through the classroom of 30 or so students. As she neared my desk, I could hear my heart thumping.

"Miss Bracy, did you hear the assignment?"
"Yes, madam."
"Why are you not writing?"

I was aware of a deafening quiet in the classroom. My body went numb. When the answer came out, my voice was barely a whisper: "I don't understand."

"What do you not understand? Do you know what 'utopia' means?"
"No." There were snickers from my classmates.
"Do you know what a composition is?"

"No." More snickering.

The teachers back at Doby High used the term "theme paper" rather than "composition." I had never heard the word "utopia" before.

Slowly and with emphasis, the teacher raised her voice: "You do not know what a composition is and you do not know the meaning of utopia… and you think you are fit to come to this school?"

The class erupted in laughter. I was so deeply shamed that I wanted to die. I had let down my mother, the teachers at Doby and the whole Negro race. Of all the mean, hateful acts directed at me, this one cut the deepest.

The taunting and terror of our first day at Wetumpka High did not subside when school let out; it continued on the long bus ride home. Black students were told to sit in the front rows of the bus for our own protection, and we did. Debra and I, Annie Pearl and the other black students on the bus made a perfect target for every possible object that the white kids wanted to throw at us. I tried to ignore the things that hit me in the back. If I turned around to see who'd thrown it, 40 innocent faces with mischievous grins stared back, erupting into whoops and shouts as soon as I turned back around.

I soon learned that the bus driver, Mr. Greer, sincerely cared about the well-being of the black children on his bus. He was in his mid-40's and had a night job at the cotton mill. His black hair combed straight back made me notice how pale he was.

Weariness showed on his face in the mornings and sitting so close to him, I noticed mill lint in his hair. A few times, I saw his eyelids droop as he fought off sleep. He was the only white friend we had at that school.

Everyone on that bus knew that some of the football types in the back of the bus were capable of overpowering Mr. Greer on some back road, stopping the bus and staging a lynching. The worst threat Mr. Greer could make was to turn around in his seat, and shout: "Sit down, and stop that throwing or I'll go back to the school!" He pounded the horn for emphasis, but his face was full of fear and his voice trembled.

Our home, in rural Redland, was only about 15 minutes from Wetumpka High by car. But the school bus route wound past farmhouses, circled back in neighborhood nooks, made frequent stops along stretches of cotton fields and on dirt roads shaded by dense pine and oak trees. It took a full 90 minutes for Debra and me to reach home and I was frightened the entire way.

The first day we were only a mile into the ride when I heard someone behind me say, "You smell a nigger? Yep, the smell of coon is making me sick to my stomach. Let's kill us a nigger." I asked myself, "Is this the day I'm going to die?

Mr. Greer turned the bus around and sped back to the school — twice. It didn't work. The taunts reached a level bordering on lynch mob hysteria. It was nearly dark when Debra and I finally arrived home and Mom and Dad were stricken with worry, wondering why the bus was so late.

This pattern continued for two weeks. Mr. Greer pounded on his horn for order, threatening to drive us back to the school. I was paralyzed with fear and only found relief halfway into the ride after the worst of the bullies had been dropped off.

There were chores to be done before school, milking the cow, helping younger siblings get ready for school, cooking breakfast, but those chores were nothing compared to trying to prepare for the taunts, ridicule and physical abuse that I knew was coming on the bus ride to school.

It wasn't only my schoolmates I had to worry about. The white farmer whose land adjoined ours was outraged that the school bus crossed his property while "transporting these niggers to a white school." He said he was going to put a stop to it, and he sounded like he meant it.

After two weeks, I let go of the panic I'd been feeling. The mind can only carry this type of fear for so long without finding a way out. For me, the calming thought was, "Okay, you may kill me, but you cannot kill the dream. Black folks will be free, and ignorance can't stop it."

"Mr. Greer, my sister is not on the bus." I spoke in a quiet but sharp voice as the driver revved the motor to pull out of the school yard.

"Where is she?" he hissed.

"I don't know."

It was 3:15 p.m., school had let out for the day. The principal and a few teachers stood outside as bus monitors.

The driver pulled the bus up to where the principal stood and leaned out the open window. "This girl says her sister is not on the bus."

"Who is her sister?"

I answered, "Debra Bracy."

The principal answered back with attitude, "The nigger is in jail where she ought to be for hitting a white boy."

A giant cheer erupted from the back of the bus. I knew how fierce Debra could be. But I also knew she wouldn't have hit a white boy without plenty of provocation. What had the white boy done to her? Even as I asked this question, I knew already in my bones that the white power structure would not answer it. White children could attack and bully us all they wanted. It was only when we practiced self-defense against whites that the law became interested, and then punishments were harsh.

My spirit was crushed. My mind turned to Jell-O and a flash of fear flooded my thoughts. Have they already killed my sister? Is she really in jail? Will we ever hear from her again?

When I managed to clear my head of these awful images, I realized that traveling the distance to our house on the bus would take too long; it would be almost dark by the time I reached home. I had to get word to my parents. They had no phone and no working car. I needed to get off the bus in town. I could go to our pastor's funeral home, try to call my Uncle Charlie— who was also president of the local NAACP—and hope he could get word to my parents that Debra was missing.

I leaned over and told the bus driver, "I need to get off the bus in town."

"It's against the rules; I can't let you do that."

"You've got to let me off," I said, "so I can get word to my parents to find out what's happened to my sister."

Again, he said no.

I started to cry; he said nothing. As we approached the street where the funeral home stood, he seemed to speed up. Abruptly, he stopped the bus and muttered, "Get off now and hurry up."

To this day, that was the kindest act that anyone has ever done for me, but it was not the last time the bus driver offered encouragement.

My parents and uncle arrived at the jail, but for several hours they couldn't get anyone in charge to talk to them. Finally, around 9:30 p.m., the sheriff came out and told them to go home. He said, "That nigger gal is going to spend the night in jail to teach her a lesson about hitting a white boy." This same sheriff was quoted in a newspaper article saying he had offered a bail immediately after her arrest but there was no one to bail her out.

My parents asked to see Debra. When the sheriff denied their request, they returned home unsure if Debra was in the jail or not and worried sick that she'd be dead by morning. You see, there were stories46 that black folk didn't fare well under this sheriff's watch.

It was a dark time for me as I boarded the bus to school, still not knowing if my sister was dead or alive. When I took my designated seat behind the driver, he asked was my sister all right? I told him she was still in jail, and my voice began to break. Only a few students were on the bus, but he turned and said in a low voice "be strong, she'll be all right, and don't let them see you cry."

Later that morning, my parents and uncle returned to the jail, bringing with them Dr. Joseph Bradford, a Ph.D. from Tuskegee Institute and a former county extension agent working at the U.S. Department of Agriculture in Washington D.C. He just happened to be in town and my pastor asked him to meet my parents at the jail.

Rural whites were always wary of doing anything that might offend the federal government and make some federal bureaucrats, or FBI men, descend on Wetumpka, messing in white folks' business. The Wetumpka police chief probably believed if Dr. Bradford worked in Washington, he might have connections to "M.L. Coon and his commies."

So when Dr. Bradford asked the sheriff why was Debra Bracy, a youngster, being held in this jail, the sheriff stammered something about she should have gotten bail last night and promptly released her.

The immediate danger of Debra being murdered in police custody had passed, but it was hardly the end of the matter. The police made it clear that they intended to charge Debra with a crime.

Meanwhile, Debra told us what had happened. The white boy was pelting her with a slingshot. She had hit the boy, yes, and she'd had a pencil in her hand at the time. But she'd never stabbed him with the pencil. The pencil had not harmed him in any way.

In the days that followed, no white people or white-run organizations came to Debra's defense.

"Though headquartered in New York, the NAACP Legal Defense Fund maintained a roster of "cooperating attorneys" willing to handle civil rights cases.  Our pastor and my uncle, both activists in Elmore County's school desegregation battles, used well-established connections to secure the assignment of a Montgomery-based lawyer to represent Debra.

He persuaded my parents that Debra's best option was to plead guilty to assault and battery, accept a five-day suspension from Wetumpka High, then return to school." Meanwhile, the Wetumpka police charged Debra with stabbing a white male student with a pencil. It was reported in a local paper the white boy had been rushed to a local hospital, and his wound had required stitches to close.

I had seen this boy late in the afternoon on the day of the incident. He said something about "a nigger" and "jail," and I had no idea what he was talking about. Had the police been seeking the truth, they could have easily checked hospital records and established that this boy had never received treatment for a stabbing, nor had even been hospitalized. But this wasn't about justice; it was about keeping black people "in our place."

For days, Debra steadfastly refused to plead guilty. But after some hard cajoling, Mom and Dad and their lawyer finally convinced her that what was paramount here was not the truth or falsity of the assault and battery charge against her, but her ability to get back into Wetumpka High.  To get back in five days would be a "win."

If she pled innocent, and was found guilty in court, she could be expelled from Wetumpka High. So, very reluctantly, Debra agreed to plead guilty to the charge of assault and battery.

The school promptly used this guilty plea as reason to expel her. Not only that, the civil rights lawyer also who had arranged the plea, and promised it would get Debra back in school, was nowhere to be found. For several months, he ducked and dodged all of my mother's attempts to reach him.

All during those months, my mother hustled rides, called everyone she knew and pursued names she got from others trying to get her child back into some high school. Twice she was successful: one for two weeks before they learned of the Wetumpka High incident, and another time for one month. My mother was terribly worried that Debra cried every day she wasn't in school.

For the next four months Debra was seething with anger toward everyone she felt had sold her out. She blamed her lawyer the most, but she was also angry at Mom and Dad. She felt betrayed.

Four decades later, in 2005, I found the American Friends Service Committee (AFSC) archives. From them I learned that the black leaders calling the shots were well aware of my sister's case, but chose not to pursue it because Debra had hit the boy and violence of any kind violated the Civil Rights Movement's principle of non-violence.

The very same lawyers and leaders who had convinced us to take this course and plead guilty had later abandoned her. Strategically, it might have been the right tactic, but it was very hard on my family.

Recalling my mother's anguish and my sister's sense of betrayal, I felt disappointed and hurt to learn that leaders for whom I had great respect could not speak truthfully about their decision with my family.

Debra lived for a time in Albany, New York where Dad's sisters Susie, Maggie and Mildred lived. She attended a junior college in Alabama but found it hard to shake the pain and feelings of betrayal after what she'd been through in Wetumpka.

AFSC staff reached out to her and Mom wanting to know how they could support her. Years later, after her return to Alabama, I asked Debra about her withdrawal and distrust. She replied, "How would you feel if each time you filled out a job application, you had to mark 'Yes' to the question 'Have you ever been arrested?' I never got the chance to explain my side of things before being denied a job."

I got just a glimpse of the huge well of pain and bitterness and sacrifice that Debra had, and I felt pained, too.

# 10

## THE BLACK COMMUNITY ROSE TO OUR DEFENSE

---

*"Let nobody stop you from achieving that which is yours."*

The abuse from my English teacher was just the beginning of weeks of insults, slights and discounts from teachers and students at Wetumpka High School. They went to great lengths to try to force us black students to fail, quit and leave. The black children in elementary school were told there were no more textbooks available, then given F's when they didn't do homework assignments available only in those books.

The County Superintendent, Ross McQueen, told our bus drivers that they could not bring black children into the Wetumpka High parking lot. We had to walk the final two blocks, often with rocks being thrown at us, and then were marked "tardy" when we were late reaching our classrooms. One white child hit a black child in the face with a baseball bat. Other whites sprayed black kids with aerosol deodorant. Often these cruelties were inflicted with white authority figures looking on and doing nothing to stop it.

But the ugliness they showed me at school only stiffened my resolve. To succumb would only reinforce the notion that we were inferior. Sticking it out at Wetumpka High became one thing I could do to change a mean and evil system that spewed out ugliness. My answer was: "I will be here every day, in your face, because that is the greatest act of defiance that I, Sophia, can make. I will be here getting the education I want."

The racist hatred made everything worse, but racism was not the only problem. I had little natural aptitude for mathematics and didn't get a good foundation at Doby High for mathematical thinking.

My father was illiterate and Mom's method of helping me with math was to threaten me with a whipping if I got a bad grade.

My Algebra teacher was stern, hard and intimidating, to white students as well as black ones. She was the wife of one of the big landowners in the area and I knew she had black people living on her land as sharecroppers. I was terrified of her. She was tall and awkward, with a military air, and would call us up to the blackboard to work on problems there with the whole class watching. I hated being put on the spot like that and my mind would go blank.

Everything about this teacher made clear that she was used to holding power. She seemed unable to imagine what it might feel like to be frightened or powerless.

"Why are you just standing there?" she'd bark at me. "Didn't you do the homework?"

After several weeks of taunting, rock throwing and other forms of ridicule, it was clear to the black leaders in the community that something needed to be done to support the 19 black kids in elementary, junior and senior high school in Wetumpka.

Meeting in the old Elmore County Training School, these leaders appealed to the black teachers from Doby High to come out and provide tutorial assistance once a week. Three or four teachers agreed, and two showed up consistently on Thursday nights.

These evenings took on the feel of a freedom rally. We sang songs, clapped to freedom chants: "If you miss me from Doby High and you can't find me nowhere, come on over to Wetumpka High, I'm in school over there." Or we sang to our segregationist governor George Wallace: "Oh, oh, Wallace, you know you can't jail us all. Oh, oh, Wallace, segregation's bound to fall!"

These boosted our spirits and helped us to see the big picture and feel connected to the larger black community.

Every Thursday, each student had the chance to share what was going on for them and to report incidents of harassment. The League's secretary captured these incidents in writing.

Then we got down to the tutoring.

Before leaving our tutoring sessions, we would regroup to sing another couple of songs to boost our morale and hear more encouraging words connecting our efforts to the struggle for dignity and civil rights.

Civic leaders spoke at the closing. They cautioned us: "Don't fall into their traps. Don't respond to the insults and intimidation in a way that could get you kicked out of school. That's what whites want.

"Blacks are reputed to be emotional and undisciplined — and you must prove them wrong."

"Do the opposite of what they expect. Stay in school, be successful in your grades — no matter how unfairly you're treated — receive your diplomas and go on to college or whatever you choose to do."

These League gatherings helped defuse some of the tension that had built up in us from being barraged with negativity, especially from teachers.

Being belittled, ignored and cast out taught me how to put up a tough front and primed me to develop a will of steel. Our mentors admonished us: "Let nobody stop you from achieving that which is yours."

I listened and I became determined to fight injustice and mistreatment of anyone. Words of the freedom song were resonating in our hearts, "Ain't gonna let nobody turn me 'round." Out of our collective experiences, this group of students was united and determined, to represent ourselves with dignity and respect and to get that Wetumpka High diploma.

Mrs. Thelma Bradford, the wife of the former extension agent who intervened with the sheriff for my sister Debra, sensed how scared I was of my Algebra teacher. She took a special interest in me and made me believe that I would pass Algebra. She helped me get past my terror of failing and being thought stupid.

Calmly, she presented the concepts, and the mental steps I needed to take. "Sophia, remember the formula. You're just nervous; you can do this." My mind relaxed and I recalled how to solve an Algebra problem. With the help of Mrs. Bradford, I passed the course.

What I held onto at Wetumpka High was that if I died, it would not be in vain. It would be in the fight for dignity and human rights. I was not seeking martyrdom, nor to celebrate myself as brave or self-sacrificing, or to be hailed by others. But I had a deep sense that, as a human being, I was entitled to spirits higher and larger than me, that I was doing what was my right... I imagine soldiers must feel this way – the dangers are real and the end may come suddenly but they accept the risk because they're fighting something far larger than a single life. That's what kept me coming back to Wetumpka High and kept me from caving in to the fears and threats of physical danger.

It came from within, from a sense of wholeness that was not always fully formed. It tapped into a well of human spirit much larger than what any person or people can give or take away.

# 11

# DR. KING HELPED ME CONQUER
# MY OWN HATE

---

*"People who took risks to do good made me realize I wanted to be like*
*them, not stoop to the level of the violent haters."*

During my bleakest times at Wetumpka High, I relied heavily on the teachings of
Martin Luther King, Jr., especially his messages of love over hate.

"There's something about love that builds up and is creative. There is something
about hate that tears down and is destructive. So love your enemies."

Dr. King had so many special qualities — his energy, his intelligence, his focus. His
extraordinary eloquence. But perhaps the quality of his which has meant the most
to me was his ability to tie the Civil Rights Movement to broader things which
white Americans respected — the Declaration of Independence ("We hold these
truths to be self-evident, that all men are created equal…") the patriotic song "My
Country 'Tis of Thee," with its beautiful phrase "Let freedom ring!"

In a 1967 speech, Dr. King said: "In the final analysis, racism is evil because its ultimate logic is genocide. Hitler was a sick and tragic man who carried racism to its
logical conclusion. And he ended up leading a nation to the point of killing about
six million Jews… If one says that I am not good enough to live next door to him,
if one says that I am not good enough to eat at a lunch counter, or to have a good,
decent job, or to go to school with him merely because of my race, he is saying con-
sciously or unconsciously that I do not deserve to exist."

Dr. King was on television all the time. The pros and cons about the march from
Selma to Montgomery were chronicled every day, as was the march itself. Until
1967, when I was in the 11th grade, we didn't have a TV at home. But coming and

going to people's houses, we saw and heard plenty about King; he was the topic of conversation. I'll never forget listening to him on the radio and hearing him say: "A man who won't die for something is not fit to live."

Dr. King helped me conquer my own hate.

One day a husky, blond, red-faced boy at school whom I'll call Ken Jones, gave me a taunting look as he announced to all those in earshot, "Does anybody want to go coon hunting tonight? Me and my uncles plan to go out and kill us some niggers."

Smirking and feeling he'd done something big, Ken slid into his classroom seat, three chairs in front of me. The teacher made no comment on this murder threat, only calling the class to settle down and prepare for the day's lesson.

I couldn't focus. All I could think about was how to strike back and hurt those who were hurting me. Rage took my thoughts to Dad's shotgun; I knew it could take out more of my harassers than the single shot rifle, especially if I positioned myself in the far left corner of the classroom. Hadn't my father praised me as a good shot? I began plotting a killing. I decided I'd need to wear my long beige overcoat to conceal the weapon and use a belt to strap it to my body. I pictured myself living out my rage. It was my lowest moment.

Within minutes, I heard a quiet voice inside my head: "Killing them would only make you one of them." I couldn't tell if the voice belonged to my mother, to Martin Luther King or to Jesus. But I got goose bumps. I vowed to myself and God never to allow anyone to make me hate.

My heroes were teachers who tutored black students, people who registered black voters, and those who housed out-of-towners coming to help, all under threat of lost livelihood or lost life! People who took risks to do good made me realize I wanted to be like them, not stoop to the level of the violent haters. These courageous people showed me what love is and how it works in the world. With the help of such messages, I managed to hold on to my faith.

Not every day at Wetumpka High was traumatic. My black comrades found music and humor to be useful tools for surviving the trauma of our second-class status.

We found ways to have fun at school, too. At first, during lunch hour, black students huddled together at one table. Whenever blacks were seated or standing somewhere, white students in the area would scatter as if we had leprosy.

One day we decided to spread out, each sitting at a different table. For several days, white students stood, lining the walls of the cafeteria while they ate, glaring as we sat leisurely eating, each at a spacious table alone.

The principal came to their rescue, ordering all black students to sit at one table. Undaunted, we did the same with the trees on campus that provided shade in Alabama's blazing August and September heat. We dispersed ourselves, one per tree and enjoyed the shady comfort while indignant white students sweltered.
Finally, whites decided that the foulness of being under a tree with a black student was better than baking in 95-degree heat.

# 12

## THE BOMBING

---

*"There was no sign of arson in the fire of the Bracy's Family home."*

Early in the evening of New Year's Day 1966, Debra and I, several of our younger siblings and a cousin had attended the annual Elmore County Emancipation Celebration – observing President Lincoln's signing the proclamation that freed blacks from slavery. We joined the crowd giving rapt attention to Birmingham civil rights preacher the Reverend Jesse Douglas. His message was powerful. His melodious voice sang out: "I told Jesus that it would be all right if he changed my name," and for most of that sermon, he had us on our feet.

The celebration had special meaning for me. I was in awe of Reverend Douglas for reasons besides his voice and inspiring presence. He was also an albino with a strikingly beautiful wife who sat in the front pew giving her husband her utmost attention. After seeing the Reverend Douglas and his wife, I realized the bias I had about Frank's pigmentation was no different than those students who ridiculed and taunted me at Wetumpka High. I resolved right then and there that I would accept Frank's invitation to start "going together."

We headed home from the Elmore County gathering full of excitement, eager to share our account of the experiences with Mom and Dad. We did, and then it was bedtime. Last I heard was Mom admonishing Debra and Cousin Joyce: "Stop that whispering and go to sleep."

Less than two hours later, at 1 a.m., I awoke to loud explosions, running footsteps and shouting, screaming voices. Dazed, I stumbled into the dining room where I saw fire blazing. Groggy, I thought to myself 'I've got to find something to put this fire out; somebody's gonna be in trouble.'

"Sophia, get out!" Debra screamed. "Get out! The house is all on fire."

Exploding flames blocked every exit but one.

Dad yelled, "Marie, get the children out!", as he grabbed his shotgun and ran out in the cold night air, chasing the lights of a disappearing car.

As I burst outside, I saw Dad running and could hear Mom screaming each of our names and crying at the same time. Even as we answered her, she started over again calling names, to make doubly sure she had heard each of our voices. All 11 of us had made it out.

Earlier that day, one of the white farmers' sons and a nephew had come and asked my father if they could come on our property and look for a lost dog in the woods behind our house. They claimed the dog had taken off the day before while they were coon hunting near our land. Dad was suspicious but, after asking several questions, he consented, as any good country neighbor would.

Homemade firebombs —Molotov cocktails— had hit our home on three different sides. Even after Dad turned in one of the unexploded cocktails that had bounced off the window screen and landed intact in our family's pickup truck, the article in the *Advertiser/Journal* reported the local authorities and Alabama Bureau of Investigation "did not see any signs of arson in the fire of the Bracy's family home."

Local white people even suggested we might have set the fire ourselves to draw attention away from Dad's poor harvest and his not having the money to pay his annual rent. News accounts failed to mention that both our home and the land we farmed belonged to my aunt and uncle, and that their own daughter, Joyce, was spending the night in the house on the night it was destroyed.

The firebombing of our home was in the same rural community where my mother was born. One could say the bombing was, in part, the result of a woman thirsting for education, progress for her race and a better life for her children. She believed that nothing important is gained without pain.

Some in our community, including my Aunt Pearl, blamed Mom for the predicament that left us homeless for over a year. These people would say "Marie, you should have known to stay out of the white folks' way."

What you have to understand is that the old 'separate but equal' system of segregated education provided jobs to black people — decent jobs, not picking cotton, cleaning houses or working as a janitor." If segregation in school went away, those jobs were going away, too. So my Aunt Pearl was active in efforts to make life better for her people but, as a teacher, integration of the schools was a direct threat to her livelihood. And because people knew she was close to my mother, Pearl's home was also in danger of being firebombed.

First my Uncle Charlie and Aunt Lacy, and later, three other neighbors, took us in even though doing so put them in danger. The civil rights activist E.D. Nixon, the Pullman Porter who was a key organizer of the Montgomery Bus Boycott, organized an effort in Montgomery that brought food, cash and enough clothing to fill my uncle's barn.

After the bombing, most of what I knew was not there anymore. Uprooted from everything familiar —clothes, photos, belongings, the landscape — my body felt numb and my mind was in a suspended state. The dread of many months had come to be. My family was grateful that at least our lives had been spared.

A week after the firebombing of our home, we were spread out across four households. We lived separated for two months. Mom and Dad and their three youngest children stayed at my uncle's. The rest of us stayed with neighbors. "As soon as y'all get off the bus, come to your Uncle Charlie's," Mom would reiterate, "and walk together." The three neighbors' homes were located just blocks apart, but Uncle Charlie's house was over a hill and nearly a mile away.

It was a tense, uncertain time, especially for Mom and Dad, with their children separated. Would we be targets again? Would those who sheltered us? No matter how severe the trauma, my parents responded: "Just deal with it."

I know today that, after a trauma, you should encourage people, children especially, to talk about what happened, to discuss their hardship and their fears. But no one told me that in 1966.

I stayed in the home of one of the elderly women I'd often visited, sometimes bringing a Sunday afternoon dessert and always admiring her petunia flower bed.

Mrs. Edith owned a large wood frame house with a raised foundation. Three rooms on each side of the wide hallway provided the solitude I needed during the daytime. But the creaks and sounds of settling wood were nerve-wracking at night. Is someone out there planting dynamite under the house? I prayed for daybreak.

Dad convinced a wealthy landowner to allow him to use an old rundown hay storehouse to bring our family back under one roof. "I talked with Mr. Phil and he said they'd have the hay out by the end of the week. You and Debra and your mama need to go and try to clean it up, 'cause I want us to move by the end of next week." Dad's words stirred excitement inside me — I would be with my family again.

The storehouse was a bare shack: no windows. Yellowed magazine and newspaper pages covered holes in the walls that let in daylight when the paper was pulled back. The floor and ceiling had larger holes. A crumbling fireplace would give way before we vacated the shack a year later. Six of us were in one room with two beds. Mom, Dad and baby slept in the kitchen. If someone wanted privacy for a bath, we went outside the house or under the hill in back. Conversations were about doing what needed to be done to "get through this." Debra and I would stay at Wetumpka High; that was never in question.

Where would we go for good water? The spring we relied on was over a mile away. Who could lend us pens and pencils, writing paper, or a dictionary or encyclopedia for our homework assignments? We didn't know where to turn next.

# 13

## GUARDIAN ANGELS

*"Many white people knew in their hearts that the whole structure of white supremacy was unjust. But they also knew working openly for racial justice would cost them dearly…and they simply weren't willing to pay that high price."*

During these turbulent times I got personal support from Frank Mitchell, and my family got support from two national organizations. Within the week of the fire-bombing, Frank managed to get a ride out to visit my family while we were staying with Uncle Charlie.

Soon after the family got situated in the two-room shack, he came again, and asked permission to spend time with me.

My sister, brother and father looked at this young man who was an albino and then looked at me like: "You can't be serious." But for me, all hesitations, reservations and discomfort were gone.

As for Frank, he seemed to have developed a layer of toughness. I didn't get the sense that people's prejudice bothered him, though in many situations he was ridiculed. With my new awareness, I felt ashamed that I had ever shunned him as a boyfriend.

The guardian angels for my family came from the staff of two national groups, the American Friends Service Committee (AFSC), and the NAACP Legal Defense fund.

The American Friends Service Committee is a Quaker and human rights organization based in Philadelphia. AFSC had an Atlanta-based office, staffed by Constance "Connie" Curry, Winifred Green and Addie Ringfield. Connie and the national office supported us from their Family Aid Fund, and Winifred Green was in the field, troubleshooting in towns around the South where black families were being harassed for having children integrating the schools. There were teachers calling black children "nigger" right in the classroom, and black families being evicted from their homes for having their children enrolled in the "white" public schools.

The NAACP Legal Defense Fund was under the direction of Jean Fairfax in New York. From 1957-1965, she'd run the Southern Civil Rights Program for the American Friends Service Committee, so she knew both organizations very well and worked with Winifred. The NAACP Legal Defense Fund is independent of the NAACP itself, and had played a crucial role in the racial integration of the University of Georgia and the University of Mississippi.

A white couple in Montgomery who were friendly to us were Virginia and Clifford Durr. They were in their 60s and I don't know exactly what made them so liberal on the race issue, but it left them as social outcasts in the white community. Clifford was a lawyer, and Virginia was a friend and supporter of Rosa Parks, who'd started the Montgomery Bus Boycott when she refused to give up her seat to a white man. Clifford, along with lawyer Fred Gray, arranged for Rosa Parks' bail the night of her arrest.

When I saw Mr. Durr one day, he asked me, "What do you watch on TV?"

Well, we didn't have a TV for 15 months because of the firebombing but Mr. Durr pushed the issue a little. He said, "When you can, I want you to start watching public TV." I told him I would.

Connie Curry, Winifred Green and Addie Ringfield, one black and two whites, were traveling weekly from Atlanta and worked frantically to ensure that we stayed in school, had food to eat and the sick ones like John and me could get medical treatment. At the same time, they were gathering resources for the rebuilding of our home.

Winifred Green, the lead AFSC staffer investigating complaints of black families involved in desegregation, was from a prominent white family in Jackson, Mississippi. I'm convinced that many white people of Winifred's generation knew in their hearts that the whole structure of white supremacy was unjust. But they also knew that working openly for racial justice would cost them dearly with their friends and family members, and they simply weren't willing to pay that high price. That was what made Winifred special. She never discussed the alienation from her own family, but we knew that she and her husband had divorced, and her mother had tried to have her committed to a mental hospital for working in civil rights. We all knew that Winifred had paid dearly for her racial justice work.

These were major losses that I believe left her with some hardened feelings about the price she paid; but Winifred readily acknowledged her gains were leading a noble life, being a Christian in the truest sense, and gaining many friendships with the people she had assisted. She was certainly a fixture in my life until her death in 2016.

Winifred assisted my mother, Cousin Annie Mae Williams, Mrs. Carrie Peavy, whose house suspiciously burned to the ground, and several others to organize the Willing Workers group. These mothers of children integrating Elmore County schools documented harassment and presented written accounts to Winifred and the Civic League.

Working closely with the Elmore County Improvement League and the NAACP's Legal Defense Fund, Winifred managed to get the U.S. Justice Department involved in Debra's case. Around December 1, 1965, my parents learned that Debra was cleared to return to school after the holiday break.

But in January of 1966, Debra was assaulted again. "Nigger, who do you think you are, getting off the bus in front of a white person?" Furious football player Michael Shan, who outweighed Debra by 100 pounds, slammed Debra's head with his fist near the front exit of the school bus. Debra had stepped in between Michael and a white girl whose purse strap was caught on a bus seat.

Debra turned and punched Michael's red face and they both went rolling out the door of the bus onto the ground. The door jammed with students straining to see the fight. Though I was sitting up front, it took me forever to make my way off the bus. My heart pounding, I imagined seeing my sister beaten to a pulp. When I got out, I saw blood on Debra's white leather hand-me-down coat. Seconds later, she was being pulled off of Michael by another student and the bus driver.

For Debra, it was off to the principal's office. The blood on her jacket was Michael's — a nosebleed caused when Debra hit him in the face with her purse. He looked stunned. He couldn't have known that Debra had just spent four months seething with rage from her first expulsion from Wetumpka High, along with dismissals from a school in Tuskegee and another in Tuscaloosa, when administrators learned of the Wetumpka fight.

Michael Shan had it coming to him, but this was only Debra's third day back in school since being expelled earlier for something she didn't even do. She was black and had drawn blood from another white kid. There was no guarantee she would be safe in the hands of the law, but fortunately when the fight was reported to the school, there happened to be attorneys from the Justice Department in the school superintendent's office, so things could have turned out even worse than they did.

As it turned out, both she and the white boy were suspended for three days, but this and other complications caused Debra to graduate after a session of summer school instead of walking with the rest of us in the spring. It was one of many indignities she experienced for being so brave and true — and for carrying so much pent-up but justified frustration and anger.

*The Southern Courier's* coverage of the firebombing of our home on January 1,1966. *Photo credit: "Fire Bomb Levels Elmore County Farmhouse". John Klein, Jim Peppler. The Southern Courier,* Jan. 8-9, 1966, Vol. II, No. 2.

At right, Bracy family home prior to the bombing with Sophia's aunt and home owner Sophia Slaughter.

The Bracy Family. Top row left to right: Sophia, Ed and John. Middle left, Charles, Katherine, Georgia and Debra. Bottom right, Aretha, Mom (Mittie Marie) and Dad (Roosevelt). Bottom left to right, Sophia's grandmother Mittie George Fleming; a senior photo from Sophia's graduation from Wetumpka High School in May 1968; and a photo from Sophia and Albert's courtship.

# 14

## THE DAY I TRIED TO TAKE
## MY OWN LIFE

*"I longed to escape the pain of being sick, and the stress of my family's circumstances."*

Not long after moving into the two-room shack, we heard that a Tuskegee Institute student, Sammie Young, was killed by whites for trying to use a white-only restroom at a service station. A few months later, my cousin, Jimmy Lee Williams was killed in Vietnam and the City of Wetumpka refused to allow him to be buried in the City Cemetery.

Jimmy Lee's brother and two sisters were among the 19 students integrating schools in Wetumpka, and his mother, Cousin Annie Mae, let the world know her outrage about this decision. In my grieving for Jimmy Lee and two other family friends killed in Vietnam during this time, I felt their ultimate sacrifice for their country had been a waste.

Later in the year, James Earl Motley, another black man, died in the same jail where Debra had been held a year before. James and a few friends were returning from a night out in Montgomery. Montgomery was a "wet" county, meaning it sold alcohol and Elmore, where we lived, was a "dry" county. Young people drove into Montgomery for entertainment and police would sit near the county line and pull over most blacks and especially black men after a certain time.

Troopers pulled over Motley's car, ordered him and his friends to get out of the car, and began to search the car for alcohol. When James asked the officers why they were being stopped, the troopers slammed him against the car, beat him with Billy clubs, handcuffed him and threw him in the back seat of their patrol car. The next morning James was taken out of his jail cell dead. The Wetumpka sheriff said James had fallen out of his bunk.

Jimmy Lee and James Earl were publicized cases but there were others—the young man who came out to court a girl that I knew from Doby High and was found ambushed in his car off the side of the road—rumors were this girl was also secretly seeing a white boy. Events like these added to my worries about safety and what life held for me. In a world where the powers that be gave my life so little value, and the justice system did not exist for dark-skinned people like me, the answer to my earlier question, "What did they do wrong?" was becoming clearer. What they did wrong was being born black.

Whether from the emotional toll or the physical surroundings, I was sicker during the time we lived in the shack. I longed to escape the pain of being sick, and the stress of my family circumstances. One day I was home from school suffering from harsh menstrual cramps and a bad cold. My siblings were at school and Mom and Dad were away. Lying in bed all alone, I wailed, "Why am I being punished for being a girl? Why couldn't I be born a boy? God, this is so unfair!"

A calm settled over me as I decided to end it all. Mom had left a bottle of over-the-counter pain reliever on the table for me to take for my cold and cramps. Not wanting to be selfish by taking all of the medicine, I counted out seven tablets —about half of what was in the container. I hoped I would fall asleep and never wake up.

Soon after swallowing these pain reliever caplets, I felt nausea setting in. Was it the pills or my menstrual cycle, I wondered? I started vomiting, and it seemed I was trying to throw up all of my insides. It went on forever. When she returned, Mom was worried that I looked worse than when she left.

But I never told her or anyone else that I had tried to take my own life. I was 16 years old when my pastor, the Reverend J.L. Jones, preached a sermon about what the Apostle Paul said about the role of women in the Church. Quoting Paul in First Corinthians, the pastor said: "Women should be silent in the churches. For they are not permitted to speak, but should be subordinate, as the law also says. If there is anything they desire to know, let them ask their husbands at home. For it is shameful for a woman to speak in church."

I had heard this message preached before. But on this Sunday, my spirit recoiled, and I thought: "This doesn't make sense, Paul." If we were waiting for my father to speak in Church, we wouldn't be there. If the women of our Church didn't pray, sing, teach Sunday School lessons, and read scriptures for devotional service when no deacon was present, we would basically have no church!

Why couldn't women preach, or lead devotion if a deacon was present, or serve as a deacon or on the Trustee Board, when women raised most of the money to be counted and kept the Church going? These scriptures made no sense to me. Only six months after the bombing, with my family living in a shack, I was doing some serious questioning of God about the fairness of things.

But remember, Mom and all of my Sunday School teachers had taught me that to disagree with the Word of God was to commit blasphemy, which would bring death and damnation upon my soul.

So the next morning, I spoke silent words to God. I told Him that I didn't agree with the Apostle Paul or with my own pastor about the role of women in the Church. I said to myself, 'God, I've been taught I have committed blasphemy against your Word and will be struck dead. I have waited all night and I am tired of being scared. So please go ahead and do it.'

It was mid-morning and I went outside of the shack, looked up to the sky with my eyes closed and waited. After ten minutes or so, when nothing had happened, I took tentative steps back inside. I was not struck dead — not that morning nor any other. In the wake of that, I felt a deep sense of relief and an amazing freedom to question God about Biblical teachings that seemed to contradict other Scriptures. My relationship with God became more personal.

# 15

## A SUDDEN AND
## FRIGHTENING DEMAND

*"How could a homeless couple with eight children, uprooted from
the land and their livelihood, come up with $7,500 in ten days?"*

Three years before we integrated Wetumpka High, the landowner who provided
the hay shack had allowed Dad to start making payments toward the purchase of 40
acres of land he agreed to sell us for $10,000. Dad owed $7,500 on this purchase of
land that joined 80 acres owned by Uncle Charlie on one side and 40 acres owned
by my Aunt Frances on the other. It was in an ideal location.

The AFSC staff prodded the Farmers Home Administration (FHA) to provide a
loan so my parents could finish paying off the land and buy building materials. But
someone in the FHA tipped off the white authorities in town, who swiftly informed
the landowner's adult sons.

The landowner came to Dad a month after we were in the house and said his sons
were upset with him for selling the land. He said Dad would have to have it totally
paid off within ten days or he would lose it. Both of them knew that was next to
impossible, and it didn't take a genius to realize that Dad might not get back any of
the $2,500 he had already paid.

This was a sudden and frightening demand.

Dad's papers, which only showed the amount paid already, not the agreement to
sell, had all burned in the fire. If it came to a legal challenge, it was a poor black
farmer's word against a wealthy white landowner.

How could a homeless couple with eight children, uprooted from the land and their
only livelihood, come up with $7,500 in 10 days? Even if my parents did so, they

would likely be kicked out of the landowner's shack. Mom and Dad were in a panic, trying to save this land, their only hope for keeping their family together. Where would we go?

Our front-line respondents were AFSC staff from field level to the top leadership. They worked like beavers to hire a lawyer, do a title search, locate funds and create a repayment plan that Mom and Dad could afford.

Within 10 days, Dad was able to present the landowner with a check for $7,500. The 40 acres became his and Mom's land. AFSC loans provided the land payment and a further $5,000 for supplies to rebuild our home. Fifteen months after we were firebombed, we moved into our new home, with running water for the first time in our lives. It took Mom and Dad seven years, but they proudly repaid those loans.

I'll never forget the devotion of these community organizers, the hundreds of hours of travel they spent on remote, often unfriendly roads in rural Alabama. They put themselves at risk from angry whites each time they came to see us and offered assistance. They treated us with great respect and dignity. Mom sent letters to the AFSC, and the AFSC staff wrote back, encouraging her to make calls to officials whom the staff had already contacted. The AFSC understood that my parents needed to learn how to ask questions of local officials and build relationships with those officials.

The generosity of the AFSC had a profound impact on me and my family. It showed the positive side of humanity and modeled caring, compassionate service. The relationships I built with the AFSC continue to this day.

# 16

## THE KILLING OF DR. KING

*"Don't give them the satisfaction of seeing you cry."*

On the night of April 3, 1968, about six weeks before my high school graduation, our family watched on television as Dr. King delivered his "been to the mountain-top" speech from the Mason Temple in Memphis, Tennessee. The message and the moment had seemed full of foreboding: "the time is near…" Mom was known to have premonitions. She kept saying, "Lord take care of him. Lord take care of him."

Just 24 hours later, Martin Luther King, Jr. was dead, and Mom sat stuffing her right fist into her left palm over and over. "I knew it," she kept saying. "I knew it. I knew it."

When Moses died, Joshua was there to lead the Hebrew people into the Promised Land. Who would lead black people to a place of equality in America? Who would be our Joshua?

The night the news came over the television that Dr. King had been assassinated, mom wailed: "Lord, what are we going to do now?" We were all crying as we sat glued to the TV.

When Dr. King started speaking out against the Vietnam War, it hurt me to hear some black folk turn against him. When he was killed, I lost a leader, a mentor, and a family member. Dr. King taught me not to act out of fear, and not to be like the oppressors we were in struggle against.

He touched me when he said in a sermon in the last year of his life: "You may be 38 years old, as I happen to be. And one day, some great opportunity stands before you and calls you to stand up for some great principle, some great issue, some great cause. And you refuse to do it because you are afraid…. You refuse to do it because you want to live longer…. You're afraid that you will lose your job, or… that you will lose your popularity, or you're afraid that somebody will stab you, or shoot at you or bomb your house; so you refuse to take the stand. Well, you may go on and live until you are 90, but you're just as dead at 38 as you would be at 90. And the cessation of breathing in your life is but the belated announcement of an earlier death of the spirit."

I dreaded the bus ride to Wetumpka High the next day knowing there was sure to be "a celebration." As the bus got closer to the school, we picked up the most obnoxious of the riders. These guys were cheering, slapping fists and one of them cut me so hard emotionally when he started a wail "Oh I am so, oh so sad."

"Why, Bobby?" another asked.
"Cause somebody else beat me to killing Martin Luther Coon."

The bus driver could see my tears starting to well up from his rear-view mirror. He turned part way said in a low voice "don't let them know they are getting next to you. Keep your chin up." Once more, this one kindness washed away a sea of insults.

All the black students decided to stay home from school on the day of Martin Luther King's funeral. When King's funeral was announced, we were suddenly informed that an oral report on Shakespeare's Macbeth, a requirement to graduate, would be due on that date and attendance was mandatory.

In spite of the threat of not being allowed to graduate, I, along with Debra and Ed, went to Atlanta. Winifred Green drove us; we could never have gotten near there otherwise. She parked her car as close to Ebenezer Baptist Church as possible. Our location was fairly close to the front door, and we saw Harry Belafonte, Bobby Kennedy and Mahalia Jackson, up close.

Next day, back at school, we were all hauled into the auditorium to make our case with the principal, who was new that semester. He went down the line alphabetically, questioning each student:

"Debra, why were you absent on yesterday?"

"Sir, I had gotten this bad stomach bug and could hardly leave my bed."

Next, it was my turn: "Sophia why were you absent? You had that bug too?"
"Yes, sir, I had that bug too!"

My brother was next, and before the principal could say a word, Ed blurted out: "Mr. Webb, that was a mean ole bug; it had all of us down like something awful."

Mr. Webb turned and asked the rest of the black students:

"You all had bugs in your houses, too?"
They responded in chorus, "Yes, sir, we sure did."
"You all are excused. Go on to class and I don't want to hear of any more bug tales."

On graduation morning it was chaos at the house: ironing clothes, curling hair, putting on make-up that melted faster than we could apply it in the Alabama summer heat. Most mornings, Dad would have been doing something outside long before we left for school. But this morning, he stayed in the house, quietly observing the flurry of activity. It wasn't his style to say he was proud of Debra and me for integrating the white folks' high school. But he didn't have to say it; I could read it on his face.

Four of us packed ourselves into the pick-up truck's cab, as mom urged dispatch. We got to the school and I made my way to the seniors' line up. "Pomp and Circumstance" started, and the march began. I remember looking over at the trees where we had held our ground, not far from where we made that long walk through a taunting sea of angry faces. What a difference three years make. I thought of all who paved the way for this moment. We made history.

Coming so soon after Martin Luther King's murder, graduation from Wetumpka High was bittersweet. The seven black graduates in the Class of '68 was the largest-ever group of black graduates from a single year at Wetumpka High. Family and friends poured out their jubilation at our success; I was ecstatic with all the well wishes and cards with money.

But the occasion was tinged with sadness on account of Debra. She still had summer school classes to take and was not allowed to walk across the stage with the rest of us.

Although many of my memories of the three years at Wetumpka High are painful, my thought of our bus driver, Robert Greer, brings a smile and affirms my belief that each of us has the capacity for kindness. Nearly thirty years after these turbulent times, I called and spoke with him, letting him know how much his kindness meant to me during this scary time. He was happy to express how he felt about blacks being no different from whites. He had grown up believing this was true and tried to live by this belief although he got flack for doing so. He added that he thought we were so brave, and he wanted to know how every black student that rode his bus was doing, calling each by name. Through tears he said I had "made his day." That call I felt was an act of kindness long overdue.

# 17

## TWO SUMMER PROJECTS

*"Sophia, you are doing the same thing to me that he did to you—
judging me based upon my skin color."*

Two weeks after receiving my diploma from Wetumpka High, I was in Brandon, Vermont. A letter from Winifred Green and Connie Curry had landed me a scholarship at an AFSC summer community service project. For the next 10 weeks, my new family was 15 youngsters ages 16 to 18. Two were Native Americans, two were African American and the rest were white.

Our counselors, a white couple in their 30s, were supervising our work as volunteers to the Vermont State Hospital for the Mentally Retarded. The program was meant to foster greater understanding and enhance racial harmony while providing a service needed in Brandon.

After getting the letter of my acceptance, it was a mad rush to prepare myself for being away for the summer. I used cash from graduation gifts to buy clothes and toiletries. I was met at the Rutland airport by a balding white male and a white male teenager. "Hi, Sophia, I'm Jim McGuire, one of your counselors. This is Bill Robb, a fellow participant this summer."

I thanked Jim for picking me up, trying not to reveal how scared I was. Clutching my two bags, I walked with Jim and Bill to the car for the 30-minute drive to Brandon. I'd never been to New England before and was amazed by the lush green mountains, pastures and wood-framed colonial-style homes. I'd only seen such things in textbooks.

During the ride, Jim chatted about the project; he told me this was his and Betty's first time as counselors for an American Friends Service Committee summer project and told me how excited they were about the group of young people selected.

I felt like a stranger in these parts, and a black stranger. Although it was called a "hospital," the buildings and grounds felt like a school campus. We stayed in a dorm-like structure with a kitchen, dining area, meeting room and sleeping quarters surrounded by a volleyball and tennis court on one side and a park with swings on the other.

Three days after my arrival in Brandon, I was rushed to the nearest hospital in Rutland, Vermont for an emergency appendectomy. I'd been sick to my stomach and throwing up since my arrival and thought it was my usual monthly sickness. What a start to my new life.

Jim and Betty McGuire tried to calm my fears and locate my parents the day before the Fourth of July. They, too, were scared; they'd never been counselors before. Several days later, my mother arrived, and stayed with me until I was released from the hospital. She was fired when she returned home; her supervisor had refused to grant her leave from her domestic job at a local hospital.

Mom was the only black face I saw while at the hospital. One day I was looking out the window of my room and a kid in a section across the wing in front of me looked startled to see me. He hurried away from the window and returned with a nurse, pointing at me as if he'd seen a boogeyman.

Back at the campus, residents would ask, "When did you have your accident?" meaning "How did you get burned?" I almost felt like I was back at Wetumpka High. The contact was not hateful, but I was treated as an oddity. It was a boost to my recovery to have Mom with me at the hospital and for a few days after returning to the camp.

A white fellow in the group from Ithaca, New York was usually the first to respond during our discussions. Most whites in our group came from families of wealth; non-whites were from racially oppressed groups in this country or another country.

We sat in a circle, in a Quaker-style meditation. Jim and Betty asked us to respond to questions about our brushes with the race issue and to tell the group what we hoped to achieve that summer. Bruce was talking when Jim interrupted to ask: "Sophia what's wrong? You seem disinterested. Are you feeling okay?"

Jolting me from somewhere, I answered "Yes." I didn't care what motivated Bruce to spend his summer in Vermont, nor what my own reasons were for being there. My face couldn't hide my feelings. Why was I angry with Bruce? He'd done nothing to provoke my disdain and seemed perplexed by my attitude. Finding my voice, I said "Bruce, I don't like you." When he asked why, I said, "Your deep red skin with rust spots on your neck and your piercing blue eyes remind me of the white man who bragged about firebombing our home."

Bruce said, "Sophia you are doing the same thing to me that he did to you — judging me based upon my skin color." That comment rocked my world. I cried because I knew Bruce was right.

Upon graduation from Wetumpka High I believed that all but a few white people in the world were unkind. My thoughts and consciousness of the world were framed around the people I'd grown up with through church, school, and work in the rural South. The exception was imaginary images and ideas caught from reading books and magazine stories.

Upon arriving in Vermont, I became ill and totally dependent on a white couple who became my surrogate parents. The other interns were my family and assisted me with healing, helping me with my bath, bringing my meals and waiting for me to catch up when we traveled.

My thinking evolved… Maybe it's just Southern whites who are mean and evil.

Lazing in a Vermont stream one day, I drifted off from the group, accidentally slid down some slippery rocks into a strong current and was afraid I might drown. When I called for help, I was rescued by a total stranger, a white man camping with his family.

I left Brandon, Vermont feeling that a large part of my injured soul had been healed. This family-like experience, my becoming ill and the support I received from Jim and Betty who also became substitute parents, started to create a balm for the injuries of the past three years.

But the mindset of white people in Alabama still seemed miles away from that kind of fairness and justice. A month later, I was enrolled in a two-year Christian college in Montgomery, because it was close to home, and met the conditions of my scholarship from the NAACP Legal Defense and Educational Fund.

This Christian college had only recently been integrated. I was thrust back into my days at Wetumpka High by the attitudes of various students and professors. In one class, a sociology professor spoke of the IQ inferiority of blacks to whites. In a Bible class, the professor, who was a minister, used Scripture to justify slavery.

When I spoke out in disagreement, he responded, "You are a prime example of blacks needing to have masters; you don't know how to obey authority." This was hard to hear, but my summer in Brandon had given me the courage to verbally challenge my oppressors.

Just as I had settled into the notion that blacks were God's chosen people, I had the chance to be part of a second summer project, this one at the Columbia Point Housing Project near Dorchester, Massachusetts.

My first night at Columbia Point, after finishing kitchen duty, I asked the kitchen helper, a white male named Jack, to walk with me to the mailbox. I was anxious to send back the $25 my mother had given me as travel money, which was all she had. Jack was a Brandeis University law student who loved reciting Robert Frost poems. He was fascinated by my life as a Southern black farm child in a family of 10; he was a doctor's only child from New Hampshire.

Another time Jack and I caught a train and walked through Cambridge Park. All the while Jack was humming "Rose, Rose, Rose, Rose / Will I ever see thee wed? / I will marry at thy will, sire / At thy will." Before the summer was over, he had asked me to go steady with him. I told him I was already spoken for. I also told him I didn't trust myself dating a white guy — there was no telling what I might do if I woke up in the middle of the night and saw a white man in my bed.

He thought I was joking.

My $25 never made it to Mom; the mailbox was blown up that night, just one of many acts of violence in a turf war between two sparring black militant groups.

Columbia Point, with its 1,500 units of public housing built in the early 1950s, was by 1969 a configuration of high-rise buildings with poor plumbing, crumbling ceilings, broken elevators and very little air conditioning. Residents tried to find relief sitting on the stoops, fanning and being entertained by kids jumping rope and running through water sprinklers.

One evening, after walking up six flight of stairs to my apartment, which I shared with two others, I noticed a guy lying face down in the hallway a couple of doors from my place. Thinking he was drunk, I carefully made my way around him and went inside, putting on both security locks. A short time later, curious about the commotion, I stuck my head out my door and was shocked to see two policemen. The man lying in the hallway was dead.

Columbia Point is no longer a housing project; it's been turned into an upscale waterfront project, called Harbor Point. When I was there the complex was surrounded by a city dump on one end and a water pumping station on the other.

AFSC was present along with other social services, religious and justice groups trying to aid residents who felt isolated, abandoned and cut off from the city of Boston. Black militant groups were in a struggle, we were told, for the heart of the growing number of black residents.

Our AFSC team included someone from Ghana, someone from Nigeria, a Frenchman, four whites and me. A Catholic church which had several nuns involved in mission work was also part of our network.

A community meeting presided over by one of the black militant leaders put to the test my secret belief that black people were God's chosen ones. Someone asked: "Who wants to share what they think should happen to help residents seize the power to change conditions here at Columbia Point?" After several comments, one of the two white nuns began to speak.

The leader interrupted: "You don't live here; what makes you think folks want to hear your____ opinion? That's the problem now; Whitey trying to run every_ thing___ and don't give a ___ about what happens to the folks who live in this _____."

I raised my hand and, when acknowledged, I said, "We all are here trying to help. You don't need to be disrespectful, even if you disagree with the lady's opinion."

"Who are you?" he challenged.

"I am Sophia Bracy."

"Where are you from?"

"I'm from Alabama, working here for the summer."

I cannot capture in presentable words his response to me, but it included sending me back to Alabama in a pine box if I ever corrected him again.

AFSC leaders worried about my safety. I was less worried, especially after coming into my apartment two nights later and finding this leader in bed with one of my white roommates. We made eye contact, and when he saw the disgust on my face, he turned his head.

I had been thinking that black people must be God's chosen ones because we are the downtrodden. After all, Scripture says the last shall be first and first shall be last. But in Dorchester, I was physically threatened by one of those working for the liberation of black people. Was this about freedom of our people or a means for power and control for themselves? I felt wounded from the verbal attack and began to distrust those calling for a black revolution.

This incident and the conditions of the housing project also left me feeling unsettled. How could people live like this, right on top of each other, garbage everywhere? Young people disrespecting the elderly, young mothers smoking weed on the stoop in front of their children. I was bewildered. In the South, we were poor and without, but there was a level of self-respect, a desire to do better. Here I saw mostly anger, hopelessness and a lack of caring.

One day, trying to escape the madness around me, I walked down toward the water, picking my way over large rocks. Finding a perfect spot facing the faded sun with only the hint of color left, I sat looking out at the water, oblivious to my surroundings. The voice of one of our leaders shook me out of my stupor.

"What are you doing down here by yourself?"

"I just needed some time alone," I said, surprised by the irritation in her voice.

"Alone? What do you mean 'alone?' Look around; don't you know you've got a thousand pairs of eyes watching you from these high rises? Sophia, you've put yourself, and this project, in danger. Don't do this again."

I felt like a caged bird. Disheartened and disillusioned, I yearned for the South. The memories of living there were painful, but my soul needed the natural beauty of my own region, and its open space.

I also believed I could somehow make a difference in my homeland.

If blacks were not God's chosen people, then who were we? To break out of my sadness, I focused on my upcoming marriage and the plans I would be making in Chicago right after leaving Boston. Chicago was another big city. Would Frank and I end up in a high rise like Columbia Point?

Midway through my freshman year of college, before I arrived at my Community Service Project at the Columbia Point Housing Project, Frank and I got engaged. We were very young and couldn't know the future. But we were wise enough to identify two qualities which had to remain sacred in our relationship. First, we had to be faithful to each other, with no boyfriends or girlfriends on the side; and we had to always be honest with each other.

Three months later, Frank left Alabama and moved to Chicago. I was against it. He said, "Sophia, I want to make a good start for our upcoming wedding by having some money saved."

"But you haven't finished college yet!" I begged Frank to stay in school.

"Sophia, once we're settled, I promise I'll finish the final two semesters." He was stubbornly determined to make some money before we got married.

Having grown up in a home where money was often short, I respected his wanting to be a good provider. With misgivings, I let Frank go to Chicago.

# 18

## FINDING ALBERT

---

*"In the summer of 1970, I was 21 years old, enjoying a new love, my
first chance to serve as a counselor, to be part of a Latino
community and having my first birthday party."*

I left Boston and headed to Chicago to make plans for a December wedding. But
two days later, I was headed home, heartbroken.

Frank had been distracted and distant in Chicago.

"Talk to me, Frank! What's going on?"
"Sophia, I don't know what you talking about." "Who was that woman?"
"What woman?"
"You ran your fingers through her hair today at the job!"
"My God, Sophia she's just a friend. Why are you trying to make something out
of it?"
"If that's the case, why was she glaring at me every time I looked in her direction?"
"You're being silly, and I don't want to talk about it anymore."

Frank's small flat suddenly felt cold and unwelcoming. With tears in my eyes, I
started to put my clothes back in my bag. It was still not too late for him to explain,
to promise he would stop seeing this other woman… to show some sympathy for
the horror of my position. I'd come expecting to be getting ready for my wedding,
and discovered I'd lost my man to another woman.

But Frank's only reaction to seeing me packing was to try to pull me into a
half-hearted embrace. I wasn't interested in that. On the plane ride from Chicago
to Montgomery, I felt my world had broken apart. I wanted to die. I remember
wishing the plane would crash, then rebuking myself for the thought, when the

other passengers had done nothing to deserve to die.

A week later, I sent Frank my engagement ring. Our four-year relationship was over. Although he made several trips home to try and reconcile, trust was broken and nothing would change my mind. His mother and I remained friends.

Seven months after breaking my engagement with Frank, I met Albert.

He and two of his buddies had come to my college, to meet some girls. Where Frank had been quiet and well read, a prolific writer who spoke of love and beauty in poetry and rhyme, Albert excelled in football, basketball, track and his favorite, baseball. He didn't like reading, had a temper and could out-curse my dad. He was handsome and a straight shooter. Not a lot of lofty talk from Albert. You always knew exactly what was on his mind, and you heard it in vivid language. "What are you trying to say?" was one of his milder statements.

Several weeks after we met, we went to meet my family in Wetumpka. Albert was from a smaller family, four children and his parents. His mother was a homemaker and his dad worked several jobs, including as a maintenance man for several law firms. Albert's folks lived in a Montgomery housing project but all of his siblings, Helen, Delores and Lawrence, had college degrees.

Wanting to impress my parents, Albert wore his latest tailoring project, a Curtis Mayfield "Superfly" outfit with a brim hat, and sported a diamond ring. When he came to pick me up at my dorm, he was overdressed for the country but I held my tongue. Albert made a poor first impression on my parents. Mom was adamant: "You don't need to be involved with this city slickster!" Dad was silent, but had to ask Albert to make a second entrance with the proper greeting, "Good evening" instead of "Hey." There was some repairing to be done.

I was attracted to Albert's honesty and directness, but spent many years trying to change the latter. You always knew when it was time to move out of his way. I was fascinated and bothered by his profanity. Early in our relationship, I pointed out that he had filled a complete sentence entirely with curse words, except for its conjunctions. I'd never heard that done before.

In the little town of Luna Pier, nestled along Lake Erie between Toledo, Ohio and Detroit, Michigan, with sprawling fields of beans and corn, Albert joined me in the final weeks of this last AFSC summer. In the summer of 1970, I was 21 years old, enjoying a new love, relishing my first chance to serve as a counselor, living as part of a Latino community, and having my first birthday party.

In the company of my summer family, Albert seemed withdrawn, but then he was one of only two black males in a group of 15. I was the only black female. We'd spent the past two months setting up a halfway house and medical facility for migrant families on the grounds of a Catholic camp. My attachment to mothers whose children were sick and adults with infected cuts heightened my sense that our efforts were needed. Still, we'd illegally occupied the Catholic camp. I had never broken the law before and it was unsettling to know that, if the camp was raided, we could all be arrested.

During the summer I had gotten to know staff working with the Farm Labor Organizing Committee (FLOC) in Toledo, whose offices were firebombed that summer. I'd joined a march in Ann Arbor, Michigan, led by Cesar Chavez. I thought to myself during the march, "You never marched with Martin Luther King but you can feel pride and camaraderie marching with this hero of migrant families and Mexican-Americans." My consciousness expanded as I saw oppression hurting another racial group.

Kalman, my co-counselor, was a Jewish law student in his final year at Oberlin College. He saw my consciousness and leadership expanding with migrant families and insisted I check out his school. Before the summer was over, I'd been offered a full scholarship to Oberlin. Kalman was deeply hurt when I chose to return to Alabama and attend Auburn University. But it wasn't just that I wanted to be closer to Albert.

I had resolved at the end of the Summer Project at Columbia Point to try to make a difference in my own state of Alabama. Albert was value added.

I started to believe that maybe the trustworthy whites were wealthy non-Southerners. After all, most of the assistance to my family came from people who lived in other parts of the country. It was there, in Luna Pier, Michigan, that this thought was challenged.

As a counselor, I confronted one of the young participants on the project who was violating a project rule. She reached for her wealth card. "You can't tell me what to do," she said, all indignant. "I bet it's my parents' money that allows you to be here in the first place." I had sensed this "charity" attitude before, but this young woman was the first to verbalize it. Her words cut deeply and left me wondering who I could trust.

I didn't know how vulnerable my sense of self was after the trauma of Wetumpka High. Now I see that my summer experiences not only showed me what service looked like, but saved me from being pulled into one-sided thinking about whole groups of people.

Without faith, I could never have coped with the harsh realities of racism. But working for three summers with Mormons, Muslims, Buddhists and Christian adherents of liberation theology, I began to see how people have used religion to support systems of race and gender inequity. This broadened my understanding of God and the role of women and created tensions in my faith walk later on.

# 19

## AUBURN UNIVERSITY

*"I was determined to graduate from Auburn, no matter what. I wasn't going to let my parents down, or give any satisfaction to those who had firebombed my house or harassed me at Wetumpka High."*

The first year in college is an adjustment for a young person, and especially for someone like me from a home without a lot of book learning and from schools that haven't provided a lot of nurturing and study skills.

To say my first semester at Auburn was rather stressful is an understatement. First of all, no dorm room on campus awaited me. I had to find a room in a private-ly-owned facility near the school, called Cox Dorm. I also managed to find a good roommate, Cynthia McMillian. But our living quarters were so bare that we had to dress them up a little or we'd go crazy. A friend gave us a lift to a department store in town and there, on a very tight budget, we picked up some bedspreads, curtains for the windows, and a few other colorful things.

A black saleslady there was very helpful, showing us merchandise and helping us see what pieces of fabric would match with other pieces. She seemed proud that we were attending Auburn University and even gave us her name and phone number and invited us to dinner sometime. When Cynthia and I got back to Cox Dorm and put the new curtains up in the windows and the new bedspreads on our beds, the room looked much more like a home.

Cox Dorm served three meals a day during the week. But on weekends, it didn't serve any food at all. I had very little pocket money and on weekends ate a whole lot of crackers and canned Vienna sausage.

I also had academic challenges to face. Two of my courses were "weed outs" for transfer students: Spanish and World History. When I arrived, slightly late, to my first day of World History, the only seats left were in the very back rows of a big auditorium with poor acoustics. There must have been 350 students in between me and the professor, a foreigner who spoke English with a thick accent. I had a sinking feeling in the pit of my stomach when I realized I could barely understand a word this man said.

My summer in Luna Pier had made me want to learn Spanish, but I saw right away it had been a mistake to try to learn the language as a college course. Almost all of the other students in my class had taken Spanish in high school. They were way ahead of me.

As a transfer student, if you did not maintain at least a C average, you could not remain at Auburn University. I was determined to graduate from Auburn, no matter what. I wasn't going to let my parents down, or give any satisfaction to those who had firebombed my house or harassed me at Wetumpka High.

So I needed a plan. I decided I was going to drop the World History class, and I was going to make friends with my Spanish professor.

The deadline for dropping classes had passed so I had to get an academic dean to sign off on my dropping World History. I assumed this would be rather easy, but it was not. When the dean asked me why I needed to drop the class, instinct told me that the truth was a luxury I could not afford. Instead, I told the dean a big fat lie that I had a job cleaning someone's house at the exact time that World History was meeting.

The dean frowned and asked me for the name and phone number of my employer. My heart pounding, I gave him the name and number of the black saleslady at the department store. As soon as my meeting with the dean ended, I was on the phone with that poor saleslady, begging her to back up my story that I was doing housework for her, and it had to be done at that certain hour! I don't know if she ever spoke to the dean, but my request to drop World History was approved. What a relief.

Now, how to make friends with my Spanish professor? I began by knocking on his office door, telling him that failing his course was not an option for me and that, despite my shyness and poor Spanish speaking skills, I really did want to learn to speak the language. I asked if he would tutor me.

Over the next weeks and months, he gave me several private sessions. But speaking Spanish did not come easily to me and the night before our final exam, I prayed to God for some divine intervention. The next morning, I came into that exam room so full of nerves, watching the door for the professor to arrive any minute, carrying an exam that just might cost me my place at Auburn University.

Five minutes passed, and then ten, with no sign of our professor. My fellow students were puzzled and then annoyed. After twenty minutes, they got up and left. I stayed right where I was. Half an hour late, the professor came rushing in, out of breath, shirttail untucked, apologizing profusely. He said he'd overslept. He seemed to deeply appreciate that at least one of his students was still in the room. I took the exam, and gave it everything I had.

Expecting that some of my fellow students might complain about the professor not showing up on the day of the exam, I wrote a note to the head of the Spanish Department saying how much I appreciated the tutoring my professor had given me. It so happened that I was able to deliver my message of appreciation about the professor directly to the department head. I handed him a note and gave my personal testimony as well. Somehow, I got a C in that course. It must have been either kindness or divine intervention!

I had to change my major from Sociology to Family and Child Development, which didn't require two semesters of a foreign language. But I maintained that "C" average and four years later I graduated from Auburn University with great pride.

Cynthia and I had both transferred from local two-year religious schools, hers sponsored by black Baptists, and we were both caregivers for siblings in our large families. But in personality, we were as different as night and day. Cynthia was a jokester, loved to party, met no strangers and went to bed late. I was serious, loved to read, reserved in making friends, went to bed early, and engaged in no sport activities. I didn't care that Auburn's quarterback, Pat Sullivan, won the Heisman Trophy.

Ten years after college, Cynthia and I reconnected and found we had married the same year, each had two children, one biological and the other adopted, and were both directing non-profit groups for children. Our husbands became good friends and for the past 15 years we have worshiped at the same church. Our friendship continues.

As a work study student, I was a credit counselor, working at the Alabama Council on Human Relations (ACHR), servicing families trying to buy federally subsidized homes through the Housing and Urban Development (HUD) program. Although I didn't know it at the time, ACHR was the first bi-racial group in Alabama and were testing Alabama's Jim Crow law making such a group illegal. Dr. Jerry Roden, Executive Director of the Council, was also the Auburn University English professor who had tutored my sister Debra when she was expelled from Wetumpka High. He tutored me as well. Jerry's wife Rebecca worked in the Graduate School on campus.

There weren't a lot of people in Alabama working for racial equality and social justice. It was a tight network of people who mostly worked warmly and well with each other. Had I been raised in a state like New York or California, I believe statewide connections in the social justice field would have come much more slowly, or not at all.

One of my most important lessons about finance and credit came, not from a course, but a financial transaction of my own. Auburn University had a vast, sprawling campus and, if I was going to arrive at my classes on time, I dearly needed a car. I had never asked for any kind of loan before but I put my pride aside, and asked Dr. Roden if he would loan me $500 so I could buy a 1956 Ford. To my surprise, he said no.

What he offered instead was to meet me at the Auburn University Credit Union, where he co-signed a loan with me for $500. I opened a savings account there and deposited the $500. After getting the seller to take a small deposit and hold the car for three months, I repaid my loan to the Credit Union from the savings account and was able to buy the car on my own signature. It was a proud moment and my first lesson in navigating the waters of borrowing and lending — a good lesson on the value of credit in our capitalist system.

I felt I had to be focused and "all business" at Auburn University, except for my weekends with Albert. We spent most of those weekends at Chewacla State Park, a few miles from the campus, or chugging the 54 miles in my balky "new" Ford, to visit my family in Wetumpka. Albert was now a student at the two-year college I had attended before coming to Auburn, and he was working part-time at an auto shop. I pressed him into service as my car mechanic.

My second lesson came as a work study student at the non-profit Dr. Roden had co-founded. I worked as a credit counselor to people trying to buy homes with federal assistance. I interviewed people with poor credit scores, to find out why. It was a sobering task. Some people simply lied about their poor credit ratings, but many had no clue that their doctor, furniture or hardware store sent data to the credit bureau that now stood in the way of their qualifying to buy a home.

When probed, they would answer: "Oh, no, I have a good relationship with that store. If I have to be late with a payment, I let them know. They tell me: 'You're a good customer, just pay when you can.'" For people who had made late payments, under hard circumstances, I often wrote letters explaining the circumstances. This might help their credit rating, but the lesson was clear: do everything you can to pay your bills right on time. Check your credit often. Complain by letter if you've received an unfair credit rating. Good credit can be crucial to acquiring major assets.

In my work at ACHR, I identified with the families I worked with. Many reminded me of my own family seeking help after the firebombing. These black families, trying to better their lives, were coming up against unjust systems, like those Mom and Dad had met when they needed to rebuild our home and were denied services by the Farmers Home Administration (FHA). For the first time, I sensed how I might work to push against these unfair systems. It reminded me of the work of Winifred Green, Connie Curry and Addie Ringfield.

Nancy Spears, my immediate supervisor and Head Start Director, would later become a founding director on the board of the organization I would direct for more than 40 years.

On another trip to the Durrs to pick up Mom, Mr. Durr asked me: "How are things at Auburn?" I said they were good. He asked: "Are you watching public television?" Knowing this was his pet cause, I said, "Yes, I am."

Clifford asked, "What programs do you watch on public TV?" He caught me! I was busted. But neither of us minded too much. That was just Clifford Durr's way of showing that he cared about me and wanted me to take every chance I could to broaden my education.

In 1971, the United States was in the eighth year of fighting a losing war in Vietnam, "the pill" was widely available and I was entering my senior year at Auburn.

My white roommate and I worked at the same organization and she had already obtained her degree and was moving forward with her career in social justice. Our relationship not only encouraged me with my writing skills but helped me to be clear about the focus of my goals. Yes, there was a social revolution taking place in the country and all around us — college kids felt they had the freedom to smoke grass, drink to excess and have as many sexual partners as they wanted. I wanted no part of this particular revolution, but became even more resolved in my commitment to the Civil Rights Movement and human rights everywhere. My determination was paramount to not get arrested, kicked out of school or have my goals derailed. Uppermost in my mind was the sacrifices of my parents and others as I was nearing the finish line of obtaining my degree.

The Civil War ended in Alabama on May 4, 1865, and nearly 439,000 slaves learned either from the invading federal army or from their former owners that they were slaves no longer but free people, free to come and go, to marry whom they chose, keep whatever money they earned, and to keep their families together.

But chains are not only physical things; there are also chains of the mind. Both white and black people had mental chains left over from the brutal catastrophe of slavery. Poverty, poor education and self-hate are some of those chains in the minds of black people, and I regard those things with great sadness.

My going to Auburn University was a tangible effort to get educated, and to learn ways to help me navigate in the larger world, a world which I would try to improve with my new intellectual tools. My values had been planted deep many years before. But I needed strategies and tools.

# 20

## A COMPELLING EXPERIMENT

*"Putting our babies in the hands of whites who don't care about them when they are too young to even speak about what is going on; we can't sit around and do nothing to protect them."*

In 1972, I was finishing my senior year at Auburn, excited and proud that I was six months from graduating with a degree in Family and Child Development. But I was also concerned about what I was going to do after graduation. I didn't want to continue in graduate school at this point but I knew I wouldn't be satisfied with my life unless I was somehow making a difference.

I didn't have enough fluency in foreign languages to do social work and I couldn't do counseling without a master's degree. I was clear that I didn't want to be a teacher. I was afraid I didn't have the creativity to really challenge the children and if I chose the safe course and taught a static second grade curriculum for 40 years, then I might become a second grader myself.

So what would I do to make a living?

Winifred Green called me one day: "Sophia, Alabama has passed a new law requiring day care centers to be licensed and folks are upset because they can't get the information on how to meet the regulation. This is your field of study, right?"

Winifred informed me of a meeting and said she thought it was important for me to attend. Yes, this was in my field, but this was very short notice, and I had a major exam the day after the meeting. But Winifred had done a lot for me and my family, and still had many connections which might be useful for me. I didn't feel I could say no.

And I'm deeply grateful that Winifred called that day because that call started a series of events which in time led to my career with FOCAL. It was a godsend call and a blessing. And yet I left the call with a tightness in the pit of my stomach. Winifred's voice was briskly encouraging but something in her tone left me feeling: "You owe me."

So on a cold winter day in January 1972, I was one of the 60 people gathered at the Tabernacle Baptist Church in Selma concerned about their children being ready for school, especially in the face of school desegregation and the uncertainty of this new child care law.

The audience was full of women: domestic workers, teachers and babysitters. They wanted training in how to give children more. They understood that Alabama's new Child Care Act required facilities to cease operating until a license was granted. They needed to know how to fulfill the requirements. In the face of their history and the recent experiences with getting the right to vote, to eat in restaurants, sleep in hotels and provide a decent education for their children, they knew they faced a challenging road ahead.

I drove to Montgomery and was happy to catch a ride to Selma with Yvonne Gannon, the white administrative assistant to David Jacobs, the new Alabama AFSC director. Jacobs's duties came under Winifred's supervision from the Atlanta office. Both Yvonne and David were former teachers and I learned on the drive to Selma that Alabama's AFSC was organizing this meeting. Winifred, Yvonne and Nancy Spears were the only whites involved in the early organization of FOCAL.

Tabernacle's structure had a majestic look with two identical entrances, each with four large columns and huge wooden double doors at the top of ten or twelve concrete steps, surrounded by stained glass windows; it was unlike any black church I'd ever seen. The rounded sanctuary and wooden pews accentuated the domed ceiling creating the feel of a theater. I made my way to the far back corner of the room, close enough to hear participants who were already assembled, but far enough away to discreetly study for my final exam.

What I did not know was that an early African-American architect, David T. West, designed these two entrances with a vision that Jim Crow laws would not last forever. When Tabernacle was built in 1922, it was located on the corner of a side street (Minter) and the main street in the city of Selma (Broad). These laws, called Black

Codes (modeled after slave codes) were designed to restrict the freedom of the newly freed blacks, controlling their movement and labor. Blacks were not allowed to walk down or have addresses on Broad Street. When Jim Crow laws were reversed with the passage of the Civil Rights Act in the mid-60s, Tabernacle's address changed from Minter to Broad, according to Sam Walker, historian for the National Voting Rights Museum and Institute in Selma.

Christine Wise, a slender woman, spoke of the challenges facing the group. Within a few months, she would become the leader of this new group. She provided challenges and sharpened my leadership skills over the next four years. A school teacher and co-director with her mother of Town 'n Country Day Care Center in Evergreen, Alabama, hometown of David Jacobs, Christine spoke with passion. "We must have a say in who educates our young children, and right now, since schools were desegregated, we have lost that control." Those present murmured in agreement.

Someone asked: "If we can't get the state out to inspect our facilities how can we meet the new law?" A woman named Thelma Craig spoke up. "We need to organize ourselves and demand fair treatment from the state. Putting our babies in the hands of whites who don't care about them, when they are too young to even speak about what is going on, we can't sit around and do nothing to protect them."

Mrs. Craig was trying to get licensed for her child care facility down near the Alabama-Mississippi line. The facility was named after a teenager who'd been run over and killed during a youth-led sit-in demonstration. Of all my mentors, and there were many, this soft-spoken woman, with a will of steel, left the greatest impression. I heard determination and worry in the voices of those present and was left wondering what could be done.

On our way back to Montgomery, Yvonne asked if I'd heard of the Southern Education Foundation (SEF). Was I interested in applying for one of its summer internships? No, I had not heard of the group and yes, I was interested. Following a few phone conversations with Yvonne and Winifred, I got my application in. Five months later, having graduated from Auburn, I started my first post-college job, as an SEF intern. I was assigned to AFSC to assist with the development of a new organization that became the Federation of Community Controlled Centers of

Alabama for Child Care (FOCAL). Forty-three years later, I would step down as its founding director.

My primary duty as an SEF intern was to learn all I could about federal child care regulations and what was contained in Alabama's new Child Care Act and then to inform communities what they needed to do to meet the requirements of this new law. The new group met four times a year to share information about our local efforts to become licensed and to learn of developments at the state and federal level and how other southern states were responding to them.

My internship hadn't gone a week before I realized Christine, Yvonne and I didn't have the same understanding of my work. I was shut out of discussions about the structure of FOCAL's bylaws, membership fees, and board composition. They expected me to make copies, stuff mailings and run errands.

When I expressed disappointment to Winifred as a friend and confidant, she replied sharply, as my employer. "Sophia, you are to do what you are told; that's life." These words cut me deeply and, for the first time in the seven years I'd known Winifred, I felt a "plantation mentality." I said, "That's not what I signed on for. I don't mind doing any work that's needed, but this internship is about learning and developing resources to help build this organization."

Her response was even more cutting: "Do you really think you earned this internship? If so, you are mistaken. The decision was already made prior to your interview." These words were the ultimate sting. I thought back on the rounds of interviews with a panel of leaders from across the south, and 15 of us candidates huddled in a hallway, waiting our turn. I remembered my sweaty palms.

I could not believe this was coming from the mouth of a woman who was like family, who risked and put herself in harm's way too many times to count. With the entire muster my deflated ego would allow, I replied, "I competed for this internship, and have earned the right to experience all the benefits to which I'm entitled. Whatever decision you all made behind closed doors is your business, but I don't plan to be anybody's gofer or flunky."

I don't believe Winifred replied, but she gave me a look which mingled anger with disbelief. That look seemed to say: "You have some nerve!" It was a defining moment in my life, to learn this mentor of mine, who cared for me and my family, had a hard side and could be dangerous to me if I crossed her. I had to protect myself, to ensure she didn't crush my spirit. So I looked in her eyes just as hard as she was looking in mine. In that moment, our relationship fundamentally changed.

As organizer, my travels took me to all corners of the state and into towns and hamlets I'd never known. One of these trips was to the town of Gadsden, 45 miles east of Birmingham, where I met Mrs. Annie B. Crook. Her first question was "What is a girl your age doing trekking around these parts by yourself? Don't you have somebody, a brother or some male that can travel with you?" Before I could answer, she added, "You're going to spend the night with me and go home tomorrow when you have good daylight."

I connected to her motherly manner and when she scolded me six months later during a conflict with Christine, I listened. "Little girl, don't ever let someone take away something you want. If it's important, fight for it. If you don't want it, move on!" I had complained about feeling shut out by the new president and was thinking of requesting a change in my internship placement. Her words stung, but I never forgot them.

Tension developed around FOCAL the "professional" organization versus FOCAL the "radical" organization. How far should we go bucking the system? What should the tactics be, especially in getting in doors where we were shut out? Christine and Yvonne favored a soft and gentle approach when confronting the system. But I believed the soft sell wouldn't get FOCAL into places where decisions were being made nor would the organization be taken seriously.

I was 23 years old, often viewed as a young girl and just as often looked to for direction on issues facing the black community in the care of our children. I was scared and asked myself constantly, "Do you know enough?"

But I did know a lot about child development, and I had a passion to offer support to people who had been wronged, who felt they'd never had a fair shot at supporting themselves. It was exciting to realize that I could give back. I could give to FOCAL's members some of what Winifred Green and Connie Curry had given my family. In moments of doubt, especially about strategy and tactics, my go-to person was Clarence "Butch" Wright, a former SNCC organizer I'd met as a junior at Auburn. Butch and Leon Hall, also with SNCC, had sought me out to organize a Black Student Union on campus, though I'd become disgruntled and left the group when our first project was to organize a Greek chapter. The BSU continues on the Auburn campus to this day, by the way.

Butch, a trusted friend in my early years at FOCAL, introduced me to Jack Guillebeaux, who became a mentor, colleague and friend for 40 years and counting. My goals were as bold as Butch's but too often my first instincts were tentative. Butch's raspy voice, passionate gestures and sharp opinions, embodied radical thinking on jet fuel.

Some struggles did not involve Christine Wise. My second year with FOCAL, I was one of five program specialists hired by the Black Child Development Institute (BCDI) to develop child care organizations in Georgia, Alabama, Mississippi and the Carolinas. The white men who ran these southern states weren't sure they wanted federal dollars being spent on childcare. If such legislation had to pass, these men wanted to keep black communities from getting any of the money.

My job as program specialist built on work I had started as an intern: informing people about policies, and coordinating board meetings, membership gatherings and policy meetings with agency officials and legislators. I was always afraid I would mess up.

Black Nationalism was a fairly new concept to me and to most FOCAL members, although James Brown's record "Say It Loud, I'm Black and I'm Proud" had provided a degree of acceptance. Calling ourselves "black" instead of "Negro," speaking of our connection to Africa, and using words like "liberation" and "Black Power", these things were foreign to blacks in the rural South. My introduction to Black Nationalism during summer youth camp in Boston had left me scarred and skeptical.

Barbara Huell, Director of the Southern Office of BCDI in Atlanta, was a black nationalist with an easygoing leadership style. Comfortable with herself, she didn't wear her beliefs to impress, or wield her authority as director. She never dominated a room but her expectations were clear. I tried to pattern my leadership style after hers.

Each month, I headed to my BCDI staff meeting in a high-rise Marietta Bank building in downtown Atlanta, to share strategies and hear about issues and trends in the five states we represented. A mix of colorful ages, personalities, and work histories; two men and three women, all black, we didn't lack opinions or struggles in our deliberations on policies, organizing strategies or the needs of black children. Underlying our debates on strategy were divergent views of what blacks needed to gain power. Martin Luther King's reforming America to achieve equality through nonviolent interracial activism? Or Malcolm X's vision of black separatism and economic self-sufficiency?

An aspect of these meetings that left me queasy was imposing my beliefs on our base, people who'd just learned to call themselves "Negro" instead of "colored" and had just begun to live through racial integration. In the late 60s, there was something about being called "black" that I was not yet comfortable with, recalling all the fights on the playground about skin tone, even with my sisters and brothers.

BCDI meetings were stimulating, and I learned a lot about my history and culture. Some discussions were painfully reminiscent of Wetumpka High; I felt put down for what I didn't know about black history, and because I hadn't read certain books and didn't wear "liberated" dress.

The influence of these discussions led me to suggest to my fiancé, Albert, that we have an African American ceremony for our wedding two years later. I remember thinking "African American" as opposed to "African" because I wanted to acknowledge my ties to Africa but also the ways that American culture had shaped who I was. It felt important to embrace all of me, as I tried to better understand both of these worlds.

Professionally, my decision was to infuse slowly my new perspectives into FOCAL. I felt strongly that these beliefs should evolve as a natural part of what the organization was about. Personally, my relationship with Albert was also evolving.

By now, FOCAL had a fully functioning board and a growing membership, with more and more calls for assistance in meeting licensing standards. One of these board members was Nancy Spears. My former supervisor, Nancy was asked to serve on the board because of her knowledge of child care policies and program administration. Prior to coming on the board, she asked me if there had there been a financial audit of the FOCAL books, and whether we had personnel policy and procedures in place.

"Nancy, we don't have staff," I replied.

"It doesn't matter, you will have staff and it's best to start right," she insisted. She was the lone white board member for the first decade. While working at her agency, she and I came to an understanding that helped define our friendship and relationship for nearly 50 years. I was surprised a few years ago when she shared the sharp-tongued letter I'd written her in 1971 about not being willing to work in a "slave plantation" environment. Nancy was honored during my retirement in 2016 as a FOCAL Stalwart, as was Winifred Green.

People ask if my memoir is my own story or that of FOCAL. How can I answer when for more than 40 years, my life and FOCAL have been intertwined? The child care providers and families became my family. They needed logistical and emotional support, much as my family had in 1965. I took on a caretaking role for the children of Alabama much as I did for my siblings in my youth, feeling pain when Alabama didn't protect its children from injury. Courageous people risked their bodies and livelihoods for the well-being of children, much as the marchers on the Edmund Pettus Bridge had risked their lives in 1965. Their sacrifices made my career possible.

To get a facility licensed you needed approval from the health and fire departments, the state welfare agency and, in some instances, local zoning agencies. There was no money to pay for renovations or equipment needed to get those approvals, so people had to hold fundraisers or pay out of their own pocket. It was demoralizing to raise the money and make the required changes, only to be told that the retardant required by the Health Department was not accepted by the Fire Department. Or one health inspector would come out in May and okay a residential-size kitchen sink but a different inspector in July insisted we needed a commercial-size sink.

Conflicts like this made it hard for our facilities to get licensed.

From the start, FOCAL members thrived on meetings that brought them together three to four times a year. Folks came from Choctaw, Dallas and Wilcox counties in the rural Black Belt. Others came from down in Mobile and Baldwin counties; in east Alabama, Lee, Barbour and Macon; and from the urban areas of Jefferson, Tuscaloosa, Madison and Montgomery.

Meetings allowed people to share and learn from each other. People who had been denied the right to vote, and had never engaged with elected officials, had to learn how to lead a political conversation, write a letter, or pay a visit to their representatives. People were able to strategize and push back against counties that were arbitrary in implementing the Child Care Act.

In one of FOCAL's first workshops, Bernice Johnson Reagon, who later helped found the superb a cappella group Sweet Honey in the Rock, challenged us to draw on our own musical heritage and pass on to children the music of our roots. She showed us the power and delight of conveying our history through song, and people left with more confidence that we could make change happen.

Fear of retribution for attending a FOCAL meeting was well founded. The Monday after every one of our weekend trainings, a state official called me to clarify what had been "misstated" at the meeting. Message being, "We have an informer at your meetings who tells us who was there and what was said." We changed our strategy and began inviting officials to the meetings. When they came, a few of our members left early, afraid they might be targeted with longer delays and stricter inspections.

When our group morale was at its lowest ebb, one of the veteran child care providers would walk the audience through the steps of holding the line for freedom. After one of these impromptu speeches, you could feel the fear dissipate. Our mandate was to stand for what is right, even in the face of retribution, and to protect our children.

My life was on a fast track, trying both to respond to a base in crisis, and to build FOCAL and its support systems. I made calls to potential resource people for the next quarterly meeting; I reached out to possible donors; set up board meetings and sent out mailings and more mailings. I was grateful to board members, Albert, or anyone else who came in for a few hours to answer the phone, make copies or stuff envelopes. I was working 16-hour days.

FOCAL's office was three small rooms in the back corner of the first floor of the Central Bank Building on Washington Avenue in Montgomery. The conference room was small, and my desk was something we bought at a yard sale. But we were in good company; our building also housed the Southern Poverty Law Center and an office of the American Friends Service Committee, and its loyal attorney Howard Mandel.

Just across South Hull Street was the county courthouse and on the second floor the city jail. A regular feature of coming to work was to see a young man in police custody hollering at me: "Hey, tell my mama to bring me some cigarettes!" or "Ooh, you lookin' fine!" Then they'd disappear behind the jail bars.

But mostly I was out in the field, troubleshooting for FOCAL members.

Driving west down Highway 80 toward Mississippi, I was sometimes crowded by 18-wheelers headed to Jackson or New Orleans. But otherwise, I was deeply happy on the road. I craved its solitude, that feeling of being alone with my thoughts in my own car. No telephones ringing, and no meetings to convene.

Headed for Wilcox County, past Lowndesboro and Benton and Sardis and Elm Bluff, out my window, I saw fields of corn and cotton on both sides of the road, and I had the time to look at them in peace. Soybean fields appeared, and memories of being a farm girl came back to me. I felt I was coming home.

Then I'd pull into the parking lot of one of FOCAL's day care centers and walk inside. This was satisfaction of a very different kind. The staff members were joyful to see, quick to offer me a glass of lemonade or a slice of cake. I felt their appreciation as I gave them a listening ear.

African Americans had only had voting rights for about eight years, and many of us didn't know how to use the political system. Day care centers had to be inspected and licensed by the state.  Many of the staff were worried that a racist inspector or a failure to master some petty rule or regulation might cost them their operating license, or a chance to receive a license. Or perhaps someone on a county commission was harassing the center.

They'd ask me "What should we do?" Sometimes I'd advise them to ignore the harassment. Sometimes I'd suggest they ask a certain local pastor to go with them when they went to see a county official, and that I would get to them in a day or so with advice that usually came after a phone call with one of my mentors. With a goodbye hug, I was off, turning my car around and driving home, knowing that FOCAL's network was growing. I was bone tired, almost dazed, but exhilarated that I had something to offer people who were just like my family had been six years before: desperate for help.

The State Department of Human Resources created an advisory committee to promulgate standards for this new child care act. It took calls to Thomas Reed and Fred Gray, Alabama's first two black legislators since Reconstruction, but we got a face-to-face meeting with Ruben King, the Commissioner of this agency to gain a seat on the committee. It was our first advocacy victory. FOCAL was becoming an entity to be reckoned with.

My Southern Education Foundation internship and the period I worked for Black Child Development had given me an army of contacts and mentors, all of them potential resources for FOCAL, but all of them needing to be cultivated.

My life was a blur. I was living in my own apartment in Montgomery and Albert and I were starting to talk about marriage. He'd received his Associate Degree from the two-year college and had transferred to Tuskegee Institute. Most of our conversations came back to issues involving FOCAL or my family.

Mom was working as an insurance agent, and Dad's health was declining again. My younger siblings were now able to take a greater role in doctor appointments and daily chores for Mom and Dad, but I still got plenty of calls for advice, or with questions about property taxes or student loan applications. Albert was supportive but, like my mother, he worried how long I could maintain this frenzied pace.

During this whirlwind existence, four people stood out for me as steadfast models of leadership: Marian Wright Edelman, John Lewis, Bernice Johnson Reagon, and Na'im Akbar.

Marian Wright Edelman, with what is now called the Children's Defense Fund, was FOCAL's first annual keynote speaker. An architect of the Head Start program and first African-American woman to pass the bar in Mississippi, Marian was a close friend of Winifred from Freedom Summer in 1964. It was Marian who convinced me that maintaining an independent voice for FOCAL would require us to not accept government funding.

John Lewis spoke to us at FOCAL about the power of the vote to uplift the race. Lewis was best known for having been brutally beaten by State Troopers on the Edmund Pettus Bridge on Bloody Sunday, in 1965 — and never losing faith or turning back. That march helped to bring passage of the Voting Rights Act of 1965. In 1986, John became a U.S. Congressman. Many in the audience knew him personally and had been part of the Selma to Montgomery March. John's courage has always inspired me.

During a BCDI staff meeting, I met Bernice Johnson Reagon, who'd been a dynamic youth organizer for SNCC in the voting rights campaign in Albany, Georgia. When Bernice spoke at FOCAL over the years, she channeled the strength and wisdom of our foremothers: "Freedom cannot wait." When she sang, the power of her voice took me to heights that melted all fear and left me believing anything was possible. Music was crucial to FOCAL meetings and provided hope when we faced great odds, much as my mother's early morning hymns had once done.

Morehouse College professor Na'im Akbar, then called Luther Weems, was the first FOCAL speaker to address the toll of distrust and self-hate which the trauma of slavery had taken on the minds of black people. I was mesmerized. His fiery, preacher style had the audience on its feet and in tears as he spoke of the "slave mind" of our current condition. Janitors and cafeteria workers left their posts to stand in the back of the conference room, listening. Hearing this man speak left me hungry to learn more about internalized self-hate and how it shaped my choices both personally and with the organization I led.

A defining moment in FOCAL's growth in Alabama came after a clash between those who assumed caregivers would have access to college education and caregivers who often had neither the time, the money nor a college in their area. Christine Wise was FOCAL's member of the State Advisory Committee on Child Day Care Standards. Other members of that committee were drawn from state agency staffs, early education professionals, and child care providers. My former Child Study professor at Auburn, Mary Lynn Porter, developed the proposed standards reviewed by the committee. Child advocates and others sat in on the discussions.

A "simple" policy decision by this body could have devastated FOCAL's base. When I objected to proposed policies that were deaf to the struggles of black providers and black families, I was criticized for "coddling" folks unmotivated and unqualified to work with children.

One proposed guideline was that those caring for children in a child care facility should have course hours of training from a school approved by the state agency overseeing child care. A black child care provider asked, "What's a course hour?" The consultant explained: "It's the same as a college course."

"Where can you get such a course?" asked the provider.

When the consultant replied: "An educational facility; a university or community college," I could feel the energy draining from our folks in the room. Many of these caregivers were older, had worked with children for years, but hadn't finished high school. Many were using utensils and supplies out of their own homes, paying themselves only if something was left over. If they had other income in their household, they received no pay at all.

Child development experts made a strong case that we needed trained staff during the critical first five years of a child's life. I understood the theory of early education; it was my field of study at Auburn. But I also knew that, even if caregivers could pass an entrance exam and enroll in a college, the cost of the course, the location of the classes, trouble with transportation and a foreign learning environment would all be significant barriers.

When it appeared this policy would be approved, I raised my hand and asked to speak to the Committee. We had a back-and-forth exchange on the ways this policy would hurt children by forcing the closure of child care facilities because of a lack of "qualified" staff. Forget "nature vs. nurture", this would be "nature vs. nothing."

The tone in the room began to shift. Over the next few meetings, we had two major victories: changing the policy from "course" hours to "clock" hours, and having FOCAL accepted as a state-approved entity to provide child care training.

These victories made FOCAL the state's largest provider of child care worker training. Our training offered insights in child development, advocacy and licensing, our reputation as a resource blossomed and our membership rose to over 500. We had to hire an office manager to help me with administration.

While the licensing committee deliberated, a conflict arose around my attending one of the Advisory Committee meetings and the BCDI monthly staff meeting in Atlanta. All program specialists had to attend these staff meetings. But I felt odd drawing a salary from BCDI and reporting to BCDI on our work in Alabama, when my deepest allegiance was to FOCAL. In August 1974, I told the FOCAL board I couldn't attend the Advisory Committee meeting; I had to attend BCDI's staff meeting.

They decided it was time to upgrade FOCAL, and a month later, I came back as FOCAL's first Executive Director. I was thrilled to no longer have dual allegiances, but heavy with the thought: "How can we afford to pay both me and our office manager?"

Just as they called me "little girl" and worried about my safety, I worried about the fate of these devoted women and their child care programs. I felt I had to be the guardian keeping the FOCAL voice independent and true to the needs of our members. I became determined to find funders who could provide that freedom.

# 21

## OLA MAE SANDERS AND ANNIE B. MOORE

---

*"Child, sometimes you have to break the rules when somebody needs help."*

Mrs. Ola Mae Sanders, mother of 12 children, directed the Nellie E. Clark Day Care Center in Bay Minette, the Baldwin County seat. Not formally educated, she spoke slowly, a storyteller, who put color and drama in whatever she said. FOCAL was in its first year of existence when I met Mrs. Sanders at a meeting at the Federation of Southern Cooperatives facility in Epes, a little town near the Alabama-Mississippi line. I was told that Mrs. Sanders was someone that I needed to know and that she'd make a good board member of FOCAL.

She was about 5'8" tall, with hair pulled back in a ball, and she looked like a grandma — a tough grandma. She was outspoken and I was a little shy, but she and I hit it off right away and she invited me to make the three-hour drive to visit her center, just north of Mobile and the Gulf of Mexico. It was my first time in Bay Minette, but there was something warm and secure about Mrs. Sanders that made me feel good about going.

For an African-American woman, traveling alone in unfamiliar territory could be dangerous. I gassed up my car and headed south. Worried that my seven-year-old Volkswagen might break down, I tried to keep to main roads so I wouldn't be harassed for the "crime of being black and female." That vulnerable feeling was the scariest part of my work.

My fears were overshadowed by the warm reception from Mrs. Sanders and her staff. I was amazed by how large the program was, with nearly 80 children. Mrs. Sanders greeted me as though I was a celebrity, introducing me to her staff, asking them to bring me a plate of food and eager to hear about my trip.

"But why didn't you have someone riding with you?" It was a refrain I heard time and time again from the older women I met. "It's too dangerous for a girl like you to be traveling alone." We settled in to talking about the issues she was having with her day care center, the needs of her people and how FOCAL could help.

We spoke about the hardship on young mothers with no child care and how contrary the state welfare agency, the Department of Pensions and Security (DPS) could be. Her talk was peppered with insights drawn from what she'd had to do to raise her own 12 children. The entire time we talked, Mrs. Sanders was interacting with children, giving direction to staff, and working on a report. She still compelled my attention.

She broke away from our conversation to speak with two parents who came by seeking child care. One mother had a job interview but no place to leave her three children. Mrs. Sanders inquired, "How much time do you think you'll need?" The mother said, "A couple of hours." Mrs. Sanders called one of her staff to take down the young mother's information and told her, "Go on, honey, to your interview. You need a job and we'll keep the kids for you."

I asked: "Aren't you worried about getting in trouble with DPS for not following the rules, having more children than you're licensed for?"

Mrs. Sanders looked at me sternly: "Child, sometimes you have to break the rules when somebody needs help. I could fill three buildings this size with the need that is right here in Bay Minette. State Welfare has to do what they have to do, but my job is to try and help these young mothers get on their feet and keep these children safe. That mama needs help to take care of her children and get off welfare. Her children need to see her working, so they can learn to work." Ola Mae Sanders lived the concept that with children, "More is caught than taught." Children learn to be responsible by watching responsible adults.

Sensing I wasn't convinced, Mrs. Sanders said "Let me take you around and show you what I'm talking about, show you what is happening with our children." She used the phrases "our children" and "my job." I found myself thinking: "This is a bold sister. She has an operation that she's navigating like any CEO of a business."

As we moved through the local neighborhoods, Mrs. Sanders drove her little car as she spoke, making sharp turns, weaving in and out of streets and packing in a lot of details. One of the stops was to a mother of five who was depressed. She greeted Mrs. Sanders warmly, and shyly invited us into the front room of her crowded, untidy apartment.

"Have you fed them today, and are the older kids at school?" Mrs. Sanders asked. The mother answered "Yes."

"You still have the books I gave you, right?" The mother nodded. "Well, read them a couple of stories later today, and I'll let you know what day you can bring them by the center this week." There was a look of relief on the mother's face that she still had this option.

We made several stops and learned something each time, but the last stop left me in tears. We walked around several car tires as we made our way across a bare yard to a half-open screen door. Mrs. Sanders knocked several times. It was at least five minutes before the door slowly opened and we stood staring into the bleary eyes of a dirty, disheveled, middle-aged man about two-and-a-half feet tall. He moved by dragging his body across a floor obscured by layers of newspaper, aluminum cans and half-full milk bottles. His niece was a working mother, who left in his charge three children under the age of four.

Shaken, I asked Mrs. Sanders, "Shouldn't this situation be reported to the Department of Pensions and Security?" She replied: "So they can be placed in the foster care system and lost forever? This mother loves her children and is trying to take care of them the best she can. There's not enough child care subsidy money; the county has no more slots. At least that's what they tell me."

From all the years of caring for my siblings, and with my fresh knowledge of child development, my soul cried, "This shouldn't be!"

By now, FOCAL was growing fast. I had met a little woman who was director of the Morton B. Simpson Day Care Center in northeast Birmingham, in the Morton Simpson Housing Project. Annie B. Moore, a retired school teacher from Barbour County, knew the value of education and became the single most important person in growing FOCAL's membership. Her "office" was little more than a storage area next to the kitchen. But the center was bursting with the sounds of happy children singing nursery rhymes, playing with Lego blocks and finger painting.

Mrs. Moore and I talked about the new child care law and FOCAL's strategies for organizing black child care providers in the state. She asked: "How will you train the caregivers? These little babies need to be taught early — and their parents need help, too."

Children scrambled everywhere in the center's ample play space. On the walls were brightly colored montages and pictures of black heroes like Booker T. Washington and George Washington Carver. The aroma of food grew distracting near the lunch hour. Mrs. Moore mentioned that the Housing Authority managed 13 other centers, and she would tell them all to join FOCAL. She thought this was the most wonderful thing that could happen to black folks.

The next week, I received a call from a woman named Ursula Reed. A German native with a heavy accent, Ms. Reed tried to intimidate providers in her network. She was curt with me: "I understand you have been recruiting child care centers here in Birmingham. Let me make myself clear. These centers do not need any help from FOCAL." She added that her program, which had a contract with the Housing Authority, could give them whatever they needed; FOCAL should stay out of Birmingham.

When Mrs. Moore learned of this call, she flushed with anger. "Ursula Reed wants to control us and dictate what should be done with black children, and I won't let that happen." It was the same feisty spirit I felt when Debra and I were told we didn't belong at Wetumpka High.

Mrs. Moore, whose face was somewhat disfigured from a stroke, put all of her 5'2", 115-pound frame to work. Within five months, she'd recruited 15 new member centers in the Birmingham area. Two were housing project centers and five were some of the largest black churches in Birmingham, including Saint Joseph Day Care, whose pastor, the Reverend Abraham Woods, had been an aide to Martin Luther King. Reverend Woods became a vice president of FOCAL and hosted many FOCAL sessions at his church.

Annie B. Moore became one of FOCAL's most recognized members; serving on the board of directors nine years before being appointed a life member, having recruited a total of 28 centers and over 100 individual members. She was a believer in educating our young children "before they become strident."

# 22

## MARRYING ALBERT

---

*"Like my father, he was very good at sensing other people's motives.  His million dollar smile drew folks to him, even if they were wary of his power."*

It was mid-July 1974 and I was getting married in six weeks. FOCAL had a quarterly meeting the first week of August, then a fundraising trip to New York. There was a buzz from people doing child care about what the state welfare agency was doing, and how soon could FOCAL provide training to help them secure a license to operate.

Albert was making dashikis for himself and his groomsmen. I told my father, "Dad you've got to participate in my wedding, and all the men are wearing dashikis. I need you to give me away."

Dad's response was classic: "I thought you was already gint away."

"Sophia, have you mailed the wedding invitations yet?" Albert asked.
"Not yet."
"What's the hold up?"
"I'm trying to get the last addresses together and plan for the Quarterly Meeting at the same time."

Albert's silence told me he was unhappy with how little attention I was giving to our wedding. I was working hard for FOCAL, finding a facility, making calls to workshop presenters, arranging food for lunch, calling on family and friends as volunteers to help on the day of the meeting, getting the program to the printers — the needs seemed urgent and endless, and I hadn't yet learned how to set boundaries.

Two weeks before my wedding day, I was on a subway train headed to Harlem from the Manhattan office of the Foundation for Child Development. I'd just finished an exciting discussion of FOCAL's recent successes and hoped it would translate into a grant later in the fall. Deep in thought, I missed my station. Dusk was settling on this cluster of skyscraper apartments. Friends told me to act like I knew where I was going. Trying to avoid eye contact, and making my way along the crowded sidewalk, I felt everyone could see I didn't belong.

I had relatives living in Harlem, but shopping on the streets of this tightly packed city I felt alone, out of my element. Time was not my friend and I was desperate to find an African center piece, earrings for my bridesmaids and me and other altar decorations. The wedding day was upon me and I had no other options. Looming in my head was my duty to my husband-to-be. I chastised myself: "Sophia, why did you wait until the last minute?" FOCAL did come first in my life because it was in service to others; giving time to my husband and our marriage, since it was in service to my own family, seemed less important. It took years of therapy to untangle my twisted thinking and reset my priorities.

Although Albert had enrolled in the two-year college where we met and he also had a full-time job, every weekend he made his way to Auburn. His mother asked me, 'What have you done with my son?' Albert, who had never liked to read and had lost a college baseball scholarship because of poor grades, now had his head constantly in books like Native Son, by Richard Wright, Jubilee by Margaret Walker and To Kill A Mockingbird by Harper Lee. The former party animal had become a homebody and had re-enrolled in college. I assured Albert's mother that all this was Albert's doing, not mine.

Albert was supportive of my work for FOCAL, so much so that many people thought Albert was on staff. He appeared at every one of our events.

Albert had a personality that left many intimidated. He had a big body, a big voice and an air about him that could be bone-chilling if he was not happy. He had been hurt by nuns in Catholic school and had trouble trusting whites. Nor did Albert care for the older black women sitting on their porches who used to overhear him cursing and snitch on him to his mother, bringing him another whipping.

He loved his mom, and she loved him, but Albert was a strident young man and his mother sometimes belittled him to try to tame him. These wounds never fully healed, and all his life Albert suffered from low self-esteem. He was extremely proud of his dad and very close to his sister Delores. His older sister Helen and younger brother Lawrence were both teachers. Albert was protective of Lawrence, even after they were adults. He blamed himself for not protecting his little brother who sustained a broken leg as a boy walking home from school.

As a husband, Albert was a romantic. To show his love, he showered me with gifts. Though it embarrassed me, all the other women loved it when he surprised me at a FOCAL annual conference by serenading me with a Luther Vandross love song and giving me a set of diamond rings. He never missed a birthday, Mother's Day, Christmas or any special day.

He was my confidant and go-to for "What do you think?" The only time I withheld asking his opinion was when I thought he would hold a grudge against someone. Like my father, he was very good at sensing other people's motives. His million-dollar smile drew folks to him, even if they were wary of his power.

I was afraid of his explosive temper, and determined not to marry him feeling that way, so a few weeks after we were engaged, I decided to test whether he felt free to hit me when he blew up. For me this would be an absolute deal breaker for marriage. I'd seen my parents come to blows too many times. I knew what would set Albert off, and called him an unmentionable epithet. When I did, I saw this man's eyes turn from white past pink to nearly crimson and the veins in his temple start pounding.

I saw that rage and, for a few seconds, I was terrified. But instead of raising a hand against me, he turned and kicked a hole in the kitchen wall. My fear evaporated —and I called him the same epithet that included "mother" again. He walked out, and I didn't see or hear from him for three weeks. I had learned not only what Albert would and wouldn't do when enraged, but also that I had no right to provoke Albert with verbal abuse.

On August 31, 1974 a sweltering hot day in Montgomery, Albert and I were married at his grandfather's church, the historic Holt Street Baptist Church.

Our African ceremony and attire made quite a buzz. When my pastor heard that we were going to exchange vows between our families, he refused to officiate the service. A few guests snickered when we took off our shoes for an African libation ritual.

After a two-week honeymoon at my friend Connie Curry's cabin in Beaufort, South Carolina, I came back to become FOCAL's Executive Director. The first seven years of our marriage was filled with the normal marital adjustments. There were also abnormal adjustments because, as Albert saw it, FOCAL was #1 in my life, FOCAL was #2 in my life, my extended family was #3, and he was #4. There was some truth to that; I was a workaholic and was overly attached to being the caretaker for my family, especially my mother.

Soon after we were married, Albert was offered two jobs, days apart after being out of work for nearly a year. One was state coordinator for the Coalition Against Hunger, a program of the Alabama Council on Human Relations, and the other, assembler for American Sterilizer (AMSCO), a Pennsylvania manufacturer of hospital equipment that had relocated to Montgomery.

The first was a dream job, doing community organizing with a respected nonprofit, ACHR, but one with shaky funding and no family benefits. The second job, with American Sterilizer, offered family benefits. It was not the type of job Albert wanted after his year as a Ford Foundation Leadership Development Fellow, but it seemed to provide security that ACHR did not. Being out of work had left Albert with a strong desire to man up to his new bride.

# 23

## JACK GUILLEBEAUX AND FOCAL:
### I WILL NEVER KNOWINGLY UNDERCUT YOUR LEADERSHIP

*"How would you feel working for a woman, especially one who is younger and less experienced than you?"*

Sitting out in the audience this morning, I overheard some grumbling and dissatisfaction about the proposed increase in membership dues from $1 to $5, and it went something like, 'Who ever heard of quadrupling anything all at once?'

"I am aware your organization is young, just three years old I believe, and you are still getting on your feet. Let me also say, I am not a member of FOCAL, just your invited guest speaker. But as a black male who's been around for a while, I can say with certainty you can hardly buy a pack of cigarettes for a dollar. Most of us will spend that amount on a candy bar and soda."

"How do we expect to be free if we are not willing to pay something for it? Freedom ain't free! Nobody is going to give us anything, and if we can't pay five dollars to support an organization that is bringing us together, providing training and assistance in operating our programs and being a voice to the power brokers, if we can't afford to invest five dollars we need to go home. We are not serious about taking charge of our own lives and our children."

This was A. Jack Guillebeaux's introduction to the FOCAL membership at its Annual Meeting at the Morton B. Simpson Day Care Center in Birmingham. When he finished speaking, folks were on their feet applauding. I never heard another complaint that our membership fee was too high. Jack, his wife Fafar, and their young child had moved to Montgomery from Atlanta, so that Jack could become the director of Alabama's AFSC office, following the departure of David Jacobs.

Within a year of making this speech, Jack and the AFSC had separated over a difference in principles. It was not a pretty separation.

In late 1977, Jack told me "Sophia, I would like to work for FOCAL."
"Jack, I am honored, but what position are you interested in?"

"Whatever you deem worthy. I'm aware of the funding situation, and I believe I can contribute to fundraising as well as program development." He added: "I'm aware that hiring me could create problems between you and Winifred."

I didn't respond to that right away. I sensed that Jack was temperamentally more radical than I was and that he could be eccentric. I probed: "How would you feel working for a woman, especially one who is younger and less experienced than you are?"

"That's not a problem for me," he insisted. "I see you as an honest leader who is deeply committed to the people of this organization. You are open to learning and have a lot to offer others. Besides, FOCAL is fresh, and has integrity. It's genuinely directed by the people it was designed to serve. I want to be a part of this new activism that's taking shape from FOCAL's presence in Alabama."

We talked about the experience and fundraising skills that Jack could bring to FOCAL. He was also a trained Vista facilitator and had been a community organizer and administrator. His skill at writing, analytical thinking and meeting facilitation might be quite useful, since those were not particular skills of mine.

Potential pitfalls were his being male, 13 years older than me with twice my experience, in a culture that defers to men. Also, he was not from Alabama, but from the Appalachian part of North Carolina. He was married to an Iranian woman, whom the black people we served would see as white. It wasn't clear whether that was an asset or liability.

I knew I needed Jack's expertise, but I was scared to bring him on. And, yes, there was friction that might grow between me and my mentor and friend, Winifred, if I hired a man she had fired. Would she see it as a betrayal? If she did, would that poison FOCAL's relations with others in the progressive world, and ruin FOCAL's future revenues?

The deciding factor to hire Jack was the agreement that we reached about how we treat each other. He said flat out: "Sophia, I will never knowingly undercut your leadership as executive director."

In return, I promised to never suppress his leadership or hold back his creativity and passion when it served FOCAL.

# 24

# BE CAREFUL WHAT YOU ASK FOR

---

*"Does the spirit leave the body? Where does it go?*
*Can the departed really see us?"*

It was our trying to start our family and enduring a first, second and then a third miscarriage that really showed me that Albert was first in my life, that he deserved to be first, and that the marriage would not survive otherwise. I made peace with that fact.

Albert was fiercely protective and did all he knew to help me carry my pregnancies. Nothing was ever enough and we both stressed over how to make things better. He cried when I cried.

"Ms. Harris, are you ready?" Two guys in green surgical dress asked but didn't wait for a response. "Let's get you on this gurney. They're waiting for you."

I was slow responding because neither Albert nor Mom had arrived for my nine o'clock procedure. The year was 1978 and I was fighting to hold on to my third pregnancy, waiting in the hospital for a surgical procedure to prevent a miscarriage. Baptist Medical Center was all too familiar with my miscarriages, exhaustion and bronchial issues.

Debbie, my young white roommate, was also having surgery and her parents were in the room. As I was being wheeled from the room, her father came over and asked if he could have prayer with me. I said yes, thinking to myself, he looks like a redneck, and has the heavy drawl of a redneck, but I'd be a fool to refuse prayer before going under the knife.

Partly listening to his words, "God bless this dear soul! Oh God, bless the hands of the doctors. Oh, God, return her safely to her family, oh God," I was distracted by his repetitious wail and thought: 'I can't wait to tell Albert I was prayed over by a redneck holy roller.' I felt a tinge of shame for making fun of someone who was praying for my well-being.

Later that evening after what seemed a successful surgery, Albert and I watched a segment of Roots, the saga of African-American life, based on Alex Haley's family history. Visiting hours ended, and Albert went home. I told my roommate I felt cold. I called the nurse's station and was brought a blanket. Three calls later, one by my roommate, and three blankets, two nurses decided to examine me. One checked my temperature, made a face, and showed the results to the other. "Take it again!" she commanded. The first reading was 105, the second was 106.

By now the room was moving, and curtains were flowing in and out of windows that didn't exist. I could hear this person moaning, and arguing with the nurses, who had a catheter.

"Ms. Harris you must allow us to insert this tube in you!"
"No! You will not hurt my baby!"
"We are trying to save your life."

More curtains were moving, and there was a frenzy of voices in the room from a nursing staff doubled in size. Frantic calls were being made, trying to locate my family. But no one was answering the phone.

"Ms. Harris, we need you to cooperate; it's late and Dr. Byrne is waiting on the line and he needs his rest. He's really concerned about you!"
I thought: 'Well, if he's that concerned, why is he on the phone and not here?'

If it was not enough, to have a moving room, hearing a pitiful soul withering in pain, protecting my baby with all the clear thinking I could muster, I was also engaged in a private war of conscience.

'Sophia, you need to ask for forgiveness for making light of that man's prayer this morning.'
'Why? He's probably a racist anyway.'
'It's not about him; it's about you and saving your soul. God is not pleased.'

Throughout this dialogue, I was resisting, swinging in and out of windows and praying that someone would come to the rescue of this person fighting the system with all her might. Where is my family? I can't die before they arrive.

I was now elevated in the room and could see where each person was standing and what they were holding in their hands. I could hear the sound of the train I was on and could see a light at the end of the tunnel, coming closer and closer. The nurses were frantic and as I completely lost consciousness, they inserted the catheter and rushed me to the operating room to abort the fetus; three miscarriages and three boys.

I lost the battle with saving my baby, but didn't lose my second resolve — I would not die before my family arrived. It would be torture for them to spend the rest of their lives wondering what had happened to me in that hospital after Albert left.

To the matter of my conscience, I finally eked out a pitiful comment to my room-mate, "Debbie, you have a nice daddy." Even on my death bed, my pride got in the way of my doing what was right and I was damned and determined not to acknowledge my wrong.

For 20 days, the doctors tried to find out what was causing my high fever. The high temperature, IV sticks and pokes were causing my body to collapse — veins would no longer hold—penicillin dosages were over the top.

One dreary, overcast day, I looked out the window of my hospital room and said to myself, "I cheated death two weeks ago, only to die because doctors didn't know what was wrong and what to do." I was covered in blisters from the high temp, and my disfigured face caused two of my visitors to pass out when they saw me.

Another visiting friend told me, "Sophia, that's why they call it 'practicing medicine.' There is no sure thing. Just lots of guess work."

On the day following my low point, Dr. Byrne rushed into my room. "Ms. Harris, I have an idea I want to try! It's a surgical procedure called a D&C." This procedure, scraping the walls of the cervix, located a piece of the afterbirth which had lodged behind my liver, keeping the E Coli infection alive in my body.

Later, I said to Dr. Byrne: "Tell me what happened." He was a man of medium height, with a broad body and glasses. His hobby was taking care of plants in a greenhouse. Sort of an absent-minded professor type, about 50 years old.

It wasn't easy for him to take out my file, look me in the eye and say, "I made a mistake." But he admitted that. He told me that during the surgery, he'd inadvertently pricked my intestine, and then had made it worse by failing to notice what he'd done. That slight nick of my intestine was enough to put E. Coli bacteria into my blood stream.

A couple of my friends urged me to sue the doctor for malpractice, but I already had what I wanted from him: he'd leveled with me. Once he did that, forgiving him was easy.

My mother always said: "Be careful what you ask God for; you just might get it." As a child, I was always intrigued with death and wanted to understand the process of dying. Does the spirit really leave the body? Where does it go? Can the departed really see us?

This near-death trauma was also intriguing. For six months afterward, I had nightmares. Finally, one of the nurses confirmed what I saw when I was elevated in the room, things that could not be seen from the bed. I learned that pride is a dangerous animal, and, in its control, one can lose what is most precious.

I learned another lesson on race, preserving our sense of fairness is our duty in the present, regardless of what history has thrown at us. Fueled by the Roots miniseries, the high temperature and my past, I had placed a wall between my humanity and my roommate's father. So many goodies I would have missed out on in life had I not come face to face with my own resentments and prejudice.

Each of us has the will to live; a powerful tool. I can't say it will be there always, but if my life is taken in an instant, I want to be living with love; not too stout-hearted, not too proud to seek forgiveness. I want to have a sense my spirit will soar unencumbered by regrets.

Twenty-five years later, a woman passing me on the street called out my name. "Sophia Harris!"

I turned and said, "I'm sorry, but I don't know you."

"I'll never forget you!" she said. "You died on me and scared me to death!" It was the charge nurse the night I almost died.

# 25

## "IF I LOSE THIS BABY, I'LL LOSE MY MIND"

*"Believe this baby is yours and you will be a mother."*

After three failed pregnancies, Albert and I were emotionally distraught on the issue of having a baby. I had internalized the idea that if you couldn't give birth, you weren't fully a woman. On a follow-up visit after my third miscarriage, my obstetrician spoke to me in a tone more like a parent than a doctor. "Ms. Harris, I understand how badly you want to give birth. Everyone has the desire to see themselves in this little person they have conceived. But what I believe you want most is to be a mother."

I sat listening to him, trying not to scream, "You don't know anything about how badly I want to give birth! You have no idea of the failure I am feeling!" As though reading my thoughts, Dr. Byrne said: "My wife and I have two beautiful children and they are both adopted. We could not have biological children." I was stunned. How could he be so devoted to delivering babies when he could not deliver one of his own?

A few days later, still recuperating, I got a call from Louise Pittman, the director of Family and Children Services at the state welfare agency. "Ms. Harris, I am sorry about your loss. I would like you to be my guest at a luncheon later this week." This was the last person I wanted to see, given our contentious encounters in the past. Nor was I ready to jump back into work. But before I could decline her offer, she added, "I am happy to pick you up around 10:45 on Thursday."

She picked me up Thursday and brought me to the Madison Hotel in downtown Montgomery to a ballroom with several hundred people, mostly social workers with a sprinkling of civic and business leaders. I was captivated by the speaker who, from my best memory, spoke of having reached her 13th adopted child. She had started the process thinking her body could not bear children, but she now had five biological children. I was taken by the large screen photos of these children who were mixed race, both genders, two of them with disabilities.

I hung on her every word of how despair had turned to triumph when she and her husband adopted, opening their home and hearts to children needing parents. My heart swelled and I was near tears. It took Albert longer to warm to the idea of adopting but, within a few weeks, he'd come around. Ms. Pittman and I became friends. We still had ideological differences on many issues, but we were united about protecting children.

Our adoption case worker helped us understand what it means to adopt a child. "You should define adoption for your child or someone else will. It's important to be honest and let them know early on they are adopted. Don't lie to them."

When she asked if we had questions, Albert asked "Is it possible to get a baby whose skin complexion is close to ours?"

I said, "Albert, you can't be serious."

"Yes, I am! I want a child that looks like she's part of our family!" I was embarrassed, but the caseworker responded, "Thanks for being honest. If skin color is important, then you should say so. The child will pick up on these attitudes."

As fate or God's intervention would have it, three months after we were approved for adoption, and less than six months since my last miscarriage, I learned, with trepidation, that I was pregnant again. This same year my oldest brother, Charles, was killed. Others who died that year included Uncle Charlie, who we stayed with after the firebombing, my Dad's father and sister, Grandfather Johnnie Williams and Aunt Susie. How could we cope with losing another baby? Albert and I were both distraught.

When Dr. Byrne suggested that just maybe we should consider terminating the pregnancy, I screamed "Why would I abort a baby as hard as I have been trying to have one!"

"Mrs. Harris, Mrs. Harris, calm down. I am concerned about your health and with the emotional strain you are under, I am not sure you are able to get through another pregnancy." He added, "Abortion is not something I suggest unless the health of the mother is at risk, but I will do everything possible to help you carry this baby if that's what you want."

The decision was to go forth and at the end of the first trimester of the pregnancy, he would perform a cervical cerclage, a procedure to stitch the cervix to prevent it from opening too soon, which could cause a miscarriage.

Dr. Byrne suggested that we keep the news of the pregnancy secret to reduce the emotional stress.

I started getting questions: "Sophia, are you pregnant?" I would reply, "Why do you ask?"

"Well, you look like you are."

"Oh, I must be gaining weight again." Albert and I had been on a weight loss program. I'd lost 50 pounds and he'd lost 75. I pretended that I had lost some of my eating discipline.

But the hardest person to hide a pregnancy from is your mother, and Mom was not buying my evasive responses. "Girl, you are not fooling me! I can see it in your face. You are pregnant."

I never confirmed her suspicion, but by the start of the third month I started spotting and the news was out. My doctor was out of town at the time and since my case was well known by other obstetricians at the hospital, I was admitted and kept at the hospital for the two weeks Dr. Byrne was away.

This was the start of five months in bed; no standing, walking, not even sitting upright to eat. The five times I did otherwise resulted in a trip to the hospital and a blood transfusion. Besides an incompetent cervix, my new diagnosis was placenta previa. My placenta had detached itself from the walls of the cervix and was positioned at the opening. The slightest movement caused hemorrhaging.

It's crazy-making when any movement you make poses a grave threat to the baby you're carrying, and after three miscarriages, you can multiply crazy by three. With every fiber of my being, I was trying to give life while fearing all the time that I would endure all this agony and end up with nothing.

"Albert, put your hands on my stomach. Can you feel any movement? Check under the cover, am I spotting?" I was frantic, listening and having him check constantly for the smallest sign that our baby was alive or might be in trouble. One night, I called Dr. Byrne around 11:30 p.m. "Doctor, it's been two hours and I haven't felt the baby move." In an irritated voice, husky with sleep, Dr. Byrne replied, "Maybe he's trying to sleep, like I am." I felt no shame in waking him.

If my life was screwed, Albert's was even worse. He was trying to keep me calm emotionally, caring for my physical needs, tending to the house, grocery shopping, cooking and coordinating with family and friends who were offering their support. On his half-hour lunch break, he had just enough time to rush home, heat my food and bring it to me. He ate his own lunch on the way back to the plant.

Things were also getting heated on the job as talks were increasing about a labor union being organized at the plant.

Jack Guillebeaux had taken over my duties at FOCAL and kept me somewhat distracted by asking my help with phone calls I could make lying flat with my legs elevated. FOCAL was in the midst of an intense legislative campaign, our first initiative with the Alabama Legislature.

With just a few days left in the Legislative session, my goal was to get our eight telephone captains to generate enough calls to clog the Statehouse switchboard. This might get the attention of legislators to vote our child care bill, HB 1077, out of committee and get it voted on by the full body.

At one point the Chair of the Appropriations Committee was so frustrated he threatened to kill the bill if we didn't back off with the calls. My call from Jack was to turn up the heat. HB 1077 passed, a bill which earmarked funds for child care. That was a high point for me.

Dr. Byrne and I hit a rough spot when I refused to go through with the cerclage procedure. "Do you really think you can carry this baby without the cerclage? You have less than a ten percent chance of a live birth even with the surgery," he said in an aggravated tone.

A week earlier I spoke with the mother of my former fiancé, Frank. Mrs. Mitchell had heard of my ordeal and called to offer encouragement. When I mentioned having the procedure, she said, "Honey, don't let them doctors touch you! God put that baby inside you and He will keep it there if it's to be." Her words had a ring of familiarity and wisdom. I answered Dr. Byrne, not with defiance but with conviction, "It's the same chance I had with the other three tries, so this time I am taking a chance without it."

Albert, Mom, my sisters and an army of friends did their best to keep my spirits up on low days, and there were many. Katherine and Charles were attending college a few miles from my house. She, and sometimes Charles would walk to my house and climb through the window to check on me.

Baptist South Medical Facility and its third floor Maternity Ward was too familiar to me. I remembered the pain of leaving the Maternity Ward in a wheelchair, after yet another miscarriage, being pushed by a nurse to the elevator. On the way, I saw couples cooing over their newborns but what I held in my hands was not a baby but a dozen red roses or a box of Russell Stover chocolates.

Silently, I prayed, 'Lord, let this time be different!' as I watched the slow drip of one of the five blood transfusions of my pregnancy. Looking out the window, seeing the cluster of cars get heavier as the evening rush hour began, I thought of the blood I'd lost and how it might hurt my baby.

My spirit was low when I heard a light knock on the door to my room.

The door slowly opened and there was my friend Martha Hawkins armed with a small Bible and one yellow rose. With her hair in its usual bump and a floral A-Line shape dress, she could have been a saleswoman or a missionary. I wasted no time in telling Martha how scared I was of losing the baby.

Martha Hawkins looked at me and said, "Sophia, you have to believe you will have this baby."

"Martha, if I lose this baby, I will lose my mind."

"Girl, let go of the negative thoughts. You have got to have the same faith a child has in Santa Claus. God did not give you this baby to take it away from you. Believe this baby is yours and you will be a mother." Through my tears I could feel my spirit grow stronger as my faith deepened.

Two weeks before labor was to be induced, Katherine had come to my house to see if I wanted her to get something for my Mom; it was her birthday. My response was "I will go with you to pick it out," and I popped out of bed and headed to the bathroom. Katherine was in tears, pleading with me to get back in bed.

About five steps from the bed, my water broke. Those five steps kicked off a frantic set of events that lasted seven hours. I learned later that after Albert got the call that my water had broken, he lifted a huge steel barbeque grill off the back of his truck that he'd needed three other guys to help him lift earlier that morning.

Dr. Byrne, wearing his usual office visit attire of white long-sleeve shirt, and dress pants, met us in labor and delivery, and ordered an IV with medication to strengthen my baby's lungs, and to slow my contractions, giving the baby the best possible chance for survival. Several times, the doctor peeked in to monitor my dilation and fluid loss. In the late afternoon, a nurse came to tell us that it was time: Dr. Byrne was waiting for us in labor and delivery. By then, an army of family and friends had gathered in the waiting room, but only Albert was allowed to accompany me into the operating room.

I could sense the hype being passed around the maternity ward. On one of my last emergency runs for a blood transfusion, one of the nurses shared that my pregnancy was the talk of the hospital. The maternity nurses joked that they were taking turns "setting hens" to ensure a live birth.

Dr. Byrne showed up in his operating greens with the energy of a coach getting ready for a championship match. During the surgery, he and five or six medical staff gathered behind the white sheet tent that obscured what was happening below my chest. The doctor kept the conversation jovial, talking about his greenhouse plants.

Every few minutes, Dr. Byrne would ask, "How you doing, Mrs. Harris? Do you feel anything?"

My answer was no, but I knew they were cutting me because the hospital lights were flecked with my blood. The lights carried the name American Sterilizer — Albert's plant.

At 4:55 p.m., my son Alden entered the world, weighing 6 pounds and 9 ounces. As Dr. Byrne pulled him from the cut of the cesarean section, he grinned ear to ear and announced, "Mrs. Harris, we have us a good one."

# 26

## ALDEN

---

*"A child is born with a baby's body and brain, but the soul is ageless."*

Alden is an Old English name, meaning "one who protects with thoughtful judgment." Our baby's middle name, Onaje, is Swahili for "sensitive one."

The joy of finally becoming a father was somewhat tempered for Albert because two days after Alden's birth, AMSCO tried to fire him for wearing a pro-union T-shirt. His performance was too good for an outright firing; to make it stick legally, they put him on three months' probation.

Albert said, "Baby, I won't go out like this. I've got my son to take care of and they are gonna have to come with all they got, and still that won't be enough to fire me." For three months Albert worked insanely hard and defied all records of performance. He was eventually fired —but that came 15 years later.

Now, for the first time, I went from being a child care advocate to a child care consumer. Should I choose for our son's child care a center, or family home care, or relative care? It was difficult to have these arrangements in place; I'd been confined to bed for five months before Alden's birth. I managed for several months by taking my newborn to work with me, but found myself growing desperate to have a permanent arrangement.

I was conscious that as a mother, I wanted to achieve everything my mother had, but without making her mistakes. She spoke openly of those mistakes: failing to get enough education; and having so many children. She would tell me: "Children are a blessing, and I wouldn't trade one of you for nothing in the world. But children cost money."

A child is born with a baby's body and brain, but the soul is ageless. I believe that a baby's soul is just as deep and as real as that of a wise 70-year-old. But that soul and spirit is housed in a tiny body and we who are its caregivers may be tempted to crush it or brush it aside.

One day when Alden was two years old, I was at the stove, cooking in our too-small kitchen. Alden was right under me, tugging at my housecoat, demanding to be picked up. Stirring my hot popping grits, not wanting him to get burned or to burn myself, somewhat irritated, I said, "Alden, go sit down."

He looked at me and said, "No."

That jarred me, so I said in a stern, slow and forceful manner: "Alden, go sit down!" He looked at me and said, with the same intonation, "No!"

It wasn't just the grits getting heated up. I could feel myself getting really agitated, thinking "This little person standing between me and the little oval breakfast table a few feet away, is not a little baby wailing anymore. He is going toe-to-toe with me, matching the power of my command with a counter response. I have to crush this, because if he's this strong at this stage, how will I ever get him to obey me, or keep him safe?" I felt both anger and fear.

This is the point when some parents snap and do drastic things to the bodies and souls of their children. With God's help, at that moment I recognized that, although I had physical strength over Alden, we were equal in spirit. His spirit matched mine. We were equals …

At that moment, Albert, who had been away, walked into the room and asked: "What's wrong?"

I replied, "I am so infuriated with this boy, I could seriously hurt him." Albert picked up Alden, sat in a chair at the breakfast table and said, "Baby, go take a timeout. I will finish cooking breakfast." I went to the quiet of my bedroom and cried.

Looking at Alden's baby picture on the dresser, lying across the same bed where I'd lay for five months pleading with God to save my baby, I asked myself: "What happened?" I was trained in Child Development; how could I have lost control of myself?

I was frightened that I had come close to being an abuser. What is it in a child that evokes thoughts of such violence? I realized with a jolt that it was the same psychosis that defiant slaves had once elicited in their "owners", fear of defiance and its possible ripple effects. That morning I lost my appetite for breakfast.

Later that day, Albert reminded me of times when I had intervened when his tone was getting too harsh with Alden. We agreed there was nothing shameful about a stress reaction that led to a fleeting urge to hurt our boy. We pledged to monitor each other for signs of extreme stress, to call for a time out when needed, and to never give in to any of those urges, not now, nor at any time in the future.

# 27

## KIMIYA

---

*"I know I'll be scared of what my daughter may learn.*
*Don't let me stand in her way."*

In September of 1983, three years after Alden was born, our little baby girl was presented, wearing a baby blue dress with a trim of white lace down the front and a white barrette in her hair. Her beautiful smile and bright hypnotizing eyes captured our hearts right from the jump.

The following day an admiring friend said, "She looks like she's just come from baby refined school." We took several days thinking it over, and then named her Kimiya Ife, meaning "pleasant spirit" and "love." Within days, she came with me to a FOCAL board retreat, and a few weeks later, made her first flight to D.C., where she was a star of the Women's Technical Assistance Project meeting.

On the night when Albert and I brought home our baby girl, I wrote a letter to her and to myself. In that letter, I prayed for the mother who had given up her child, knowing that in years to come she would pass girls on the street and wonder if any of them were her girl. I asked God to ease the pain of this child's birth mother.

I knew that one day this precious little girl would want to know her family of origin and why she was "given away." I asked God: "Please help me feel secure enough as a mother to support my baby's search for her birth family when she is ready. I know I'll be scared of what my daughter may learn. Don't let me stand in her way." Each time I came across information connected to Kimiya's origins, I tucked it away in a private folder.

When Kimiya came into our lives, Cousin Maeteria shared her secret wish that our new child's skin color would be darker than Alden's because she didn't want him to feel slighted. She was the second one to raise the skin complexion of our new baby.

Although Cousin Maeteria was not Kimiya's caregiver, she was quick to caution me about leaving my girl child when I traveled. "Sophia, be careful with who is keeping her. You got to protect your little girl."

We placed Kimiya in a childcare center serving infants and preschoolers. Joan Ford, the director, was a pediatric nurse practitioner and became a family friend. Joan said Kimiya was a great comforter of the babies. Joan kept her with some of the younger ones until Kimiya was two years old, because the little ones liked her so much. Joking with Joan, I said: "You should be paying us for childcare!"

Albert enjoyed the travel that being married to a FOCAL executive brought. He liked the hotels where we stayed on the road, but his concept of sharing did not include the TV remote!

He was proud of our family being involved in the community, standing for something, helping people.

He loved being a father but, like my own father and so many black men, could never earn as much money as he would have liked. Albert had to endure racist supervisors, several of whom he had trained, and he couldn't support the family on his income alone.

Also, his colleagues in the factory teased him about some of the roles he played; taking care of our children while I was traveling out of state, and his frustrations at being a "hen-pecked husband" popped out from time to time.

"Albert, were you able to get to the grocery store?"

"Sophia, I am tired. I leave home at six, drop Alden off, work my job, pick up the kids in the afternoon, come home, fix dinner, give the kids a bath, go to sleep and wake up and do it all over again. When will you stop running all over the country and come home and be a wife and mother?"

Exhausted, guilty about being away from Alden and Kimiya, I wondered myself sometimes whether I was leading the life I should be. Was I being selfish?

If I could change one thing as a parent, it would be to have spent more time with my kids, especially attending their baseball and basketball games. Albert almost never missed a game, and I tried to tell myself that was enough.

When Kimiya was young, Albert taught her how to think about the game of basketball. He sat in a lawn chair watching, as Kimiya endlessly practiced her three-point shot, and he helped her prepare for each season. In her senior year, she was team captain.

On the rare occasions when I made it to one of Kimiya's games, I realized what I was missing. The gyms were mostly full. The players ran up and down the court, their sneakers squeaking. The points went up on the scoreboard, the clock ticked down toward zero, the fans screamed, and the referee's whistles blew and with all those eyes watching, my daughter was so poised, so complete. But then I'd miss the next game, and the next… Kimiya seemed to feel my absence more than Alden. At 14, she told me: "Mom, when you travel everything is different at home. Alden goes in my things more and Daddy spends a lot more time in his room, and sometimes I hear him crying."

Oh, I felt guilty hearing that! I would race home from a trip but only get to a basketball game in the last quarter. One evening, when my plane was delayed, I missed the entire Little League awards dinner. Therapy helped me sort through my fears and refine my vision. Those years were gratifying, but never easy.

One evening near dusk, the white toddler named Ennis who lived next door came close to the backyard fence dividing our two properties, and was talking with Alden, who was almost exactly his age. Ennis's father pulled into the driveway and came out of his vehicle while taking off his belt. I told Alden to come inside. I knew Ennis was about to be whipped and the tightness in my chest told me it was because this kid, no more than three years old, was at the fence treating his black neighbor as a friend.

The next day, I was hanging clothes on the line. Alden, tagging along behind me, went to the fence to wait for his friend. Ennis came outside and started towards the fence but abruptly stopped and backed away. He must have remembered the beating. I went inside and cried, both for Alden and for Ennis, for the pain of racism that my child would endure during his lifetime and the hatred that Ennis would have to carry in his heart for those whose skin was a darker shade than his own.

Out of all the growing-up struggles we encountered, perhaps the most shocking was Alden coming home at age six saying he hated Martin Luther King.

"Why, do you hate Dr. King?" I asked.

"Because he prayed to God for black people and that made us Black. I don't want to be black."

Who do you want to be?

"I want to be like Tammie. I want my hair to be like her hair and I want to be white like she is."

I was stunned. Our household was one with educated parents, and positive black images proudly displayed. Our children had black dolls, and watched the civil rights documentary Eyes on the Prize… And now my son stands before me saying that he hates being black?

When I told Albert, he asked: "Who is filling that boy's head with that stuff?" My answer was "No one, and everyone. He's learning it in subconscious messages from us, television, magazines, at the grocery store, school and church; all around him." This six-year-old was being fed images and messages that being white was good and being black was bad.

I would learn later the syndrome was called "internalized superiority and internalized inferiority." I dealt with the pain by sharing this story with as many childcare providers, parents and community leaders as I could. Racism is so insidious.

Kimiya, attractive, athletic and talented, with a fair complexion, was faced with another set of challenges: how to grow up feeling good about herself as a smart, intelligent and, yes, beautiful woman, when the constant messages from men, black and white, young and old were "Little sweet thang, come let me do you."

I was trying to raise an emotionally healthy girl child; not bound by the heavy labels I'd had to bear as a girl: "Know your place. Don't be sassy. Don't do something to get yourself in trouble. Don't speak to an adult with a certain tone of voice. And, by all means, keep your legs closed."

How could I provide Kimiya with protection and freedom, set boundaries but offer space so my beautiful daughter could grow up to feel self-assured? Could she be confident in her intellect, able to pursue her dreams, yet savvy enough to spot the dangers lurking on every corner?

Kimiya has been stopped by the police as much as Alden has but the conversations have been quite different. They involve no threat of an altercation but more of the subtle "I'll let you go this time," with a wink or even, "Give me a call sometime." The sexual innuendo can distract young women and undermine their self-confidence about their skills, ability and character.

As parents of color, we try to provide each of our children with survival skills to face a brutal world. I believe my daughter is less equipped than my son because her looks provide a false sense of value. She will have to work harder to be viewed as serious.

When Kimiya turned 18, she said, "Mama, will you help me find my birth mom?" Then for the first time, I presented Kimiya with the folder I'd been keeping, and she started her search through the State Welfare Agency. Her first exploration didn't turn out as we had hoped. Kimiya was crushed when she found her birth mother wasn't ready to connect with her.

Kimiya kept searching for information about her family of origin and, when she was 34, she called me on the phone, exuberant: "Mom, I've just gotten off the phone with my great aunt and she told me everything! All my aunts, who my daddy is, and I've got a bunch of sisters and brothers and nieces and nephews..." My daughter had found the part of herself that had been missing.

I asked God to please protect my adult daughter from being disappointed by folks she didn't know, but who were kin by blood. But I said a prayer of thanks that the prayer I'd made 34 years before had been answered. Since that day, I've been able to welcome Kimiya's very large family of origin. When they gather with the Bracys and the Harrises, it becomes quite a large extended family. Kimiya's birth family has become my family.

# 28

## AUTUMN FRIEND

---

*"You work too hard. When you're old like me your body won't be kind*
*to you because you didn't treat it kindly when you were younger."*

Separated in age by 35 years, Cousin Maeteria and I became best friends. We shared it all: our hurts, our joys and our dreams, both those fulfilled and unfulfilled.

When I asked her what it was like to be 70-some years old, she replied, "Aside from the aches and pains of a worn-out body, I feel the same as I did as a young girl. Maybe with a few more disappointments because now I know that I will never get to visit New York or go to Paris, but there is still the desire to go to these places. I feel just like a girl inside; I want to be loved and look pretty. You know I still like pretty things."

She encouraged me to take care of myself and said, "You work too hard. When you're old like me, your body won't be kind to you because you didn't treat it kindly when you were younger."

One day, as August was turning into September, she spoke of autumn sadness and how she felt it as a young girl. She was from a large family and was a big sister and caregiver to her younger siblings. One September, out of nowhere, her mother fell ill and died. Later, she would lose a brother and uncle at this same time of the year.

As September turned to autumn, I rode her out to view the foliage, the array of colors, the cattails. She oohed and ahhed at the fiery reds and the bursting orange and yellow trees.

She told her wonderful childhood stories. I encouraged her to keep dreaming and not give up on that New York trip she spoke of so often.

One Sunday afternoon, we went riding. She wanted to look at houses. Four blocks from my house was a new subdivision with a mix of one-story brick and wood-framed homes. They were built in a mix of styles; some with front porches, square and oval-shaped windows, some with two carports. All had lovely, manicured lawns on a sloped, curving street that disappeared into a forest of pines.

Cousin Maeteria was enchanted, looking at several homes before saying, "Stop, stop, Sophia! This is the house of my dreams!" She pointed to a yellow house, with white window frames, near the base of the sloped street. It could have been an extra large doll house. I thought to myself, "She can't be serious about buying this house. Her Social Security and limited savings would never be enough. Even if she sold her present home, it would be a financial strain."

But how could I dampen her childlike excitement with realism? Instead, for a quarter hour, I admired this 'doll house' alongside her. When we returned to her place, before getting her stiff knees out of the car, she turned to me and said: "Thank you for dreaming with me." Her hug was tender, and there were tears in her eyes.

Three years after delivering my three-month-old to her care, I noticed that while she still had spunk and all her memory, her body was losing ground. Albert and I decided to put Alden in nursery school, though we knew this would hurt Cousin Maeteria, and might even shorten her life.

I dreaded telling her. When I did, she cried as though someone near and dear had died. She pleaded: "Don't take my baby away; he's added years to my life!" But for several weeks she thought it over, and when her doctor told Cousin Maeteria that her heart was wearing out, she consented.

Alden went off to nursery school.

Within a month, Maeteria had started to pack up and give away her prized possessions. She walked into a lawyer's office and put all of her papers in order, identifying which of her possessions would go to her daughter and which to her son. She asked me what I wanted, and I chose two gold-trimmed ceramic egg dishes.

A week later, the movers came and she went to visit her son Grover in Talladega. When I'd asked her what she would do when she gave up her house, she said she was moving to Chicago to live with her daughter, Alice.

I pressed her: "You told me you would die if you had to live in Chicago; it was too cold for you up there. Are you going to Chicago to die?"

She remarked, "You really think you know everything." She never answered my question.

After 10 weeks in Talladega, she headed to Chicago. Ten weeks later, she passed away. I got the call on a Sunday that she was near death. I hopped a plane the next morning and arrived by mid-day.

When I walked into her room and called out to her, she was lethargic and spoke to me as though I'd arrived at her house to pick up Alden: "Sophia, go check on my biscuits, don't want them to get too brown. That boy 'n a half is something else. Check my bread again; it should be ready." Fifteen minutes after my arrival, all her vital signs began to drop and the medical staff summoned her immediate family.

When she was returned to her final resting place in Alabama, I spoke at her funeral about friendship and the gift of a difference in 35 years. Her life lessons to me included parenting, friendship, work and family. She poured affirmations into Alden and rivaled my mother on becoming his "grandma." In fact, for several years, every heavy-set, white-haired woman, regardless of color, became "Grandma" to Alden. Every time a breeze blew the back door open, I wondered if Maeteria was stopping by, a comment I had shared earlier when my young son asked who was at the door.

Every September is tinged with a sadness that is soon flushed away with the beautiful colors of autumn. I remember my friend and caregiver and treasure our sharing of joys, triumphs, fears and dreams. With her I knew the depth of true friendship and love, a gift that I pass on to my children, and carry with me in all seasons.

At top, marriage ceremony with Albert's parents Albert and Iola Harris and Sophia's parents Roosevelt and Mittie Marie Bracy in African American ceremony dress. Center, left, Albert and Sophia on their wedding day. *Photo credit: Author's personal collection.* Center right, Sophia and Thelma Craig at a FOCAL Conference. *Photo credit: Craig Dwight Coleman*

At right, Sophia with a group of children that appeared in the textbook, Building Bridges Psychology and Public Policy, published by Houghton Mifflin, 1993. *Photo credit: Wekesa Madzimoyo*

The late civil rights icon and U.S. House Representative John Lewis speaks at FOCAL's 2nd Annual Conference in 1973. At center, Jack Guillebeaux, Deputy Director and FOCAL Life Board members Mary Jones, Clara Card and Nancy Spears were honored with Legacy Pioneer Awards at Sophia's Retirement Tribute, 2016. *Photo credit: Author's personal collection*

At bottom, Sophia with philanthropist John D. Rockefeller, III, center, after receiving the Rockefeller Public Service Award in 1977 in Washington, D.C. Accompanying her at the event were Pearl Sattiewhite, husband Albert Harris, Loutricia Wilson, Ed Bracy, Marie Bracy, Christine Wise, then-FOCAL board president, Sophia Slaughter, and Rosetta Jackson, then-FOCAL board vice president.

Left, bedtime for youngsters Alden and Kimyia in their first home in Montgomery East. *Photo credit: Author's personal collection.* At right, Sophia with John A. Griffin, Southern Education Foundation; Ingrid Reid, Princeton University; and Freida Mitchell after receiving the John A. Griffin Award.

Left, Sophia, Albert, Alden and Kimyia with "Cheers" actor Ted Danson after Sophia received the Gleitsman Foundation Award. *Photo credit: Gleitsman Foundation.* At right, The Harris Family: Albert, Sophia, Alden and Kimyia.

# 29

# SOPHIA'S DECLARATION OF INDEPENDENCE

*"I will not be controlled by the men in my life, whether it be my husband or colleagues. And I will not define myself by the expectations others have of me —as daughter, sister, wife or mother."*

I was grateful to my deputy director Jack Guillebeaux for running FOCAL during the last stages of my pregnancy with Alden. But when I came back and started working those long days again — 6:30 a.m. to 7:30 p.m. — I felt split between FOCAL and motherhood and not being good enough at either. How do you supervise your mentor and best friend, meet the challenges of being a wife and new mother, and serve the members of 300 childcare facilities in crisis, all at the same time? I was completely off balance.

Had Jack been the only addition to FOCAL, the office dynamics would have shifted, and it would have taken some time to get used to. But we also had a new organizer, Wekesa Madzimoyo, and he and Jack were always in conversation. Wekesa was as radical and eccentric as Jack, but 20 years younger. They energized and fed off each other, and intellectual sparks would fly.

One week they were discussing whether African Americans were facing "internalized oppression" or "racial scripting." The next week it was "Should we call ourselves 'Blacks' or 'Afrikan Americans,' with a 'k'?" Were we creating a "movement" or a "revolution"? Wekesa loved to label things and both Jack and Wekesa could write as well as they could talk.

There were aspects of this to celebrate, and I was pleased that Jack and Wekesa were so engaged in their work. But the two of them transformed the office dynamics from three women and two men led by me in a structured way, to a free-wheeling, male-dominated workshop on "black liberation." We were becoming a "think tank."

I felt personally disempowered by this dynamic and, more importantly, I felt there had to be more balance, to have all voices heard, in order to best serve FOCAL.

Some of my discomfort I could release by teasing. I called Wekesa Madzimoyo "Mr. Black Nationalist Extraordinaire." But the plain and painful fact was that Wekesa and Jack had created a firewall of ideas, strategies and testosterone that left little room for the women in the office, including me, their executive director. My work hours, mindset and confidence plummeted.

In the world outside FOCAL's office, it was a painful time, too. In 1980, Ronald Reagan had been elected president and he made clear both during his campaign and after he took office that he felt government was over-spending and that race relations were none of his concern. Alabama had double-digit unemployment and many of our people were losing their child care centers and their jobs.

The Reagan people had also made clear they were skeptical that we were abiding by the rules for tax exempt 501c3 organizations, and this was scaring the hell out of our major funders. Overt racial attacks were also on the rise, including the lynching of Michael McDonald, an 18-year-old teenager in Mobile. Morale was low.

As the leader of my organization, what should I do? What could I do to help my people regain the hope and inspiration of the 70s?

Jack and Wekesa were inside our office bouncing ideas off each other about internalized racism and the lack of vision among our members. But I didn't want FOCAL to be an office think tank; I wanted to get out in the field, to connect and hold the hands of those who were hurting.

We sparred and disagreed on what was most effective. "We need to challenge people to take responsibility for their communities," Wekesa said. Jack believed proactive planning was the answer. In my view, people needed a safe space to share their fears and hopes. The responsibility issue became "responsibility for what?"

But Jack, Wekesa and the rest of the staffers agreed that having vision was a key. Although painful, this tense period opened the door for our producing some powerful results.

We got through this tense period. Jack helped me in many ways and was always my friend. His support during my pregnancy with Alden holds a special place in my heart. Jack was the chief architect of our first miraculous victory at the State House, which few believed was possible.

Jack also helped me to see that I was discounting my own needs, that my obsession with caretaking and "fixing" things for everyone else was exhausting me and landing me in the hospital once or twice a year. Jack not only confronted me about my dysfunctional behavior, but encouraged me to seek counseling, which was a life saver. His constant reservoir of positive strokes reminded me of the way I'd been treated by my older brother Harvey.

Jack's skill in facilitation and analysis, and energy for principles lifted FOCAL's work beyond run-of-the-mill community organizing. Yes, we led protests, started letter writing campaigns, conducted role plays and other tools from the movement directed at policy change. But we also determined that race, prejudice and discrimination had left some impacts that couldn't be changed by public policies and institutions. These things required personal transformation.

As an employee and friend, Jack was fiercely loyal, and did whatever I asked, never rejecting anything as impossible or complaining that he had other deadlines to meet. He expressed his passions beautifully in writing and offered support and guidance on every issue FOCAL was facing. Jack deserved my trust, and I gave it to him, though it took me several years to give myself credit for doing that.

I struggled to claim and reclaim parts of myself. It was a time of stress, confrontation, self-examination and growth. But I can say now that Jack and Wekesa's presence at FOCAL catapulted our influence to new heights, as we began to address the superior/inferior narratives in this country, and the internalized oppression that has been created.

Over the next few years, we evolved an organizing strategy. It included bringing into consciousness the impact of historical injustices. We also built on my recent discoveries with women organizing in support groups as a tool for igniting hope. This approach would later become a basis for our community development curriculum, "More is Caught Than Taught," the centerpiece of our organizing, training and advocacy work.

Part of my struggle to claim and reclaim parts of myself was to focus on my identity as a woman. Like so many people, I had tended to see inequity in terms of race, and also of class. But now I started to see much more clearly than I had before, issues of gender.

My involvement with women's organizations gave me the chance to try out this new approach and to regain my confidence as a leader.

"I will not be controlled by the men in my life, whether my husband or colleagues! And I will not define myself by the expectations others have for me—as a daughter, sister, wife or mother." As I spoke these words, my voice cracking with emotion, the audience of 200 women cheered. I had arrived 15 minutes late for my presentation at the Southern Rural Women's Network meeting in Selma, after a morning of turmoil with Albert over childcare arrangements and wearing the burden of a fight the day before with Jack and Wekesa over program strategies.

As I took my seat after my speech, I thought to myself, "Do you know what you've just done? Now at least half the women in this room think you are having a breakdown and all of them know your business." I could not recall a time where I felt more vulnerable from sharing with an audience. My mind was a roller coaster — jubilation in the freedom of outing my repressed feelings about gender oppression, and fear of what it all meant and what the consequences might be.

"Sophia, you spoke my truth." "You were great!"
"Girl, I could feel you."

These were some of the comments, along with hugs, I received at the break, following my talk. The most affirming was Billie Jean Young, a mentee of Thelma Craig and organizer of the first convening of southern rural women to my knowledge. It was clear to me this was a defining moment.

Several weeks after my Selma presentation, a tall, broad-framed white woman showed up at my office. Her name was Eileen Paul, and she reminded me of the nuns who had helped my family during my childhood. In fact, Eileen was a former nun, working for the Center for Community Change as a women's organizer out of D.C.

Eileen had heard about me through the Southern Rural Women's Network. She wanted to share the latest women's rights developments in the South and to invite me to join a new women's organization, the Southeast Women's Employment Coalition (SWEC).

Having had several not-so-positive encounters with white feminists, I was shy about accepting her invitation. I asked, "Are there other black women on the board?" My heart sank when she said no, but I agreed to meet with the board. To my surprise, the next board meeting was at a beach house in North Carolina.

"Folks, we are interested in expanding diversity on our board, but want women whose views are compatible with SWEC's mission." This proclamation came from the board chairperson, a heavyset woman with a masculine haircut, dressed like a farmer in denim coveralls.

"What is the mission?" I asked. She replied, "We are about advancing employment opportunities for women, especially in non-traditional jobs, such as road and housing construction, utilities and engineering."

I was one of three black women being considered for board membership, but to be "compatible" with SWEC, we would have to take a positive view of homosexuality. When the three of us returned to our rooms before dinner, we burst into a laughter that masked our discomfort about being grilled on an issue we weren't accustomed to discussing in the open.

Our laughter also covered the sting of being interrogated about possible prejudice with questions that totally discounted the prejudice and inequality we'd faced all our lives as black women. We joked about how black folks would never meet in the hot sun — we didn't need a tan. Despite the white privilege on this board, we agreed, with trepidation, to accept appointment to the board if it were offered. We wanted black women to have these kinds of chances.

At the same time, Gardenia White, Sarah Fields Davis and I challenged the white women on race and class attitudes. At that very first meeting we each told them a version of the same truth:

"You assume the issue of equal rights for women is as important or more than the issue of race, but you don't know what our experiences have been as black women. Yes, women have been kept out of non-traditional jobs in construction, engineering, aerospace, and leadership roles in the tech industry, but black women are still trying to get a foot in the door of traditional jobs as nurses, office managers, teachers and supervisors. We still have to prove ourselves doubly. And often white women are our harshest critics. You presume we want what you want, without the courtesy of asking."

"An example staring us in the face right now is where we are meeting. As white women, you are relaxed and excited to be on this lovely, sandy, hot beach. As black women, we are miserable, and certainly not dressed for the environment. The best thing we can do is to use this time together to get to know what our particular experience has been and how we might forge a collective agenda that benefits us all."

This became an opening for deliberate, conscious dialogue. Over time, we learned that all of us were prepared to "push" the others to recognize certain aspects of injustice, and all of us were willing to be pushed.

But all this took time and tears. On one tough afternoon, a white woman began to cry when she felt her position was threatened. I heard myself say, "Your tears do not move me." Others seemed surprised to hear this from me and I had to follow up by pointing out that, for centuries, white women in the South had used their tears, both real and contrived, to get many a black person whipped or even lynched.

I grew as well during my three-year tenure on the SWEC board. Some of my deep-seated beliefs about the rights of people to love and live with whomever they chose were challenged and uprooted. I learned that I was "homophobic." It would be another 15 years before I became congruent with my religious beliefs on same-sex marriage.

That laid the groundwork for experiences we shared for a decade on other boards and other collaborations, most notably the attendance of six of us at the world conference of women in Nairobi, Kenya several years later.

Top, Sophia with Winifred Green at the dedication of the Marian Wright Edelman library in Bennettsville, SC. At right, Sophia with former Alabama Senator Hank Sanders. *Photo credit: Marty Makower*

At left, Sophia's husband Albert was known for dressing well, as he was here in this photo. At right, Jack and FaFar Guillebeaux at the Bracy Family Reunion, September 2019. *Photo credit: KT Event Creations*

# FOCAL, INC.

3703 Cleveland Avenue
Post Office Box 214
Montgomery, Alabama 36101
Phone: 205/ 262-3456

August 11, 1987

Dear FOCAL Members, Supporters and Friends,

## We did it, again!

Last year's lead **UPDATE** article read, "**WE DID IT!**" That "it" referred to our having caused the legislature to shift 40 million dollars to Human Services programs in a special session of the legislature. This, of course, saved hundreds of Day Care programs from closing and prevented a crisis in child day care for poor working families in Alabama.

While this was a significant victory, it was still stopgap "last minute rescue" funding. What we've really wanted was some assurance that Child Day Care wouldn't be treated as an unwanted child of the DHR at the whim of whoever occupied the Governor's chair or DHR commissioner's seat. We wanted to know that day care funds wouldn't be cut in favor of some other program. We wanted some relief from our yearly begging, writing, shouting, and protesting to maintain subsidized child care for indigent Alabamians.

## We Wanted Child Care to exist by legislative mandate!

Friends, you have wanted this for a long time, you have worked for it for years. I can scarcely remember how many meetings, how many strategy sessions, how many letters in this concentrated effort since January of 1986! I am so very proud to say that on August 3, 1987

## We Got It!

H. B. 536 passed both houses of the Alabama legislature and was signed into law by Governor Guy Hunt. This act makes Child Day Care a legislatively mandated service.

Chills come over me and I'm moved to tears. I'm so very proud of **FOCAL**, so very proud of you, each and every FOCAL member, supporter and friend. I'm also very happy and proud of the newly formed Alabama Alliance for Child Day Care. Their work was invaluable. Some said it couldn't be done, but you kept on calling, kept on writing, kept on visiting your legislators, motivating your communities and kept on sending me the spirit which sustained me and the other FOCAL staff, here in Montgomery.

I'll never forget this experience, this victory. I'll never forget the feeling that came over me when, with just 5 hours left in the entire legislative session, the votes were taken and Senator Hank Sanders looked at us in the Senate Gallery and said with a broad smile: "You can all go home now." I was humble and jubilant at the same time. In my head all I could say was: we did it, we did it, we did it.

Folks, take time to thank yourselves, your staffs, your parents and your community supporters. Please don't forget to send notes of thanks to your Representatives and Senators too. This is the first time ever that the Alabama legislature has taken such a forthright stand for early childhood education in Alabama. You and they made history on August 3, 1987. Celebrate!

Sincerely,

*Sophia*

Sophia Bracy Harris
Executive Director

Sophia pens a letter in 1987 to FOCAL members and supporters announcing the organization's leading role in the successful passage of legislation that provided $40 million to child care programs.

USA TODAY · TUESDAY, JUNE 18, 1991  **NEWSMAKERS**

# Day-care advocate wins $260,000 grant

By Patricia Edmonds
USA TODAY

Sophia Bracy was threatened by white students, and her home fire-bombed, when she dared enroll at the segregated Wetumpka (Ala.) High School in 1965. But she stayed because she cared so passionately about equality and good education.

And today that passion pays off as Sophia Bracy Harris, 41, receives a $260,000 MacArthur Fellowship for her work bringing day care to poor black children.

An imposing woman with a no-nonsense style, Harris says her struggle for education moved her

"to dedicate my life to providing and creating opportunities for people who were basically like me."

In 1972 she helped found the Federation of Child Care Centers of Alabama to help black-run day-care centers in poor communities receive funds and meet licensing standards.

Since Harris was appointed executive director in 1974, FOCAL's service area has grown from 15 day-care centers to 110, and the group has spurred state legislation providing more than $41 million for child-care and other services.

In addition to helping the day-care centers with funding, training

and regulations, Harris says, FOCAL has encouraged day-care children's parents to "be a part of the policy-making process" that shapes their children's education.

State Sen. Hank Sanders, whose district includes Alabama's eight poorest counties, says Harris "has done a tremendous job fighting for the rights of young children" in a state where he says "day care for poor and minority kids is almost off the list" of priorities.

"She's a very strong individual, very intelligent, very capable, and she has vision."

Harris isn't sure what she'll do with the $260,000 prize. But she

**HARRIS:** When thinking [of the] grant, a 'smile starts in my h[eart]'

says it may free her to take a [...] leave and spend time with her [...] children, Aiden, 11, and Kim[...] and her husband, Albert.

## Other MacArthur Fellowship recipients

Annual fellowships given by the John D. and Catherine T. MacArthur Foundation are "no-strings" awards to support creative people for five years.

No one may apply for the so-called "genius grants." Names are proposed by more than 100 anonymous nominators.

The foundation board makes the final selections.

**1991 MacArthur fellows:**
Jacqueline Barton, 39, San Marino, Calif.; chemistry professor, California Institute of Technology; $250,000.

Paul Berman, 41, New York City; literary critic; $260,000.

James Blinn, 42, Pasadena, Calif.; computer graphics animator, California Institute of Technology; $265,000.

Taylor Branch, 44, Baltimore; historian/author; $275,000.

Trisha Brown, 54, New York; dancer-choreographer; [$...]

LANE: Investigates the language and culture of the deaf

By J.D. Levine, AP

By Lisa Davis, AP
FELD: Anthropologist got mask during study of rain-forest sounds and culture in New Guinea.

W. Lewis Hyde, 45, Gambier, Ohio; writer; professor, Kenyon College; $260,000.

Church; $335,000.
Patricia Locke, 63, Standing Rock Reservation, S.D.; exe[cutive] International Native Ame[rican] Language Institute; $369,000.

Mark Morris, 34, Brussels, [Bel]gium; dancer-choreogra[pher]; $225,000.

Marcel Ophuls, 63, Neuilly [sur] Seine, France, documentary [film]maker; $369,000.

Arnold Rampersad, 49, P[rince]ton, N.J.; English profe[ssor]; $300,000.

Gunther Schuller, 65, N[ewton] Mass.; composer-condu[ctor]; $374,000.

Joel Schwartz, 44, Washi[ngton] D.C.; environmental toxico[logist] $275,000.

Cecil Taylor, 62, New Yor[k;] pianist, composer; $365,000.

Julie Taymor, 38, New [York] theatrical puppeteer; $245,0[00]

David Werner, 56, Palo [Alto] Calif.; advocate for health c[are in] developing countries; $335,0[00]

THE OPELIKA-AUBURN NEWS, Sunday, July 4, 1993  COL[...]

# Harris honored with Dartmouth degree

By Ethel White
Special to the O-A News

Sophia Bracy Harris was one of seven honorary degree recipients from the prestigious Dartmouth College in Hanover, New Hampshire, during the college's 223rd commencement exercises in June, where she received the Honorary Doctor of Humane Letters award.

Mrs. Harris joins a list of very accomplished degree recipients including Bill Moyers, nationally acclaimed journalist; novelist Carlos Fuentes; Irish poet Seamus Heaney; businessman and Dartmouth alumnus George B. Munroe; Cornell University President Frank H. T. Rhodes; and biochemist, Dr. Maxine Singer.

Sophia Bracy Harris has received numerous honors, including a MacArthur Fellowship in 1991 and the Gleitsman Award for People Who Make a Difference, in 1990.

She is the founder and execu[tive ...]

Sophia Bracy Harris

**Ethel White**

found in 1972 as a training, advocacy and technical assistance agency. FOCAL has evolved from a small, grassroots community-based organization, to a training and organizing development center for child care providers across the State and [...]

dedication and expertise in child care reform, as well as her personal empowerment and community organizing, have been an inspiration to many. The Honorary Doctor of Humane Letters award was bestowed upon her in acknowledgment and reflection of the work Sophia Bracy Harris has conducted throughout her career.

An Auburn University graduate, with a bachelor's degree in family and child development, Sophia Harris is well known in this community by members of the local child care facilities.

Making the trip with Mrs. Harris to receive the award, was Clara Card of Auburn, currently [...]

Top left, Billie Jean Young, a dear friend and a 1984 recipient of the MacArthur Fellowship. Right, Sophia featured in *USA Today* after receiving the same award in 1991. *Photo credit: Young family.* Article is from *June18, 1991 USA Today* by Patricia Edmonds. Center, Sophia was one of seven recipients in 1993 to receive an honorary doctorate from Dartmouth College in Hanover, New Hampshire. *Photo credit: Opelika-Auburn News, July 4, 1993. Ethel White*

Orchard House Women's Retreat at Washoe Valley, Nevada. Pictured are Jan Gilbert, Karla Bush, Fannie Etheridge, Amy Moorer, Sophia, Michelle Nash, Kit Miller, Christian Lee and Marty Makower. *Photo credit: Marty Makower*

Albert, left, showing off the bounty of his beloved community garden, which was often visited by school children to whom he spoke about gardening. *Photo credit: Author's personal collection*

Sophia's niece Lequita Mayes, and sister-in-law Delores Harris with Sophia at Retirement Gala, 2016. *Photo credit: Marty Makower*

Above, sisters Aretha and Katherine with Sophia and Marian Wright Edelman, second from left, after receiving Children's Defense Fund's Children's Advocate Award. *Photo credit: CDF*

At left, Sophia's parents Roosevelt and Mittie Marie Bracy in later years. *Photo credit: Author's personal collection*

# 30

## YOU CAN'T GET ENOUGH OF
## WHAT YOU DON'T NEED

*"I felt a new determination springing from my soul; a determination to strive, not just survive; to live with dignity; and to share with others what I had seen and done, so they could lay down their own burdens, and begin to soar."*

Before 1980 I carried — locked inside — doubts about my worth and intellect. Nice things were said about my intellect and talents as I received the Herbert Lehman college scholarship and the Southern Education Foundation internship to work developing FOCAL. But I discounted the compliments and affirmation others gave me. I thought they were deceived, that I was really not a very bright person.

In 1977, when I received the Rockefeller Public Service Award for Outstanding Service as an advocate for children, I dismissed myself as unworthy of this tribute. In some ways, I'd never stopped being the girl in bed for a year with rheumatic fever who felt — despite her swollen knees and trouble walking— that she wasn't really sick, that she was faking her illness, and had fooled the doctor and her parents. Now I felt I had fooled the people who had chosen the Rockefeller Public Service award. How could I be a good advocate when I had to psych myself for days before any meeting where I had to take a difficult stand?

A doubt I did not have was my passion for helping people to fight injustice. Somehow the pain and hurt I'd received early on fueled my energy to make things right for the poor and disenfranchised. A series of events introduced me to the concept of "internalized oppression" and raised my awareness of messages I had internalized about my worth.

As I've mentioned, a major event was Jack Guillebeaux coming to work for FOCAL in 1976. A second major event was my attending, along with more than 2,000 other black women, a conference held by the National Black Women's Health Project at Spelman College in 1983. I had no idea how my life was about to change.

Atlanta was familiar to me from my monthly trips for staff meetings with the Black Child Development Institute, but this was the first time I'd ever set foot on the campus of Spelman College, so often praised by my teachers at Doby High. I was awestruck by the beauty of Spelman's manicured lawns, by the pristine Sister's Chapel and the other halls of scholarship. My mentor Marian Wright Edelman had graduated from Spelman and had been arrested during a Civil Rights protest. Spelman adjoined Morehouse College, where Dr. King had studied.

A buzz was in the air as the conference approached: What was our event convener Billye Avery planning? Since it was about black women, would there be friction and "cat fights?" How would the agenda of this event differ from that of the National Association of Women (NOW) which focused on reproductive rights, the Equal Rights Amendment to the U.S. Constitution, and equal pay for women? The United Nations declared the 1980s the International Decade of Women, which gave us an opening to focus attention on abuse and violence against women, health issues stemming from the stresses of poverty, racism, sexism and second-class treatment in ethnic and cultural traditions.

Presenters in the opening session stated the goal of the conference: for black women to learn to care for ourselves and to take charge of making the changes that were needed. Billye Avery spoke of the early death of her husband, leaving her to raise their three young children, as the catalyst for her focus on health issues.

There were around 2,000 women in attendance, far more than organizers had expected, and we came from everywhere, in all shapes, sizes, ages and complexions; dressed from plain to fancy, and from all parts of the country. As a breakout session, I chose "Black and Female: Reality vs. Myth," led by Lillie Allen, a family medical educator from the Morehouse School of Medicine. About 250 women crowded into a large, oval-shaped room. When the chairs were all filled, attendees sat on the floor. Women were to my right, left, behind and in front of me.

I'd never felt so proud of being black and female. I'd believed my Bible teachings — we had been cursed from Eve disobeying God and eating the apple in the Garden of Eden. Black females were, as Zora Neale Hurston called us, "the mules of society." Whatever our background or station in life, we had to carry the load of our husbands, children, mothers, fathers, aunts and uncles, as well as of white ladies and white men and, often, white children. We were the backbone of the church, the school and the home.

Lillie Allen helped us call out the myth that we should never be tired, needy or sick. We had cooked, washed and cleaned, held outside jobs and been expected to cheerfully meet the needs of our men, no matter how tired our bones felt. It was powerful and rejuvenating to realize that my shame for "being," my exhaustion and pain were not mine alone. A world of women felt as I did, and we were connected.

Women told of being sexually molested by their fathers and blamed by their mothers, of being routinely beaten, of fearing they'd be killed or left without money to survive. A chorus of women spoke of feeling trapped in the role of caretaking for elderly parents or belligerent children. Make-up was smeared, tears flowed freely and tissue boxes were passed like collection plates. I heard women confess to thoughts of suicide, just to escape the pain. I'd thought I was the only one who held that secret weapon to deal with the ultimate madness of living.

It was at this meeting that I first heard the phrase "internalized oppression." The only person I knew in the session was an older woman with whom I'd had several run-ins at Auburn during my work study job there. It's fair to say we didn't like each other. But when our paths crossed as we were leaving the session, we hugged each other, and wished each other well. Our decade-old resentments had vanished.

I left Atlanta knowing my life had been shaken up and all the pieces emptied out. The overwhelming feelings were of joy and relief. The joy sprang from belonging to a group — discovering there were so many others like myself. The relief came from feeling the mask being lifted. I no longer had to pretend to feel joy when I felt sadness nor to hide my anger for fear of upsetting someone.

I felt a new determination springing from my soul; a determination to strive, not just survive; to live with dignity; and to share with others what I'd seen and done, so they could lay down their own burdens and learn to soar.

# 31

## STEREOTYPES AND SCRIPTS

---

*"Unless we truly believe we are equal, structural systems of discrimination will remain forever."*

It's crucially important to identify the superior and inferior scripts that surround us.

"I can't write well."
"I don't like reading."
"Girls aren't supposed to do this."
"You can't trust black folks."
"You got to involve white folks to do it right."

These internalized messages were barriers to the development of healthy children, adults, families and communities and secret messages I had carried inside myself for as long as I could remember.

The amazing discovery was the staff and others shared similar thinking and attitudes. The question became: How to shine a spotlight on changing attitudes in the same way program objectives were used to change poor educational systems, unfair taxes between the haves and have nots, mistreatment of immigrants and low wages?

Unless we truly believe we are equal, structural systems of discrimination will remain forever. I realized my greatest tool for effecting change was to examine my own self.

Allen's "self-help" concept led us to form the Black Women's Leadership and Economic Development Project (BWLEP) in FOCAL. She spoke of the need for a support group to provide safety and accountability to tackle long-held beliefs about our worth. Ten women made up the core of BWLEP and included domestic workers, Ph.D. educators, child care providers and administrators, and organizers.

During the five years we were together, we peeled back layers of fears we carried that blocked our leadership and hurt our economic wellbeing. Coming together, nurturing and supporting each other, sharing what we wanted, let us begin to know that our feelings, intuition, morals, and hopes were valuable, and had to be part of any strategizing around making the world better. The ultimate question of evaluation for anyone in the Project was: How close are you to realizing your vision, and what is needed to make it happen?

Martha Hawkins, a mother of four and on welfare, spoke of her dream to create her own restaurant that would provide for her family and offer employment to other women. Martha's vision became our "Project" and out of BWLEP, Martha's Place restaurant was created. Thirty years later, Martha is known around the country as a mental health advocate, restaurateur and motivational speaker. Her book Finding Martha's Place has inspired a lot of people.

On a recent visit to the restaurant, Martha was speaking with an older white couple from Kansas on their way to Florida who felt they had to find Martha's Place. The woman had come across Martha's book in the Kansas City Library, was touched by her story and wanted to meet her. Tour companies around the country often make Martha's Place a stop on their tours.

The Atlanta experience helped shape my sense of self as a woman but there were others that also deepened my understanding of my own prejudices. The Southern Rural Women's Network (mostly black women in the South), the Southeast Women's Employment Coalition and Women's Technical Assistance Project brought together black and white women, Hispanic and Native American women and expanded our view of oppression.

These associations gave us the chance to push against issues of race, gender and homophobia. I could clarify my thinking on values I cared about, confront my own prejudices and stereotypes, and try out some of the tools that were evolving in FOCAL. These were also ways for me to assume leadership roles away from my mentor, Jack, and focus more on gender scripts.

As I'd been trying to emulate Jack's style of leadership in facilitation and supervision, I was losing myself. The harder I tried, the more incompetent I felt. Jack's nudging just created more fear. When someone asked for our help, I referred them to Jack. Being in women's groups helped me to venture from Jack's tutelage and discover my own style, one that better fit the issues and mindsets of women. It took me a while to hear folks say, "We want you, Sophia, not Jack."

At the same time these events were taking place through my service on boards of these various organizations, there were discoveries taking place inside FOCAL. The staff still consisted of three females and two males. As we sought to confront the wave of conservatism on the national level, and the passive response of black leaders, we called for a consultation with black leaders to address the lack of vision and the urgent need for an agenda to confront Reaganomics.

Using our best organizing skills, we held a series of meetings leading up to this event that included key leaders from various sectors of the community. On the day of the meeting, to our surprise and dismay, all leaders but one canceled. We learned that a call had gone out suggesting that they not attend. One of our funders received a call from one of Alabama's highest black elected officials, saying we "needed to stick to caring for children and stay out of the business of politics."

Undaunted, we pressed forward to organize black women through the Black Women's Leadership and Economic Development Project. All outside experiences were brought to the table at FOCAL staff meetings, which were chances to get feedback, modify our strategies, nurse our hurts and practice new behavior.

The staff went through its own visioning session, and each person was asked to develop an Individual Growth Plan (IGP) that stated where the person wanted to be within a given period, and the knowledge, skills and qualities they wished to develop. Staff served as a support group; each person would identify their areas of growth and specify the support they needed from the group.

The Cooperative Mode borrowed from Transactional Analysis and the principles of cooperation versus competition and abundance versus scarcity formed the basis of the group's contract for "how we want to be together."

We were each responsible for our own learning and asking for what we wanted, or didn't want, from the group. The process was as important as the product.

This arrangement had its strengths, but a major weakness was that staff meetings took longer. We missed some deadlines. In the early phase of our work, we didn't realize that for everyone who is "process-oriented," someone else is "product-oriented." We were "birthing" these concepts, and I leaned more towards process, which left some folks feeling disempowered.

We struggled to evolve these concepts into program strategies. It was hard to separate planning from implementation. Our staff became subjects in our experiment, as we tried to create a model for sharing this work with our constituents; it also became one of our strongest assets. Sharing examples of my personal struggles with empowerment helped make it safe for women to open up about their own fears. More than once I was confronted by women from our base: "You need to practice what you preach Sophia. Take better care of yourself." Being called to task was challenging and helpful.

I can't overlook the staff women at FOCAL, whether serving in positions of Organizers, Office Managers, Coordinators of our various programs or volunteers. They were 95% of the personnel for the 43 years I served as Executive Director.

These women were like sisters: "Sophia can I get lunch for you? It's getting late and you've been here since early this morning and haven't eaten. Why don't you take a couple of days off? You really look worn out; we can handle things, I promise." Passing a note to me as I am on my third conference call: "Do you need me to pick up Kimiya from school?"

This emotional support doesn't begin to account for the professional support of late nights and weekends away from their families as we planned Quarterly Trainings, Legislative days at the Statehouse, and working against report and proposal deadlines to our financial supporters and potential funders. We cried with our losses whether family or work; we pushed and disagreed on strategies and nurtured each other when we fell short.

Male staff had introduced the concept of scripting and internalized barriers. As we engaged in debates about how to use this work with our members, men did most of the talking and women most of the listening. When women did speak, we were timid and hesitant.

This invited males to assume a "teacher" role: "What are you trying to say, Sophia?" or "What would you like to see happen?" I resented their questions but was confused about what I really wanted. A nagging voice in my head said, "You are executive director and should be providing the leadership. Stop abdicating to the men here!" My defense was: "It's their concept so they know best how it should work."

Men had more permission to pick up the magic marker when it was time to run a discussion and they had more permission to debate and even filibuster when they were uncertain about an outcome. On the other hand, it was easy for us to sit back and critique how the guys did it wrong. We wouldn't risk putting ourselves out front.

I was also aware that I wasn't confronting Jack and Wekesa as much because I needed them to do other things that I hated to do, primarily writing. Though they had writing of their own to do, I sometimes asked them to take on my own writing assignments.

It took years for me to develop facilitation skills enhancing my leadership because I could not bring myself to practice this craft at the table. Oh, the "labor pains" and shame of that time! But these were also invigorating times. It was an atmosphere of invention, discovery and promise. The shame of not knowing changed to the joy of learning. Lights came on daily as we uncovered thoughts and feelings and we were learning how to apply those new concepts to our work. Most staff who came through FOCAL learned to apply these discoveries to their lives.

I feel proud that Afiya and Wekesa, who met as FOCAL staffers, have now been married for 32 years and are co-directors of the AYA Educational Institute in Atlanta.

One evening in the early spring of 2019, on an impulse, I called Maria Dacus, a former child care organizer at FOCAL, who is now in Child Care Quality Enhancement at the State Department of Human Resources. When she took my call, I could hear the weariness in her voice from a full day of meetings.

I asked how she was doing, and she replied: "Sophia, I am proud of what I learned at FOCAL and how it informs so much of what I do now." I lamented about missing her and so many of the women that I had known for years. I hoped they were staying strong, through all the changes taking place in the ever-evolving world of child care.

Instantly, Maria's energy was full throttle and there was pride in her voice as she said: "Don't worry, I hear comments when I'm in the field like, 'Honey, they don't know I've got some FOCAL in me and I don't plan to give up.'" She added, "I am proud to let my colleagues know, I am a product of FOCAL."

After chatting about her daughter, a college sophomore, and about new programs on the horizon in the Early Care and Education field, she added lovingly: "Sophia, you will always be my mentor, so please take time for yourself and be grandma for Timiya and little Al." Our roles had switched and she was now offering counsel to me. I climbed into bed with a warm glow in my heart and a sense that all was well.

Cynthia Brown worked in finance in the evenings at FOCAL to provide income for herself since her newly formed organization could not pay her a salary. Heritage Training and Career Center provides support to young mothers and fathers to enter the workforce and better their lives. "Sophia, you've been on my mind. Do you need anything? I know you're traveling to Birmingham a lot for medical treatment; if you need me, with a couple of days' notice I'll be happy to take you."

"Cynthia, you are already overloaded, I can't ask you to take off from work." She reminds me of myself during my time at FOCAL.

"What you have given me Sophia as a person and a leader, it would be an honor to give back." While I've never taken her up on the offer to drive me to the doctor, her office is just a few miles away and she has run by at lunch to unjam my printer or offer me computer advice. Retirement has its perks and disadvantages.

Pamela McCorvey, our former office manager, is a comptroller for the City of Montgomery and uses the FOCAL "being together" approach in her staff meetings. Our very first white employee, Marti Rodwell, operates a "More Is Caught Than Taught" non-profit in Michigan.

Tania Burger, our first full-time development director continues her development work with a Community Development Corporation Agency in Massachusetts; and Wanda Lewis started her work as a bookkeeper in a child care program and held three positions on the board before becoming a FOCAL Parent Support Specialist. Wanda took her experiences back to her childhood hometown and for over 20 years has served as Executive Director of the Boys and Girls Club for Greater Lee County. We continue to connect and collaborate as friends on the issues of our families and the larger community. Deborah Thomas, Program Director and Teumbay Barnes, Child Care Coordinator, continue their work in leadership development of women and girls.

The most wonderful gift to me is being able to call on these women and other FOCAL staff, to be received with warmth, and to know that our work at FOCAL lives on.

I was committed to creating a workplace I would enjoy being part of no matter what position I held. I grew as a person, which changed the way I operated in the office, at home and elsewhere. This process of growth was exciting, scary, and frustrating. I had become so focused that every interaction was filtered through the superior/inferior lens. At times this was aggravating because I just wanted to take things at face value.

For the most part, I was fully energized, and felt the freedom to experiment, to expose my raw feeling, to seek truths and to live in the moment, even with strangers. I had always been rather reserved and disciplined, respectable and predictable.

As my system of values and norms were challenged, I observed that I was becoming compelling, passionate and bold. In the past, during travel if a white person was sitting next to me, especially a male, even if I was reading, writing or napping, they would very often try to strike up a conversation. My response was to accommodate, to talk or mostly listen, even when I preferred to do otherwise. It was a holdover from the days when there was nothing more important for blacks to do than be available to whites. When I became conscious of this, I changed my behavior. The white person would try to get a conversation started with a question:

"What are you reading?"
"I see you are working, what type of work do you do?"
"Wow, I can't wait to get home to my little girl, this has been a hard trip; do you have children?"

I learned to use body language to quiet the questions, and if that didn't work, I would make a polite reply, then say: "I'd like to chat but I have work to finish" or "It's been a tiring trip and I need to refuel." It was liberating to take charge of my personal space.

I no longer needed to psych myself to confront people who were asking too much of me; I no longer worked at hiding my feelings. Nor did I stifle myself out of politeness. I decided to "not abandon me" for any reason. Holding on to this thought was my most powerful tool. "Sophia, I will not leave you, I am here for you and we can get through this together." I learned to be my own best friend.

The decade following the women's conference in Atlanta, I examined my life and restructured all of my key relationships. At first, Albert was hands-off. He wasn't with all this "feeling and emoting" stuff. But as my life changed, he made two major changes.

First, he decided to attend group therapy with me. Also, without my knowledge, he read every book by a black female writer that I brought home. Maya Angelou, Zora Neale Hurston, Alice Walker, and Toni Morrison soon became a way for him to identify more with what I was living, and what was going on in my head. This was a blessing and I appreciate the courage he displayed risking doing something that most black males would see as "wimpy." But he decided he would not be left behind.

I wrote an open letter to my family letting them know what the present "way of being" with them was doing to me, and how, with my new resolve, I would be different. I told them I'd learned recently that my caretaking in the family was driven by feelings of guilt, that my commitment to helping others in the family was still strong but that I would now need to be an advisor, no longer always the person responsible. I said that, in the long run, I hoped this new approach would be better for them, as well as for me.

No one responded to my letter, and I later learned that Mom had told everyone they should be careful with me because I was "nearing a breakdown."

In a way, this was true. I was "breaking down" old dysfunctional patterns and charting a new course. For several years, my relationship with my family was fragile and strange because, despite my brave words, I didn't know how to be with my family without being their caretaker. I deeply appreciate my therapist, Fafar Guillebeaux, for her gentle guidance during these years. I still, at times, care take for my family of origin. But now it is my choice, not an expectation. A good therapist can be essential in the process of healing, escaping old scripts and learning new ones.

A key element of my growth was the black women's support group. It gave me a place to unveil, to share my feelings of inadequacy without judgment. It was a safe place to reveal all the negative thoughts that competed with my feeling good about myself and know that I was not alone in this struggle. Each person in the group had their own issues, their own struggles, and we learned and grew from each other.

There were also four women friends, each of whom served a special need as I struggled with various issues. They were Martha Hawkins, Wanda Lewis, Deborah Walker and Eileen Paul. My two youngest sisters, Katherine and Aretha, were always there, nurturing me during my illnesses, caretaking my children and giving emotional support to my husband when I was away. They asked for little and gave much. I need to identify all of these internal supports, because I couldn't make change happen in my life all by myself.

The most rewarding part of all of this transformation was discovering my own gifts. I allowed myself to recognize and value my strengths and accept my weaknesses. Discovering my true self made me feel more real and alive than I'd ever felt before. There are still pockets of hidden negative messages waiting to be uncovered.

There is in me potential not yet realized, truths waiting to be told and lies still to be exposed, but I am on a journey toward wholeness.

This quest to address internalized oppression and superior/inferior scripts took us on the journey that ended with "More Is Caught Than Taught" (MCTT) and "Communities Act to Create Hope" (CATCH) a decade later. These publications captured our thinking and experiences with uncovering and changing internalized messages about our worth and offered a step-by- step process as a tool to others.

Engaging parents in visioning often begins with a question no one ever asked parents before: "What do you want for your child? What are the qualities you want your child to have?" They often start with, "I want their life to be better than my life," and we ask, "What does that mean for them to have a better life?" They might say, "I don't want them to work as hard, to be treated the way I am at work, and not have an education. I want them to be able to speak out for themselves."

So we ask them, "Do they see you speak out for yourself?" If a parent says no, we ask them why not. We get answers like, "Because I don't have an education," or "I don't speak well." But at that point, they're already involved in the change process.

It was encouraging when we began to hear of others using the term and speaking to the superior/inferior narrative and scripts supporting this belief. I happily accepted an invitation to share our CATCH tool at a White Privilege Conference in Albuquerque. I took every chance I had to make this work visible in grassroots organizing circles.

The entire focus of the conference was examining and pointing out privilege and entitlement and the impact of "whiteness" in our country. One role play in particular left a big impression. Six persons were fitted with labels that everyone could see except the wearers. Their task was to spend 10 minutes planning a party (place, type event, food, invitees) and as they worked on the task, treat each person as society saw them.

Having lived in black skin for all these years, I know all about stereotyping, but I was astounded that people with concealed identities could always name the label they'd been wearing. Some of the clues were: the gay person was asked to decorate and maybe invite a friend to help, but when she asked to bring a friend to the party, others said no. The immigrant was asked to prepare the food. The poor person was asked to help clean but denied the chance to greet guests at the door.

Observing the group's response to the "invisible" person was most painful. Each time he tried to join the planning discussion, his comments were ignored; even when someone looked his way, they quickly averted their eyes. When the young man wearing this label was asked what he thought his label was, he replied "Someone invisible, or maybe mentally ill."

It was also painful to hear the person wearing the label "black" say; "Either I am black or someone marginalized." It happened that a young black male wore the label of rich. When asked to guess his label, he replied, "I am either a white male, or rich." During follow-up discussion of this exercise, two themes resonated: the starkness of scripts, and how quickly people become a pack, upholding scripts and labels, even when they dislike doing so.

# 32

## LEAVING HOME AND GOING HOME

*"The jealousy, the unease with black independence reminds me of adoptive parents whose child has started searching for her birth parents."*

"I am from Alabama in the United States. My hometown is Wetumpka, and my community is called Redland. Growing up, every fifth Sunday, the community came to what we called the District Center to praise and worship and fellowship with each other. Being a part of you today, hearing you share your hopes and aspirations — achievements and struggles — I am humble and touched by your gestures of love, given so freely and unselfishly. My tears are tears of joy because in each of you, I see the faces of my cousins, aunts and uncles, sisters and brothers. I feel the presence of your encouragement and affirmation, the same as I felt from my home community during those moments as a child speaking shyly before the congregation. I am at home, you are my family."

Even before the translations were complete, I saw smiles and nods and heard applause, just as I had as a child. It was 1985 in Kenya, but for a moment I was a child again, back in Redland. I was speaking to 50 women and men in Githunguri, 50 miles north of Nairobi. My journey there had started a year before, at FOCAL, when each of us had shared a five-year vision. I said that I'd like to travel to Africa. I soon received a call from Eileen Paul. Would I like to present at the World Conference of Women in Nairobi in July? I laughed and said "Yes, if I can do it from Alabama." But when I was invited to apply for a Ford Foundation Woman of Color Scholarship to attend the conference, I did. I was one of 25 women, half of us women of color, who won a scholarship.

It would have been easier not to win the scholarship! Now I had to resolve some conflicts: Was I being selfish here? Who would take care of my children? How would Albert manage? Would my going hurt FOCAL in some way? How could I leave my ailing mother? And was my own health strong enough to make the trip?

I resolved these conflicts, one by one, and decided "Confusion be damned, I am going to Africa!" I had four weeks to get a passport, a visa, six inoculations and $2,000.

I was first amazed, then amused, by how folks responded when I told them I was flying to Africa. My white physician said: "I can't understand why you would want to go. All they have over there is disease, beasts, and racists." From the waiting room, my mother called out: "She's got all three of those right here!" My black nurse commented: "Girl, you must be crazy. What about your children?" She was worried I'd bring diseases home from Africa and expose my kids. The postal worker processing my visa application felt that Africa was full of starving, diseased black people, and why would anyone in her right mind want to go there? These people seemed to make mental exceptions for hunters, safari visitors and gold-seeking investors. During an anxious phone call to the post office two days before my departure, the man there told me the President had warned us that no one should travel to Africa while TWA was dealing with a hostage crisis. When he conceded he'd located my visa, I could not contain my delight.

What I realized is that many whites still perceive blacks as children, people who need to be directed and guided. An attitude persists of possession or ownership. The jealousy, the unease with black independence, reminds me of adoptive parents whose child has started searching for her birth parents. As blacks, we sometimes try to protect whites by denying our roots in Africa. But I thirsted to connect with these roots, to push through the barriers and stereotypes, including my own, and to experience Africa!

Amid the confusion of Immigration, Customs, baggage checks, possible hostage crises, bomb scares and poor travel instructions for 35 women traveling together, the "togetherness" frayed. By the time we reached Nairobi and the New Chiromo Hotel, we'd split into sub-groups by race and, within race, by region and political ideology. How sad that we were only united once after arriving: to vent our anger at group leaders we felt had abandoned us. We were all charged up to be in Nairobi with a chance to connect with women from around the world, but we had very little interest in connecting with each other as members of the American family.

I was determined to focus on seeing Kenya: its peoples, cultures, lifestyles, freedoms, oppressions, beauty, ugliness, its riches and its shortcomings; to connect with women from around the world, to share my insights and to learn from others. The city of Nairobi was beautiful, thronged with palm trees, flowers, fruits and handsome people, like the marketplaces I'd seen in Sunday School pictures as a girl. My ingrained images of Africa were from TV clips of "Tarzan," (jungle savages and half-clothed people in tents) and famine coverage (starving children with bulging eyes and bloated stomachs.) I was taken aback by how modern Nairobi was: skyscrapers, big banks, sleek hotels and more Mercedes automobiles than I'd ever seen.

Why were there such extremes of wealth and poverty? Did the middle and upper classes of Nairobi ever connect with those living in the shanties, in mud, cardboard and tin huts? Then again, when was the last time I had emotionally connected with someone that lived on the fringe — lonely, penniless and near starvation?

Mary, the housekeeper, washed and sunned my clothes, and brought me extra soap, towels and toilet paper. She looked poor, spoke little English and appeared to be living in a shanty slum outside of town. She seemed overwhelmed by all of the hotel room's frills and trinkets: toothpaste, perfume, clothes, shoes, jewelry. One day, I returned to the room early and found it filled with the aroma of my perfume, and Mary brushing her teeth with my toothbrush. She knew exactly which of my clothes fit her and, a few days before we were to leave, asked me to give her some of my belongings. I offered her food when she looked hungry and tipped her for cleaning the room; she soon started asking for money for sodas and bus fare.

Was it my fault for leading her on? Was the rich American being taken for a ride? I knew the frustration I felt was less personal than cultural, but I couldn't help feeling Mary was acting selfish and greedy. At the same time, I recalled how it had felt being "without" as a girl — without new clothes, new shoes or a lunchbox, when other children I knew had those things. For several days, I debated, then decided the only way to defuse my anger was to let Mary know how I felt. I did and, after that, we became much closer.

There was a spirit of ingenuity and craftsmanship in Nairobi. The city was full of small entrepreneurs — so rare in black communities in the U.S. But tradition and custom had allowed men to escape shouldering their share of the work. One local leader told us: "The women still carry the loads, working in the fields and caring

for our children and our 'big babies.'" She meant the men. Some men tried to justify these inequities, insisting women enjoyed their role. We were told that women
were the laborers for the family, and men the protectors. Women seemed to know
the system was unfair — but perhaps not the psychic price they were paying for it.
The hard dues they'd paid had taken a clear physical toll on their bodies, yet they
rejoiced in a unity of spirit. Kenyan women seemed not content, but more peaceful
than their American sisters. I was saddened by how willing women were to mutilate
the genitals of young girls to make them acceptable wives, less likely to cheat on
their older, polygamous husbands. But it was a misplaced disdain that American
women showed toward Kenyan women who supported this practice.

The opening of the woman's conference was like an Olympic opening ceremony.
Everything had an air of excitement, adventure and unity. Nearly 10,000 wom-
en packed the Jomo Kenyatta Center in the heart of Nairobi. We were every size,
shape, color and form of dress, armed with camera and translators. As dancers
from many Kenyan tribes performed their welcoming dance, as the drums roared
and the African women responded in their native tongues, I was proud to be a
daughter of Africa.

The workshops, held indoors and out, on lawns, under trees, in tents, in hallways,
and lobbies and on sidewalks, all celebrated the power and value of women. We
saw ourselves in the struggles of others. We felt each other's pain, recognized each
other's fear of war, poverty, hunger, violence and self-oppression. Would this be just
a spark, kindled once a century? I kept wondering how we could keep this flame
burning. I knew we had to believe in ourselves, and in our power to create a world
reflecting our hopes and dreams. To do that, we had to remove the barriers of distrust, suspicion and insensitivity that stood in our way.

They were the same barriers that prevented some women from feeling the pain and
loss expressed by native women as we left the New Chiromo. They were the barriers
of "I am better than you" or "You are better than me." These barriers plagued all of
our deliberations, and forced us to have two women's conferences in the first place,
Nairobi Official on one side; and NGO on the other.

I was touched by the giving nature of Kenya's people and their openness and offers
of friendship. We left Nairobi with far more than we had given. As the NGO group

stood for a group photo, bunched tightly to fit everyone in the picture, New Chiromo people looked on in front of us. Some had to be pried away. Rosalind was standing near me, tears streaming down her face. Instinctively, I handed her my camera. Excited, she stepped up to take a picture of us — but one of the NGOs chided her and forced her aside; Rosalind was interfering with the professional photographer. It was like slapping a child who'd asked for a hug.

We boarded our skydecker bus laughing and waving to New Chiromo and its residents. Women on the New Chiromo staff who'd made sacrifices to see us off at the airport learned they could not ride the bus back but we foreigners didn't seem to care. We were delayed 10 minutes after boarding as our driver tried to maneuver the huge bus out of New Chiromo's little parking area. Kenyan men graciously lifted cars out of our way, while on the bus my fellow sisters were clapping and cheering to be done with New Chiromo, with its lack of hot water, poorly cooked eggs and diarrhea. How could these women be so insensitive?

There to greet us at Nairobi Airport were Susan, Rosalind and Sufrose, who'd paid a taxi driver half a month's wages to drive them there. Again, I was deeply touched — but struck that I was the only one in our group who thought to help these Kenyan women with the cab fare. I borrowed 200 shillings and gave it to them. Had this been Mexico, Nicaragua or India, would I have cared as much? I think I would have. To care about each other is the only way to create a world where we are all one.

This was the spirit of the conference: women of the world coming together. What's still missing is an understanding that our world agenda, all of our resolutions and platforms are like sounding brass and tinkling cymbals, if we cannot love and appreciate each other. Women have the foundation for this kind of love but we must first feel good about ourselves. We must examine the worldwide scripts that say that women are not okay. These negative messages cloud our minds and separate us from our humanity.

We can all do better.

# 33

# "I AM SERIOUS AND I MEAN BUSINESS"

*"This is one of the greatest moments of my life!*
*I am so glad to be alive to see it."*

A span of 30 years existed between us in age. Her demeanor and presence called for a handle when addressing her. It was in the Tabernacle Church meeting that I first laid eyes on Thelma Onita Craig, soft-spoken and with a complexion fair enough to pass for white. She had a passion for voting rights and the education of black children. "Call me Thelma," she commanded.

"Mrs. Craig, that's hard for me to do. It seems disrespectful."
"Not if that's what I want," she replied.

I was puzzled and after several unsuccessful attempts to call her "Thelma," asked why it was important for me to call her by her first name?

"Sophia, you are a young leader and I don't want your leadership to be marginalized by your age. You should feel a peer of any of us in this room." This was progressive thinking for the Deep South in 1972.

Thelma Craig was not only advanced in her thinking about leadership development, but a visionary as well.

Mrs. Craig put her commitment to education and becoming a voter into action. When the 7th of her 12 children started school, this small-framed woman boarded a school bus with her children and returned to finish her high school education. She joined in a lawsuit against the county for its discriminatory practices in zoning and issuance of equipment to black schools, and refused to be dissuaded by the tactics used to keep blacks from voting.

We teased Thelma by calling her "the velvet-covered razor" because of her quiet, nonchalant way of leading policy makers to her point. "Mr. Lee, what is the State's process for reviewing fire inspections of exempt facilities? So if there is no process; who is in charge of this area? If no one is in charge of this area, does that mean exempt facilities are not being inspected?" Never raising her voice or appearing adversarial, her questions cut to the chase and spotlighted key issues to be addressed, whether at a State agency or a FOCAL meeting. I trusted her wisdom deeply.

I came to her with a political quandary. Our two strongest supporters in the state legislature were battling fiercely for a Congressional seat. 'How should I handle this situation?', I asked Mrs. Craig. One of these politicians was like a son to her. Her reply was vintage Thelma: "Your job is FOCAL and doing what you can to ensure these children are taken care of. These are big boys and they can take care of themselves without your help."

My life as a black woman, wife, mother and leader of an organization during the early 80s was at an apex one moment and fairly low at other points. I struggled to make sense of my place in the political climate that had catapulted a new movement for black women and created financial peril for child care facilities and black families as a whole. I wondered whether there was enough of me to meet all of these demands.

A person key to my leadership at the Alabama State Legislature and at FOCAL was Clara Card, Director of Joyland Child Development Center in Auburn. Ms. Card climbed the ranks of leadership on FOCAL's Board to become President, and held the rare distinction of life member.

Clara's quiet spirit was buffered by steel and fortified by raising her two siblings and 10 children as a single mom. In my first meeting of memory, we were in a workshop discussing how to address difficult staff issues. She talked about feeling that she was held hostage by one staff person who had a relationship with her funding source; but was doing her job poorly and had a poor attitude toward her co-workers.

Clara cried tears of frustration. I offered some advice from my limited exposure to problem-solving, and she would later thank me for helping her confront a situation she had long avoided. It was the start of our relationship, and the favor over these 30 years would be returned many times.

Clara had a quiet, yet stern manner. She had no formal education and had started out as a housekeeper in the local Catholic church, which helped her launch Joyland Child Development Center. A local white director of a child care program in the housing project that housed Joyland invited Clara to accompany her to the state Legislature. This brought her into the inner circle of a group of white child care provider advocates from east Alabama.

While we were all there at the legislature working side by side for the benefit of children, this group, which had the ear of Governor George C. Wallace, negotiated a contract to use state funds as a match to draw down federal funds. This was done without FOCAL's knowledge. This contract led to large disparity: seventy-five percent of the dollars used for child care were supporting twenty-five percent of the children, mostly white. A mere twenty-five percent of funds were left for the majority of children, mostly black, receiving child care services. Clara Card was the person to let the cat out of the bag about this covert holdover from Alabama's past.

In the early '80s, FOCAL succeeded in having this unfair funding practice thrown out. Clara's whistle-blowing did not sit well with the group members and, for a while, relationships cooled. Clara would later be the catalyst for bringing most sides together. Clara was somewhat familiar with the legislative process, and had enough staff to allow her time away from her center without violating state child/staff ratio requirements, so she became my regular cohort at the statehouse.

It was during one of these statehouse trips that I had my "life changing" encounter with two black senators. These were not just any senators; they both were friends of FOCAL, and men I admired a great deal. In fact, one was more like a personal friend because his mother was a FOCAL board member and center director and his wife was a leader in our women's organization.

The question that prompted what ended up being a "screaming match" between the three of us was this: "Senators, when do you think is a good time to introduce our child care funding bill?" One responded, "Sophia you are stressing yourself. Why don't you go back to work, or better still, go home and get some rest and let us handle things?" The other chimed in, "That's right, because you're looking rather fatigued."

Had they told my white colleagues the same thing when they visited earlier in the day? Their paternalistic, patronizing tone was infuriating. I responded with more than a little sarcasm, "You're overlooking or not detecting that East Alabama contract which has taken most of the money for white providers is reason enough for me be here looking out for my constituents."

"You are out of line, Sophia Harris!"

"In what way?" I asked. "Is it because I'm a woman talking to men — or is it because I'm a citizen, talking to my elected policy makers?"

The words spoken that day, on both sides, were loud, passionate and at times shrill. In my anger and disappointment, I started to cry, and headed off to the ladies' room to compose myself. Ms. Card was in an adjoining office and heard the whole thing; she followed quietly behind me.

In the restroom, I repeated over and over: "I am just so mad at myself for crying, I don't want them to think I am weak; I am so mad!"

She allowed me to rant for a moment, then started laughing. "This is one of the greatest moments of my life! I am so glad to be alive to see this moment. Sophia, those tears are not at all a sign of weakness. You have just put both of those men in their place and called them out for patronizing you."

By then, I was laughing, too, and thinking: "Wow, I have just confronted two well-known civil rights attorneys regarding their sexism."

I emerged from the restroom, ready for the business at hand: obtaining child care funding. The first and more familiar senator apologized as soon as I returned. When I went to the office of the second senator and asked, "Where do we go from here?" he looked up slowly from his computer and said: "Sophia, we can work well together as long as you understand one thing: I am serious and I mean business."

I replied, "I am confident we can work well together—as long as you understand me—I am serious and I mean business." Later that year, this same legislator requested the "honor" of presenting me with the distinguished service award by the Alabama Black Lawyers Association.

I still love and respect both of these men, and my heart hurts deeply that one died suddenly, several years after this incident.

Protecting children both physically and emotionally was Clara Card's mission, starting with her own siblings, after her mother became mentally disabled. Once, she overheard a teacher tell a child in the classroom "You make me sick." Instantly, Clara summoned that teacher to the office. "I want you to go home for three days and think about what you said to that child. After that time, let's talk about the impact of your words."

All of her sons played sports and one coached at the university level. Once, when Clara overheard a degrading remark by the head coach to one of her sons, she went to the coach and told him her son was transferring to another university the following day and if the coach failed to make an announcement wishing him well on his decision to transfer, there would be a press conference to report what she had overheard. The coach wished Clara's son well on his decision to transfer.

Parents of Joyland childcare program trust her because she is a wonderful nurturer to their children and to them as well. Probably more than any child care program that I am aware of, Clara Card has had more parents to complete their GED, and many go on to college. She is invested in their well-being and the entire family.

Her children treat her as if she were a precious stone. When I traveled to New Hampshire to receive an honorary doctorate from Dartmouth College, Ms. Card accompanied me along with Albert and my sister, Katherine. While there, Ms. Card became ill from something she ate. I had never been so scared, remembering the face of her son Nigel, himself a university basketball coach, who had instructed me at the airport, "Don't let anything happen to my mother."

She is a treasure to many, and a child care stalwart in Alabama. Ms. Card never sought the spotlight; she was willing to be the backup. Her quiet resolve and devotion to her children, the children of Joyland and the state were a source of strength and encouragement to me. She was my rock and go-to source for board business and in a few instances, personal advice. I trusted her wise counsel and knew she would not hesitate to give it to me straight.

There are not enough pages to capture all the impact on my life of stalwarts like Clara Card, Annie Moore, Ola Sanders and Thelma Craig. Clara, who loved those babies so dearly; Annie, a small and quiet woman who looked frail but was feisty; Ola, always willing to defy the system for the sake of children in her care; and Thelma, soft-spoken but with a will of steel. There have been many more models for me in my life and career; and the lessons of endurance, commitment, bold leadership and sacrifice are some of the takeaways I strive to live by.

# 34

# FAFAR GUILLEBEAUX: TRANSFORMATION

*"For me, transformation is to move beyond every barrier that blocks one's sense of okayness."*

At the heart of my transformation as a woman and a person was Farzaneh "Fafar" Guillebeaux, wife of Jack Guillebeaux. Fafar came to the U.S. at age 20 as a student from Iran, married Jack when interracial marriages in North Carolina were still illegal, and was a devout Baha'i. Since the fall of the Shah of Iran in the late 1970s, many of Fafar's family members have been persecuted and even killed for their Baha'i faith.

What is it about this small-framed, attractive, soft-spoken woman who speaks four languages and has been close by during every major challenge and celebration in my life since I was 27? She fashions beautiful creations from flowers and other art forms, she reads Baha'i teachings, but her all-time favorite practice is to offer wisdom to a person about who they are and what is their purpose for being.

"Sophia, what was the update from your doctor's visit?" Fafar asked me. "There has been no change, Fafar. I will need surgery. I am anemic which has weakened my immune system and lowered my resistance to catching colds and other respiratory infections."

This counseling session in late 1989 was one of many since Fafar became licensed as a psychological therapist in the late '70s. I'd agreed to be part of her practicum group as she earned her degree.

In those days, I was working so late that I'd start to fall asleep at the wheel and only be jolted back to consciousness when my car hit the shoulder of the road. I'd jump in my car after a fight with Albert and speed down the interstate in tears, not aware of a bridge until I was halfway through it. At least twice a year, I was landing in the hospital from illness brought on by exhaustion.

But I was so deeply in denial that I was insulted when Fafar asked why I was trying to kill myself. "Fafar, what are you saying? I've never told you I was trying to take my life."

She replied, "No, you have not spoken the words, but your actions have spoken loudly what may not be in your awareness." How could she know about my early attempt with the seven pain reliever tablets at age sixteen?

It took several sessions and some resenting of Fafar's words before I came to terms with her assertion and agreed to a "no suicide contract." She convinced me to close the door on behavior that would leave me feeling discounted and demoralized. She pointed out that death is not an escape.

"Sophia, repeat your contract with me: 'I will not unintentionally or on purpose, take my life.'" I agreed not to eat myself to death; and not to overwork myself to death. I hated the exercise of double chairs, when you talk from your perspective, then change chairs and speak from the perspective of the person you are challenged by. I also hated going around the room asking for affirmation or stating, "I will not kill myself." But these things were helpful to me.

I recall an instance of Fafar's intervention while serving of the Board of the Ms. Foundation for Women. Although the Ms. Board was diverse in color, wealth and a mix of women who were like me, a grantee of the Foundation, I felt that some of the women of wealth, did not see a black, grantee from the South as peer. I will hasten to add that those were small in number and I felt privileged to be in deliberation with top women leaders in the country. Gloria Steinem, Board Chair, opened her home to each of us for overnight stays to learn more about our families and work. A black CEO now leads the Foundation.

During this particular meeting I was asked by Gloria to head up a new committee.

"Gloria, I will need to get back with you," I responded.
"Do you need to check with your board?" another member inquired.
"No, I need to check with my therapist," I replied.
There were raised eyebrows and some turned toward me in surprise. One repeated, "Your therapist?"

My response was curt and laced with sarcasm. "What's wrong? Are you all surprised that a black woman from the South has a therapist? I bet the majority of you in this room have therapists." At that point, I wasn't sure if the patronizing tones were classism, racism or both. Out of regard for Gloria, I didn't pursue it further.

As a way of combating my inability to say "no," a major culprit in my chronic exhaustion, I had promised Fafar I would not accept new board service or projects outside of FOCAL without consulting her. This practice would strengthen my resolve to turn down commitments and take better care of myself, rather than handing over my power to others.

I felt the attitude of some women on the Ms. Foundation board, most of whom were white and well-to-do, fed into a dysfunctional belief held by many in the black community that to pursue counseling was to admit you were weak-minded or crazy. Why else would you place someone else in charge of your mind?

Fafar had a remarkable practice for over 20 years — consulted with physicians, conducted sessions across the U.S. and in Israel, Turkey, Australia, and China, primarily speaking on women's empowerment. During the 18 years since she had to shut down her office due to illness, my admiration for her has doubled. I have seen her faith put to the test, and her skills and sense of purpose become even sharper. Her book, Spiritual Transformation: Reclaiming Our Birthright captures the transformational tools and principles of her Baha'i faith.

What has made Fafar such an effective transformative healer is her willingness to be a peer in the learning process. Acknowledging her growth and challenges and the continuous process of peeling the onion of discovery in life's choices is a powerful tool. She is a listener and takes to heart each of her clients.

When I confessed I had a grave fear of receiving blood transfusions, she advised me to donate my own blood for surgery. I spent a year receiving iron injections prior to my surgery and was able to donate my blood in case it was needed during surgery.

Then, just two days before surgery, I learned that my donated blood had been contaminated and was unusable. Since childhood, I've had trouble overcoming the superior-inferior relationship of doctor and patient. In this case, my fears were elevated by the attitude of my doctor of 15 years.

With Fafar's assistance, I was able to sort through my feelings and identify what I needed from my doctor. In essence, I wanted to be treated as a person, not a slab of meat on an operating table.

I summoned my courage and told him: "Doctor Byrne, we've been through some challenging times these past 15 years. Even when things didn't work out as I'd hoped, I felt you cared and had given your best. But my fear right now is that I don't feel that sense of caring. You seem distant, matter of fact... I don't feel a connection. Before going under the knife with my life in your hands, I need to know that you care about me as a person."

It took courage on his part to confess that my perception was correct. He felt jaded. A mean-spirited lawsuit from a former patient had left him wondering if he should shut down his obstetrics practice. He apologized for letting this affect his professional behavior. I knew from my own life that it can be hard to separate the two. Fafar used to say: "If it doesn't come out straight, it will surely come out crooked."

I came through the surgery fine and went home on the third day. On my second day home, I was rushed back to the hospital and had emergency surgery for a life-threatening infection.

As I was being placed on the operating table, before being put under, I overheard this debate about a blood transfusion between my doctor and the surgeon who was called in for my case.

The surgeon said, "This patient needs a transfusion, before surgery."
Dr. Byrne replied, "No, she doesn't want blood. I promised her she would be transfused only in a life-and-death situation.
"What do you think this is?" asked the surgeon.

In my foggy state of mind, I wished that someone in my family was hearing this. I awoke to Dr. Byrne sitting by my bed, saying "Mrs. Harris, you are going to be fine.

We did not have to give you a transfusion. Do you like grapefruit?"

The next day and two days following, he came bearing grapefruit and sat for at least 20 minutes by my bedside.

During the hours prior to the second surgery, I was only semi-conscious as doctors tried to figure out the cause of my massive infection. I could hear Fafar praying in Farsi. At one point, I heard "Sophia, Sophia, you've got to come back! I have prayed every prayer I know." Moments later, the doctors came and said X-rays had found the problem.

For me, transformation is to move beyond every barrier that blocks one's sense of what I call "okayness." Whether that obstacle is embedded in messages about race, class, gender, religion, sexual identity, whatever, it's about becoming aware and peeling back the layers of those things we've been taught to believe about ourselves since childhood and replace them with new information. The second step is having the courage to act on the knowledge that's been unveiled.

I have deep trust in the woman who has played a huge role in my learning to know, love and appreciate Sophia. She showed me how to recognize and value my strengths and to acknowledge my weaknesses, and in doing this I found I felt more real, more alive.

I have seen a woman who came to this country 50 years ago and adjusted to an income status, marriage and culture that were completely foreign while still advancing the Baha'i faith for which her family has been persecuted in her homeland. Fafar incorporated the tenets of this faith in her practice, "the oneness of mankind." As a therapist and women's rights advocate, she has shared her own transformation and invited me and others to join her on the journey.

# 35

## GROWING UP

---

*"The Sophia who once couldn't write a composition on "utopia" was now presiding over a body of people at a statehouse where lawmakers once wouldn't dignify my presence by looking at me when answering a question."*

"What did you mean when you said between 1980 and 1986 you grew up?" my writing coach asked.

"It was not about becoming an adult, that's for sure," was my first response. During this period I became a mother, FOCAL went broke and, within a couple of years, received its largest grant. I became a caregiver for my mother who had a stroke, and I became a women's rights activist. I traveled abroad for the first time, lost and found my confidence as executive director of FOCAL, and finally realized that if I was going to survive, it was up to me to make my own way.

It was October 1986, and I was en route to Atlanta for a board meeting of the Southern Regional Council. My heart was as heavy as it is when someone has died. My mother was hospitalized in a semi-coma following a stroke. For the first time in my 36 years, she couldn't say "Hey, baby, how you doing?" or offer me guidance on a problem or just pray for me, as she did whenever I had to get on the road. Would she be alive when I returned to Montgomery?

I didn't want to make this trip, but my siblings told me, "There's nothing you can do for Mom but worry. At least you'll be making a contribution by going. That's what she would want." I didn't know it then, but Mom's stroke would set in motion a care giving provider/coordination role that would last for 19 years. During this period, until his death in 2000, Dad played a key role in mom's caregiving.

In late summer of 1985, we were informed by the Human Services Commissioner that the Child Care Subsidy Program would be terminated by early spring of 1986. When the Commissioner was confronted about what this would mean for working families, she said: "If you all want something different, go to Legislature and get more funding; in the meantime, I am going to do what I have to do."

My response was: "You are absolutely correct. You do what you have to do and we will do what we have to do!"

Miffed by the Commissioner's arrogant, uncaring attitude, our group of five, mostly FOCAL board members, left resolved to address this crisis.

"We will see who has the last word." We could not allow this vital program for our people to be eliminated. We planned a strategy meeting for the following week.

In the fellowship hall of Dexter Avenue King Memorial Baptist Church, across the street from the Capitol and the offices of Governor George Wallace, about 25 people gathered and put together a strategy, setting into motion one of FOCAL's most triumphant advocacy campaigns.

"One with a vision will marshal all available resources," says the African Proverb, and that is exactly what happened over the course of the next five months. We joined forces with the Adult Day Care advocates, other child advocates, and community leaders.

In a speech at our annual meeting, which was turned into a strategy session, we were encouraged by State Senator Hank Sanders who told a story: "My brother was trapped under a car that had fallen off the jack as he tried to repair a flat tire. His muffled screams of pain were heard and two guys came to help. After several failed attempts to lift the car and realizing that my brother's chest was being crushed with the weight of the car, they were frantic, trying to figure out what to do next.

"At that moment my brother's wife, hearing a commotion, came over and saw the dire situation. With a force that defied nature, she positioned herself and the three of them lifted the car enough to free her husband."

Hank Sanders finished by saying: "They saved my brother's life. And although the task you all are facing seems insurmountable, if you are determined and willing to draw on all of your resources, you will prevail."

We launched the Movement to Save Child Care that included rallies and marches at the State Capital and a letter writing campaign that resulted in 10,000 letters being delivered to the desk of Governor Wallace's secretary.

One night my young daughter answered the phone and said "Mommy, somebody's on the phone that don't talk good." When I answered, the person said "Mrs. Harris, this is George Wallace." He went on to say something like, "I have always stood for the little people."

He paused, began to weep and said "I know what it's like to be poor, and I am not against young mothers trying to feed their children; I'm not trying to take away their livelihood; I've always stood for the little person. Whatever I can do as governor to save day care, I will. You can count on that."

When I hung up the phone, my mind flashed back to the Wetumpka High years when Wallace, in his heyday, would give a speech to fire up the segregationists. Mailboxes in our neighborhood would be shot up the next day. Taunts and ridicule from white students flared. I wondered if he realized who he was talking to, that I was one who had integrated a white school?

Memory of that painful period swept over me, yet I felt relieved that I held no hatred.

My thoughts went to Psalms 110:1: "Sit thou, at my right hand until I make thine enemies thy footstool." During the next month, George Wallace would make several more such calls to me. I was told he was quite lonely. Making calls was one of the things he enjoyed doing.

Five days before termination of child day care was to take effect, the Legislative Black Caucus and the Governor's Office made a deal to extend the program until further state funds could be found.

By now, I was vice chair of the Governor/Legislative Task Force on Child Day Care. We were meeting day and night with advocates, business leaders, agency heads and community leaders to stabilize this critical funding base for low-income families. In between, I was running to take Mom to physical therapy, checking on FOCAL and checking in with Albert and the kids. My life was a maze of meetings, drafting bills, negotiating with policy makers, confronting child advocates on strategies that didn't work for black providers and parents, coordinating care givers and doctor visits and feeling a ton of guilt that I was not around to support my mother in her recovery of this devastating stroke that had taken her memory, most of her speech and left her right side paralyzed.

On one of my "run by" the office visits, Jack showed me a letter from FOCAL's newest and largest funder, the Bernard van Leer Foundation from The Hague, requesting I attend a seminar in Lima, Peru the next month.

I said "What! I can't travel right now. There is just too much going on."
Jack answered, "You've got to go, Sophia."
"Why can't you go?" I asked.
"Because they want FOCAL's executive director; this is too important, you must go."

Thoughts running through my mind—Mom's recovery is still in a delicate place, we're at a critical juncture with the Task Force, Alden's asthma has been flaring up… How can I be out of the country for two weeks? Even as I pondered these thoughts, I knew I couldn't turn down a request from this new lifeline to our work.

Developments with the Task Force were racing through the Legislature. Eighteen resolutions and a bill to mandate child day care were being readied as we moved to present the report to the governor and legislature, as legislation required. I was humbled to see words I'd written turned into policy.

The Sophia who once couldn't write a composition on "Utopia" was now presiding over a body of people in a statehouse where lawmakers once wouldn't dignify my presence by looking at me when answering a question.

With our strong coalition of advocates, child care was getting the attention it deserved.

"The lady from Alabama has had her hand up for a while, Mr. Chairman." Yes, my hand has been up several times. Each time I've been overlooked at this western hemisphere symposium on early education in Lima, Peru. Besides my frustration of being discounted, there was the language barrier; not being a Spanish speaker, I've had to adjust to listening to speakers through translation equipment.

It was no coincidence that I was ignored by the chair of the proceedings who was president of the foundation that had just funded FOCAL. In a smaller workshop discussion the day before, he'd heard my position of bringing all the key players in a child's life to the policymaking table. I got the clear impression that he disagreed.

When finally acknowledged, I said, "Mr. Chairman, I am in support of all the principle issues raised that are paramount to a strong early education and development, but I also believe it is short-sighted not to include the value of advocacy both by practitioners and parents to ensure quality programs."

My remarks were out of line with the rest of the conferees and sponsors, but I had to represent what I knew to be true in my life, and I didn't think the countries represented were that different from the United States, especially where poor children and families were concerned. Later, FOCAL's program officer told me in a joking tone: "You Southern blacks have to make trouble wherever you go."

When I burst into tears, he quickly added that he was delighted I'd pushed the issue of advocacy; it would later become a key component of the foundation's principles for early education.

Peru was my second trip out of the country; my first had been to the World Conference of Women in Nairobi, Kenya the year before. In each instance, I found myself promoting justice; advocating for those who were discounted and left out of decision-making—women in Nairobi and parents in Lima. My work on the Task Force added momentum and clarity to my beliefs.

It was 1985 before I realized that the Decade of Women, declared by the United Nations, was ushering my own growth into womanhood. I bore my first child in 1980 and adopted my second one in 1983.

Life threw me some curves, and there were more discoveries to be made, but one thing was certain: I had grown up.

Top, Sophia marching across the Edmund Pettus Bridge in Selma, Alabama during the annual Bridge Crossing Jubilee Commemoration in 2014.

Center, Equal Justice Initiative founder Bryan Stevenson with Sophia at 2014 FOCAL Annual Conference, where he served as keynote speaker. *Photo credit: Joe Keffer*

Below, LaTosha Brown, co-founder of Black Voters Matter, Sophia and writer, political activist and feminist organizer Gloria Steinem, at a New York Gala held in honor of Sophia's work in 2016.

Sophia with dear friends Marty Makower (writing coach) and her husband labor rights organizer Joe Keffer, while visiting them in California.

The Bracy Family Reunion, September 4, 2019. *Photo credit: KT Event Creations*

Sophia's brother-in-law, Rev. Lorenza Moore, granddaughter Sacoria Brown and Katherine at her graduation. *Photo credit: KT Event Creations*

Sophia's niece Kim Evans, her husband David Evans and brother Harvey Fleming at Sophia's Retirement Gala, 2016. *Photo credit: Marty Makower*

Sophia with daughter Kimiya, granddaughter Timiya, son Alden and grandson Alden, Jr. after church service, March 13, 2017. *Photo credit: Author's personal collection*

THE WHITE HOUSE
WASHINGTON

December 8, 2015

Ms. Sophia Bracy Harris
Montgomery, Alabama

Dear Sophia:

It is a pleasure to join your family, friends, and colleagues in congratulating you on your retirement. As you celebrate this milestone, I hope you take pride in the contributions you have made over the course of your career.

I send my warmest wishes for a rewarding retirement and the best of luck as you set off on the next stage of your life.

Sincerely,

Letter congratulating Sophia on her retirement from
President Barack Obama

FOCAL staff and volunteers at the organization's 2014 Annual Conference:
Back row, left to right: Cynthia Brown, Deborah Thomas, Grace Okia, Teumbay
Barnes, Natilee McGruder and Maria Dacus; Front left to right, Aretha Bracy, Sophia,
Marty Makower, Katherine Moore and Destiny Bracy. *Photo credit: Marty Makower
and Joe Keffer*

Sophia's brothers at parents' 50th wedding anniversary celebration. From right to
left: Charles, Harvey, Edwin and John. *Photo credit: Author's personal collection*

Sophia with her sister Debra in 2010. *Photo credit: Marty Makower*

# 36

## MY FUNDRAISING YOKE

---

*"Money is power and when someone has something you need or want, it creates a superior/inferior dynamic regardless of color."*

One late summer day I took a call from a woman visiting the Highlander Training Institute in Monteagle, Tennessee, a social justice institute that had provided leadership development training to Rosa Parks, Martin Luther King, Ella Baker and many SNCC leaders.

"Sophia, I am Andrea Rabinowitz from Seattle and learned of your work at Highlander. May I come over for a visit to see what the work looks like on the ground?"

I learned later that Andrea was a retired clinical child psychologist and her husband, Alan, a well-known economist. They were both involved in social justice funding, and Alan had been a founder of the National Network of Grantmakers.

The FOCAL staff had just kicked off its fall fund drive and was facing all the demands of our annual training conference and election. My agreeing to her visit was a bit hesitant. Andrea wasted no time; she hit the road with contacts and places in the Black Belt she wanted to visit. She was most interested in our Peer Education sites where we were trying out our internalized oppression model.

Back at the office, Andrea rolled up her sleeves, stuffing envelopes, making photocopies and phone calls for our fundraising drive. Several years later when our funds ran out for publishing our "More Is Caught Than Taught" early childhood education manual, Andrea put up the funds and her Peppercorn Foundation supported our work on Race and Child Care Matters. Andrea and Maya Miller were exceptions in my 40-plus years of fundraising. A complaint I heard often from funders was that grassroots community groups don't operate with strategic plans and clear governance structures and can't show clearly the impact of the grants they receive.

In the early years, funders told me that FOCAL, as a statewide group, was too small in scope; they wanted to fund regional or national groups with a greater reach. One funder wanted a more locally-based group with more hands-on support. Years later, when our "More Is Caught Than Taught" model was published and we looked for funding to move beyond Alabama, funders asked what hard evidence we had that our model would work outside the state.

Their skepticism had some merit, but with no development staff, and wearing many hats, I found myself on the defensive, struggling to meet deadlines. I knew that reports and timely follow-up were needed to build and maintain trust in our funder/grantee relationships.

It took me years to see that poor funding hurt further fundraising, a problem much bigger than my leadership style.

In 2015, our Southern Rural Black Women Initiative study, Unequal Lives, revealed that less than one percent of foundation dollars support work led by African-American women in the rural South. How can these groups meet the standards of foundations and other donors without start-up grants, seed funding and planning grants?

What happens when overextended staffs are putting out fires with policy threats to our constituents, writing required grant proposals and reports, networking with community partners and advocating at the legislature all in the same week? For years, I carried this feeling of incompetence for not being able to do all these things well. I beat up on myself for not having the funds to hire the needed staff.

A long-time funder and supporter of FOCAL's advocacy and leadership development work was Mary Reynolds Babcock Foundation (MRBF).

Babcock observed through its work in the region the need for stronger support of effective organizations in the South. In its study, So Goes The South, Babcock spotlights the impact when national funders overlook the South.

I observed many of my colleagues following the money. Whatever the trend, that was their focus. As tempting as it is to go for the money, it can create a loss of trust with one's constituents. In the early '80s, when we started to do the "racial and gender scripts" work, many funders shied away from FOCAL, saying we were "out of our league." On a fundraising trip to New York, Jack and I had a meeting with Dr. Colin Greer, who had moved from Program Officer to President of the New World Foundation, following the departure of the Rev. Dr. David Ramage. To put it mildly, FOCAL was operating on air, and Jack and I knew we didn't have many other options. After laying out our organizing model based upon racial scripts, we were tentatively holding our breaths for Colin's response.

"I don't believe it, this is fascinating! You all have put together a strategy for organizing around internalized oppression." I jumped up, gave this small framed, soft spoken Englishman a bear hug and burst into tears. I remember saying, "Colin, your affirmation is as important to us as money."

It was our first of three periods where we didn't have the funds to pay staff. The organization was broke. Board members brought supplies, paper, and toilet paper, and the members started to hold bake sales and raffles as fundraisers to keep our lights on. The church where we were tenants, Beulah Baptist, allowed for a six-month suspension of our rent. It was a painful time, and I felt guilt and shame for not being able to uphold FOCAL's commitment to pay its staff.

The second period of austerity happened in the late '90's. We underestimated a deadline for finishing a major project. We had taken on too much and promised more than we could deliver. Our largest funder told us they were moving on. Within three months, our staff dropped from ten down to three. Only one of the three remaining received sixty percent of their salary.

Our morale was at rock bottom. The stress was so great I was praying daily to make it through the day without having a stroke. During this time, FOCAL was offered the chance to become a subcontractor of the State to the tune of $300,000. There we were, on financial life support, and offered employment from the very source that held the lifeline to our base, child care providers.

The wise words of one of our founding members, Thelma Craig, summed it up: "Sophia, FOCAL has had a great run. Don't wither on the vine. If you can't find funding that allows you to maintain a voice for the people, close the doors and hang up a shingle that says: Well Done!"

After consulting with the board, the President and I announced to our members that if we could not find funding in the next six months, we would close our doors. These child care providers, struggling for funding themselves, turned into bake sale and fundraising beavers. Several new sources opened up, including Oxfam America U.S. led by Hubert Sapp, a former director at Highlander and an old friend. By December's end, proceeds from our local fundraising totaled $110,000, and we ourselves became our organization's largest funder that year. A board member and local donor, Laurie Weil, was instrumental in guiding the board to our fundraising success, mainly by identifying local corporate donors. In his wise, quiet way, Hubert Sapp told me that funders didn't want to hear a litany of the trials and tribulations of poor folk in Alabama; they wanted to hear what FOCAL had achieved, and what more we could do with their dollars.

It was also following the summer that we attended the Southern Organizing Project's five-day development training in Maryville, Tennessee. We built all these strategies into our annual fundraising activities. Our response to this funding crisis, a focus on local and membership fundraising, gave me a great sense of independence.

In my 43 years of work, nothing challenged my confidence and sense of self like asking for money. Several friends said I should approach prospective donors thinking: "It's a privilege for you to invest in FOCAL." I never quite got to this way of thinking, but I did learn a few lessons that may help others who struggle to make "the ask."

Relationship building was a two-way street. The funder had to want to understand FOCAL and to learn something about me personally. It was just as important that I be prepared for the conversation, that I understood the funding organization, and knew something about the person I was meeting.

As the meeting began, I tried to get a sense of how much time the funder had. I hated to leave a meeting feeling impotent because a funder left for another appointment before I'd shared key parts of my presentation.

A few minutes of chit chat helped build the relationship, but not at the expense of what I came for: a request for funds. I found that a friendly funder didn't mean automatic funding, nor did a salty personality guarantee a rebuff. Laurie Weil taught me the value of quick follow up, whether with promised information or just a thank you for the visit. When we got a grant, I made sure to telephone the funder on the same day we got the good news and to send out a written thank you letter inside five days.

It took me five years or more to gain the courage to respectfully disagree with a funder on something that was unworkable. In a few instances, that honesty helped deepen the relationship.

Around 2005, I was invited to join a session called Speaking Truth to Power at the annual conference of the National Council on Foundations. I was excited but apprehensive. I asked the organizer: How honest do you want me to be? She replied, "We want a candid discussion and I've been told you're a person who would do so."

My message to the audience of foundation staff was: "If we want to empower people and communities to create a more just and equitable world, it starts with modeling the values we seek to create. As funders your money can pay staff salaries, provide office space, supplies, telephones and travel so we can meet with our constituents.

"When I come to meet with you and have to pretend that you know what's best for my community, and I don't, even when you haven't taken the time to learn the nature of the problem, that's disempowering. This kind of relationship perpetuates the very system we're trying to fight, by preserving the superior and inferior hierarchy.

"If I'm not careful, I leave this meeting feeling unworthy and one down, and take it out on my staff. They, in turn, take it out on our childcare providers — who pass it on to their staff and the families they serve. A parent in one of these families takes it out on one of her children, and the ugly system of superiority and inferiority stays intact."

I was asking white people for money to support mostly black people. Money is power and when someone has something you need or want, it creates a superior/inferior dynamic, regardless of color.

But the extent of the dynamic varied with the funders. Some were difficult and reserved, others open and personable. Many had a sincere commitment for change; others had an axe to grind and we were the immediate target. It took some time to learn that my work, integrity and worth were mine to hold and preserve. It required me to stay with myself; to be truthful in representing our work and to avoid bad-mouthing other people or groups. Getting a grant is wonderful, but not if you have to sell your soul or sell out your constituents.

Fundraising taught me to take advantage of every chance I had to make visible FOCAL's work, and expose to others our tools addressing racial scripts and internalized oppression, which led to my accepting every board invitation I was offered. One element of our toolbox was "how to be together" in settings of diverse gender, race, class and professional backgrounds. The goal was to have our organizing strategies become a norm by other organizations and fundable by foundations.

My skill at fundraising led to recognition and a number of awards and board service on several foundations. Serving as a trustee and later Chairperson of the New World Foundation provided affirmation, personal growth, and physical restoration. Colin, the Board and staff had incorporated the Being Together process following my question at my first trustee meeting, "Do you all want to hear from me or is my being present enough? If the answer is yes, then the culture dynamic has to change to make space for my voice and perspective." This accommodation created space for professors, lawyers, community organizers, grantees and donors to bring to the table their visions and offerings for change. It also offered chances for me and others to seek the truth alongside leading national advocates for justice.

Under the leadership of Colin, New World created the Alston/Bannerman Fellowship, named for two New World Trustees, Charles Bannerman and Dana Alston, whose deaths left a void in the progressive community. The Fellowship was designed to advance progressive social change by helping sustain long-time activists of color. I was proud to become a fellow in 2009, where I started in earnest to write my memoir. New World was known for shining a spotlight on developing leaders and their accomplishments in social change work through recommendations for Board Service and awards. One of FOCAL's spotlights, Mother Jones' Heroes for Hard Times recognition was from a New World Trustee. I was the beneficiary of Colin's recommendation for the Gleitsman Foundation People Who Make A Difference Award and recommended for service on the Calvert Group's Advisory Board.

My service as a trustee of the New World Foundation connected me to activists involved with South Africa's anti-apartheid struggle and heightened my interest in the parallels of the two countries. In one, the majority enforced a system of white domination on its minority of African descent. In the other, the minority enforced a system of white supremacy over most black South Africans.

In the mid-90's, Haywood Burns, a fellow trustee of the New World Foundation, invited me to come to South Africa. Haywood was revered for his civil rights activism and legal acumen. A former dean of City University of New York School of Law, Haywood co-founded the Lawyers Committee on Civil Rights and was helping South Africa to develop its new constitution after the defeat of apartheid.

It was a trip I could not take at that time—but longed to make. Soon I would have that chance.

# 37

## TWO HISTORIES: AMERICA
## AND SOUTH AFRICA

*"We need truth and reconciliation to ensure that no race, religion or creed can succeed in elevating itself at the expense of others."*

"Okay folks, we need to head to baggage claim for our bags and to meet our guide. If you need to convert U.S. currency to rands, please do so now. Take someone with you. We'll meet back in this section in 45 minutes for transport to the Fire and Ice Hotel."

We were a delegation organized by Shared Interest, a New York-based non-profit devoted to helping guarantee bank financing to build housing in rural areas. Fourteen of us had just arrived at the Johannesburg Airport to spend two weeks meeting people and seeing projects supported by the finance group.

Haywood Burns had been killed in a car accident while visiting South Africa in 1996, not long after the constitution he worked so hard on was adopted. When I had the chance to make this trip, the loss of Haywood and my admiration for his work made it a pilgrimage.

I wanted to witness the changes two decades had brought. What parallels could be drawn between South Africa's civil rights struggle with apartheid and our Civil War in the United States? What could I take away from this visit to inform my own life's passion for justice? What could I learn from South Africa to help inform future generations of Americans?

South Africa is a country of many faces. It is old and new, joyful and sad; filled with wisdom from its history yet immature in its present state. Walking through the prison on Constitution Hill in Johannesburg was jolting in its contrasts. I found it chilling to see the buildings that had been the women's prison, the isolation cells where Albertina Sisulu and other African National Congress stalwarts were confined, as well as the site of the treason trials of revered political dissidents including Oliver Tambo and Nelson Mandela. It was scary to realize that apartheid had been the law of this land for more than half of my lifetime.

The fort and prison buildings, the institutional gray walls, the rolled barbed wire still present as they were under apartheid, are now open, full of photos and prisoner's accounts, and the pressed uniforms of prison guards, a museum that people still living have known firsthand. One of the prisoner accounts described how women in prison were denied proper sanitary napkins, then beaten when they could not conceal their menstrual bleeding. These buildings cry out to all who see them: "Do not forget the disgrace that was apartheid!"

But the most astounding sight on Constitution Hill stands just yards away: the new Courthouse. The building is constructed on one side of bricks salvaged from the prison to memorialize the horrors of the apartheid past. On the other side, its design and building materials are modern, sleek, open and inviting, to honor the present and shape the future.

The courthouse is populated by a judiciary made up of men and women who represent the gamut of South Africa's people — the tribes, languages, sexual orientations, religious beliefs and races of the country. In step with its Constitution, South Africa is advancing in the challenge to overcome its racially divided history.

In South Africa, the white minority controlled the nation's vast wealth of gold, diamonds and minerals. Black South Africans were pushed off their land, forced to live in shabby housing, undernourished and left out of the governance of their country. Apartheid segregated people by township and color, and forced them to carry identification passes at all times. These buildings on Constitution Hill reflect the former government's attempt to crush the anti-apartheid revolution by jailing its leaders.

South Africans are clearly proud of the struggles that led to their liberation. Yet a national commitment to equality cannot simply make it so. People still carry internalized oppression. One incident involving a middle-aged hotel porter and the young man driving us around Johannesburg makes the point. In an exchange that should have taken five minutes but stretched to 45, the two men could not reconcile their misunderstanding.

The young man explained: "He was from my township and we spoke the same language. Because he knows where I come from, he didn't think I knew my way around the hotel and airport terminal. He just didn't listen, and you got delayed, for which I apologize. "

I was reminded that we often devalue those who look like us when we don't value ourselves.

Perhaps this country's greatest challenge in the aftermath of apartheid is finding the difficult path to healing. The Hector Pieterson Museum stands as a symbol of the nation's pain —and a reminder of the need for forgiveness and unity. It is named for a 13-year-old boy gunned down by the apartheid government police on June 16, 1976, at the beginning of what became the Soweto children's uprising.

On that day, Soweto school children organized a peaceful march to protest apartheid's mandate that they study the white Afrikaans language, not their own. Government police opened fire on the unarmed children, and for days the conflict escalated. A photo of Hector's bullet-ridden body being carried by his despairing brother is credited with helping to turn world opinion against apartheid, though it would take another 18 years of struggle to defeat it.

The Hector Pieterson Museum touched many of us personally, even our guide, Refilwe. She spoke of her grandmother's grief at never finding the body of her grandchild after the June 16th uprising. Her grandmother died without taking her grievance to the Truth and Reconciliation Commission over the loss of her child.

Refilwe's story showed us there is something powerful about a national and international body assembled to hear the grievances of citizens. This process of giving respect to accusations, acknowledging the wrongs inflicted under apartheid, and formally condemning white supremacy, opens the wounded places so that healing can happen — psychological, physical, and economic. The South African Constitution creates the national mandate to achieve equality; the Truth and Reconciliation Commission is the process of preparing old enemies to live in harmony.

In the home of white Anglican priest and anti-apartheid activist, Father Michael Lapsley, we learned more about healing. As a young priest from New Zealand, he was assigned to South Africa, saw apartheid, was appalled and fought. His enemies fought back, sending him a letter bomb that blew off both his hands and destroyed the sight in one eye, all just months after Mandela was released from prison.

Father Lapsley survived, his disfigured body a symbol of the ugliness of apartheid. In his book, Redeeming the Past: My Journey from Freedom Fighter to Healer, he tells his story of faith, and of the power of love and forgiveness in finding healing and wholeness.

Listening to Father Lapsley speak of healing, I found myself tallying the vast undertaking we have yet to begin here in the U.S. Every day, as an African American woman, I am confronted with my race and gender, reminded of the myriad ways inequality goes unacknowledged. The U.S., to this day, refuses to account for the human and material costs of inequality. We have never accounted for the wrongs done in slave times, or in the Jim Crow laws that lingered long after the Civil War. Nor have we held our public institutions to account for the fact that children of color attend under-funded schools and African American men populate our prisons, far out of proportion to our numbers, not to mention inequities in access to health care, asset accrual, places to live and employment. We seem oblivious to the connection between high black-on-black crime and the evil of a system when individuals were forced to hate themselves and those who looked like them.

My takeaway from South Africa is that people shape institutions and institutions shape people. The South African economy is skewed; many are living a bare subsistence. Yet South Africa has given far more than the resource-rich U.S to the struggle for justice and equality. South Africa has outdistanced the U.S. in its repudiation of racism, sexism and other prejudices. The Truth and Reconciliation Commission has provided a place to acknowledge wrongs and let go of anger. As a companion to the Commission, South Africa's much debated, forward-looking Constitution defines and provides for equality.

I am determined to share the legacy of Haywood Burns, taken from us too soon in South Africa; to continue the struggle for acknowledgment from the highest levels of government of past wrongs and of continuing inequities; and to insist that blinders do not make prejudice tolerable.

We need truth and reconciliation to ensure that no race, religion or creed can succeed in elevating itself at the expense of others. In April 2018, I was able to see part of this dream come true with the opening of the Peace and Justice Memorial and Legacy Museum in Montgomery. These historical monuments were the vision of Bryan Stevenson, Executive Director of the Equal Justice Initiative, inspired by his visit to South Africa and viewing the Holocaust markers in Germany.

I had the honor of introducing two of my mentors at the opening ceremony, Marian Wright Edelman and Gloria Steinem. There is nothing in the world quite like helping to collect soil at a lynching site. It is heartbreaking work, and yet... When we remember a lynching victim and call out the shameful violence that stole a life, we honor that person and we do something noble, and especially powerful when you share it with grandchildren, great-nieces and great-nephews, as I did.

# 38

## MY LIFE COMING FULL CIRCLE

*"I have been aware of you (Sophia) and your family since the days of the fire-bombing of your family's home. I was a member of the American Friends Service Committee's Family Aid Fund and have kept up with you over the years."*

"Maya, this is Sophia, how are you?"

"Fine, is this Sophia Bracy Harris?"

"It is and I am calling to ask if you would consider making a grant to the work of FOCAL?"

"Of course. I wondered what was taking you so long to ask."

Maya was my very first "ask" of an individual donor, and I was thrilled by her response.

Maya Miller owned a ranch outside of Carson City, Nevada. We first met at a National Network of Grantmakers meeting. We were introduced during a workshop where I was presenting FOCAL's work on internalized messages. This small frame, soft spoken woman sat on the first row in this hotel meeting room and listened, although I recall she asked no questions.

I was surprised to meet her again later that year, as we both came on the board of the Ms. Foundation for Women, an organization co-founded by Gloria Steinem to build collective power of women for justice. In the six years we worked together as board members, Maya was a fierce advocate for women and children. She fought for clean air and water and the rights of indigenous people here in the United States as well as in Central America. It was clear Maya had money in the way she was treated by staff and others, but you couldn't tell by her worn khaki pants. Maya had close relationships with Gloria Steinem who had joined with her in the Welfare Rights Campaign in Las Vegas, and with Wilma Mankiller, first woman chief of the Cherokee Nation.

Maya said little at the table about herself, but others spoke of her 1974 candidacy for the U.S. Senate from Nevada; being a co-founder of EMILY's list to encourage and support women running for public office; and driving a truck carrying medical supplies in an embargo during the Iraqi conflict in the 90s. We didn't have a close relationship, but I admired her comfort level with opposing her friends at the table.

Maya was deeply connected with liberation movements, putting great stock in the leadership of women. Maya saw the child-rearing instincts of women as key to building peace. She sought to support women from Nicaragua to South Africa, and from Iraq to the Mexican border. Maya relied on personal observation and close communication, and she put her money where she had confidence in the leadership.

When our tenure ended on the Ms. Board, grantees had to wait a year before approaching a current or former member seeking funds. For 25 years I have jumped through all kinds of hoops for any amount of money, so I asked Maya if she was really going to give FOCAL $5,000 with no questions asked. She answered, "I know you and your work."

I was confused, especially given I had not approached her for money before. Sensing my hesitancy, she added, "I have been aware of you and your family since the days of the firebombing of your family's home. I was a member of the American Friends Service Committee's Family Aid Fund and have kept up with you over the years."

I was astounded and near tears. This was the Fund that was life support for my family for several years during the most turbulent period of my life. Why didn't you tell me, I asked? She responded, "I didn't need to tell you anything. I do what I do and don't need to talk about it."

The following year, Maya made a trip to Alabama, spent the night in my home, and visited a number of FOCAL member communities. My ten-year-old son saw her worn khaki pants, took me aside and whispered, "Mom can you and Dad buy your friend some clothes?"

I said, "Baby you don't understand, Maya has enough money to buy clothes for all of us. In fact, her money helps to pay my salary." It was a chance to reinforce our discussions on consumerism and spending money.

Even after Maya's death, her support and legacy lives on through her daughter Kit Miller and the Orchard House Foundation. It had been more than 16 years since that first grant from Maya, and I would open a card and find a gift and note, "Loved the newsletter," or "Great report," or "Thanks for the update and I hope this helps." Maya's gift usually came at a time when I was praying to have enough funds to meet payroll. Thankfully, Kit continued her mother's pattern of giving.

# 39

## CONFRONTING MY OWN HOMOPHOBIA

---

*"I am sick and tired of the hypocrisy of black folks. You sit in judgment of me but have no problem supporting a preacher and musician who are on the 'down low' so long as they don't acknowledge their sexuality."*

Serving on the Southeast Women's Employment Coalition in 1982, I came face to face with my homophobia. I was surely not in the camp of those who quoted Scripture about the abomination of the act of homosexuality; I had learned that lesson when I heard Scripture quoted in a college class to justify slavery.

But I was ambivalent. As a mother of two young children, I could not in good conscience teach them that a gay or lesbian lifestyle was okay, and that it was all right by me if it was their choice.

I came down on the side of advocating for the right of people to choose without discrimination or retribution, but stopped short of advocating homosexuality as a lifestyle just as proper as heterosexuality.

Yes, I was conflicted, and my position seemed contradictory. I was not ready to support something until it was congruent with my heart and values, but I was making progress.

Twenty years later, I found myself standing up in a contentious church meeting and saying, "I am proud to be a member of a church where an openly lesbian pastor can stand and give her testimony of her love for Christ.

It is not my place to judge her any more than I would judge the gay musician or someone else who may be engaged in a lifestyle that is different than what I believe. Given our history of having been discriminated against, we must be careful that we are not perpetuating the same mistreatment."

For months I felt shunned by some members of my congregation, but felt congru-ent and proud of my transformation. It was my colleague and friend, Alex Burger, who was a catalyst for my change of heart. He acknowledged at a board retreat in a session on race as a "target group" that he felt like the "other," being a gay white male in a mostly black organization. At the time of this sharing, he had never told us he was gay, though I suspected he was.

It was quite a scene with his tears, and this group of mostly middle-aged, church-go-ing black women. Alex had a tendency toward theatrics and laid it on strong.

The positive of this experience was the upfront and real pain of discrimination regardless if it is race, gender, class or sexuality. Alex was also a Harvard graduate from an upper income family and loved by the people of FOCAL. It was another eye-opening moment for the board and staff.

I couldn't help wondering how this "outing" would have been received had Alex been a black male. My moment of truth came a few years later when I confronted Alex about his lifestyle choices and how they might reflect badly on FOCAL.

His response left an indelible impression. "I am sick and tired of the hypocrisy of black folks. You sit in judgment of me but have no problem supporting a preacher and musician who are on the 'down low' so long as they don't acknowledge their sexuality."

He insisted that some of the best-known churches in Montgomery were pastored by gay preachers.

"How do you know that?" I asked.
"Because they are propositioning me on Saturday night!"

I had no response to Alex, but I continued to search my heart for an understanding that was consistent with God's will for my life.

I confronted my ambivalence and moved quite a distance towards accepting gay relationships. I visited with an old friend with whom I had spent time in her home, traveled together with her and her partner and admired their advocacy of people with disabilities. When I inquired about the health of her partner, her response troubled me greatly. My friend shared that she had been away on a remote consulting trip six months earlier, and her partner had a brain aneurysm. There was no fast route home and in the days waiting for a flight, her partner's father was contacted. He had been estranged from his daughter for 25 years.

When my friend finally arrived at the hospital, her partner's father refused to allow her access to her partner. Fortunately, the doctors stepped in and told the father that if his daughter was to regain consciousness and recover, she needed the presence of her partner.

Three days later, she was able to be at the bedside of her love. Her partner had recovered from this life-threatening episode and was back at work, teaching. With changes made in the Sexual Identity laws under the Obama Administration, this couple is now legally married.

I was profoundly moved by her story and thought of two scriptures, "Do not judge or you too will be judged." (Matt. 7:1); "Love ye one another; as I have loved you." (John 13:34). The evolution of my experiences and soul searching helped me to be at peace with my position several years later at the contentious church meeting.

# 40

## THE PASSING OF DAD AND MOM

---

*"He's your Dad, and treat him with respect."*

One of Mom and Dad's proudest moments was the renewal of their vows on their 50th wedding anniversary, surrounded by friends and family and all the children, grandchildren and great-grands that had been produced by the remarkable union of two very strong people.

Dad had smoked a lot of cigarettes and he developed emphysema. Later, I learned that his doctor had told him: "Your heart is weakening." But he never mentioned that to me.

I remember him grumbling: "Lord have mercy, this is so hard trying to breathe." I tried to gently tell him to stop his complaining. He was acting as if he didn't have long to live, and I reminded him that his own father had lived to be 89.

He retorted with some heat: "You get so you can't breathe, and then tell me about it!"

Not many months before Dad died, Mom was totally incapacitated and required around-the-clock medical care, feeding, turning, and she could do nothing for herself. She overheard my speaking to Dad in a tone that was a bit chastising for something he had done.

When I came back to her bedside, Mom had this glare in her eyes that instantly had me respond, "But, Mom, he knew better." She never uttered a word, but the message was clear "He's your Dad, and treat him with respect."

Dad kept on saying "Lord, have mercy on my soul." One Tuesday, he walked very slowly over to the phone and he called my brother in Atlanta.

He said "You need to come tomorrow and come here to see me and come see about your mother."

My brother said, "Dad, I can't come tomorrow. But I can come Thursday, the day after tomorrow."

Dad said: "You need to try to come tomorrow."

My brother didn't get there that day or the next. I was there with my parents the night before Dad's passing and he kept saying, "Lord have mercy, Lord have mercy."

The following morning, the last time I ever saw Dad alive, he said, "Before you go, hand me that basket with all of the telephone numbers. Bring it over here." It was clear that moving was very hard for him now. When I handed him the basket, he looked up at me and said: "I appreciate all you've done for me."

I was taken aback; praise or direct thanks was not like Dad. He was a firm believer that children should obey their parents and there was never a lot of thanking us for the work we did. But now he had expressed what was in his heart.

I said "Daddy, of course. You're my Daddy." That was the last exchange we ever had. I kissed him on his forehead and said, "Ed is here," and I left.

My sister Katherine was with him at the very end. His last day on this earth was January 15, 2000 — the birthday of Ed and of Martin Luther King. Dad always loved sweet stuff and now he wanted a teacake. Katherine got it for him. Then he said to her "My breath is short. Come sit with me." Dad complained a lot and directed us a lot, so you heard but didn't hear. Katherine said "Daddy, I'm cleaning up the floor over here where it's sticky. I'll come over in a minute."

When she came over he was lying crosswise on the bed, barely breathing. She heard him take his last breath, a little gasp, and then he died. But at least he enjoyed that last teacake before he went. It was a hard life he had, but all of us in the family did our best to try to sweeten it for him.

On the eve of the fourth anniversary of Mom's death, I awoke with her memory fully present in my spirit and I knew the time had come for me to put words to paper on this remarkable life and its influence on me and those around her.

I felt overwhelmed by the magnitude of her many dimensions and how to do them justice. The part of her that intrigues me most was her ability to love hard with an intensity of emotions that ranged from total devotion to a death defying will to obliterate anything and anyone who threatened something she loved.

During my senior year of high school, Mom had started to work as an insurance agent. She had gone back to school, received her GED and completed a trade in upholstery. She was excited now and wanted more. Her manager at the agency was John Henry Baker, who pushed Mom to become one of the best known agents of the company in this area. It was right up her alley, because it allowed her to become that social worker that she had long dreamed of.

Mom knew people in a five county area and many spoke at her funeral of her being the source of feedback for their problems, advisor on papers they could not read or didn't understand and transportation to the bank and even grocery store before they could pay their premium. For some, she paid their premiums when they didn't have the money, reducing the size of her commission. Mr. Baker understood the joy and fulfillment my mother received from her involvement with the people on her route. This job gave mom a chance to serve and a sense of being valued beyond her family and neighbors.

She knew that Mr. Baker was cutting her slack on her collections and she loved him for it. He was the best thing since sliced bread, though Dad didn't care for him one bit. Dad could tolerate the others Mom had fallen for because they were women, but Mr. Baker was a different story, a male recipient of mom's affection. Mom was not in the least bit daunted by Dad's issues. For her, if he didn't know her by now, she could not explain her fidelity to him. After a while he gave up his objections, but it was as though he said, "I will put up with that man, but I don't have to like him.'"

In fact, Dad was always a bit reserved with Mom's lovers. For him, it was affection taken away from him, although it never appeared to me that mom loved him any less. I learned after Mr. Baker's death of his involvement in the Montgomery Bus Boycott.

Mom loved Jesus, family and friends who provided her the outlet for affirmation of the intelligent, creative and caring qualities that she possessed. She chose her mate and loved him hard. At times her marriage was turbulent and she and Dad were challenged to find within this relationship ways to meet their divergent needs. She made the decision to stay in the marriage to provide the greatest support she could offer her children: being raised by their father. In doing so, the other outlets she found allowed her to sustain her love for Dad even beyond the 55 years of their marriage.

My mother gave me permission to love hard and intensely and she also modeled a moral compass. If I were writing about my love affairs, she would top my list. She inspired me and gave me wings for life. I tried to emulate her ways, her values and her passion for justice.

And, yes, in my life I have done things and gone places that she could only dream of, but I've tried to take her along with me—always. In my teen years and young adult life she consumed my every thought and I prayed that I would not have to experience life on this earth without her. In the early years of my marriage, my husband and I had to make accommodations for her in our relationship until he fell in love with "Mama Bracy." If you could see me now you would notice a sparkle in my eyes.

In the early '80's, Mom came to my office in a somber mood. "Sophia, I need your help. I want you to help me open up a checking account and help me pay my bills." Mom and I had a heart-to-heart talk a month before about my not being able to give money to help pay her bills when she had given her money to her children for their needs even though they were working.

I said "Mom, you know I will do whatever I can to help you but this is unfair to my family and not teaching your kids responsibility."

When I took her to the bank to open the account, she told the clerk, "I want my daughter's name on the account, because she will be handling my bills."
I said, "Mom, are you sure?" She responded, yes, that she needed my help.

When we left the bank and returned to my office, she said there was something else she wanted to ask me. "Will you help me plan my retirement? I think it's time for me to give up my insurance route." This worried me, because I knew what a lifeline this job was for her. She talked about the specifics of what she wanted and when she wanted the event to happen. I knew my mother's health was declining, being on the road and not eating properly in a car without air conditioning in the southern heat was taking a toll on her diabetic condition and her mind wasn't as sharp.

Her children all worried about her being in an accident. She'd had a couple of hospital trips as doctors tried to get her blood sugar levels regulated. What did all this mean? I asked "Mom, what are you coming home to do?"

She responded that she wanted to learn to play the piano. Mom's retirement was a highlight—all her children, dad, two surviving sisters, co-workers and special friends were present and poured love and lavished her with praise. She was ecstatic!

# 41

## LOSING ALBERT

---

*"Albert and I struggled, as most couples do, but we loved hard and were faithful to each other."*

My thirty-eight year partnership with Albert was filled with all the ups and downs that you would come to expect from a long marriage relationship, but his commitment and support of my personhood and dreams fit nicely the definition, "I've got your back!"

Albert didn't wear the label of feminist, and although he would jokingly call himself that, he most likely wouldn't care to be described as one. Regardless of the label, I'm not sure there are many men who would support their wife's work to the extent that Albert did. That included travel out of state several times a month; being both daddy and mommy to their children; preparing meals, giving baths and helping with homework; and transporting children to childcare, elementary and junior high school, all while working a strenuous factory job. Plus, Albert volunteered at least one weekend a month for the myriad of tasks associated with FOCAL's training workshops.

Everybody understood that Albert was a straight shooter when it came to saying what was on his mind. Don't 'front him, don't spank his children, don't hunt on his land or go into his gardens without his permission, and don't raise your voice too loudly when talking to his wife in meetings.

Albert was a big man with an even bigger personality. He was a good judge of character, with an ability to size up people's intentions and situations relatively quickly—and most of the time he was right. He could be the life of the party, but he could also be quiet and reserved, too. He had a way of simply taking things in.

As a young man Albert had kidney issues which prevented him from being drafted in the military. With the onset of diabetes, high blood pressure and being overweight, his family genetics began to take a toll. He also had survived an earlier open-heart surgery.

Albert had diabetes, which we treated as best we could. Albert didn't want me to go with him to the doctor, and didn't want me asking questions about his health. He most definitely did not want me to nag him about eating the proper foods. That was hard for me because asking questions and helping him to eat right was one way to show my love.

My mother had suffered with diabetes and I knew quite a bit about this disease. I knew Albert was not supposed to be eating white potatoes and rice and hamburgers. I was saddened and bewildered because Albert was intelligent, well-informed, and a good cook. He knew what to do but he wouldn't do it.

When his kidneys failed, he had to go on dialysis. It was a setback, but it did give him a "Come to Jesus" moment. He thought, "I better get my act together." He became much more attentive to what he was eating. He was still working as a machinist and could still outrun most of my skinny brothers. He was on his feet a lot as a gardener, too.

A year after the dialysis started, Albert was hopeful he'd be able to get on the kidney transplant list. He had an outstanding surgeon who'd performed his open heart surgery three years prior to the dialysis. The surgeon told us he was amazed by how strong Albert's heart was despite the blocked arteries. For three months, Albert was actively doing physical therapy, conscientious about exercise and eating right.

But one day he learned that his heart surgery would disqualify him as a candidate for a kidney transplant. Then, everything changed. Albert said, "To hell with this! I'm going to eat what I want to eat!" Back to hamburgers he went, and Alden and Kimiya became his partners in crime.

We could see he was laboring. He could barely climb into his truck to get to his beloved garden. When he bought a new big, bright red Ram truck, I told him, "You have lost your mind!" But he knew he wasn't long for this world and he dearly loved his vehicles. He also got himself a scooter, which he tried to ride everywhere — even into one of my FOCAL meetings.

One day, I pleaded with him: "Albert, let me call the doctor." He already had a bad right foot, a toe had been amputated, and his leg was very hot. I said, "Albert, you're not in this by yourself. It's the both of us."

When I confronted him about all of the hamburgers he was eating, I got the longest, most elaborate cursing-out I'd ever gotten from Albert. That man could have held a doctorate in profanity!

I cried and cried after my husband's explosion. I was ashamed of crying. But my therapist said, "That's all right, David cried out." Fafar reminded me, "You can't keep Albert alive but you can take care of yourself, the temple that God has given you."

Earlier in the day of his death, I spoke to the doctor who told me that Albert should be brought to the hospital immediately. He was certain they would need to amputate Albert's right leg below the knee. With deep guilt, I kept the part about the amputation from my husband because I thought if he knew that, he would refuse to go to the hospital. This man with this huge presence was not ready to leave us, but I also knew that he would define his quality of life for himself.

Death was imminent, but Albert was clear about what he wanted. For him, a leg amputation would not be an option.

He started crying a lot as his illness slowed him down. He knew that he didn't have a lot of time left, and there were still things he wanted so much to do. The community gardens, especially. He used to leave the center where he got his dialysis and go straight to one of those gardens. When he wasn't strong enough to work there anymore, he would sit and direct his faithful volunteers. The collard greens, squash, watermelon, turnips, okra, corn and peas in those gardens helped to sustain him. When there wasn't enough outside money to fully support the gardens, he spent money from our own family bank account, and that wasn't negotiable.

His garden in Montgomery was on Fairview Avenue, a main thoroughfare that had been the last leg of the Selma to Montgomery Voting Rights March in 1965 and home to St. Jude Educational Institute, a historically black private Catholic school that both he and Kimiya had graduated from.

Directly across from the garden was a senior center, formerly St. Jude Hospital, the only hospital for blacks in the Jim Crow era. Passersby could see the garden from a half-block away and were often amazed by the size of the collard leaves. It made Albert so happy when seniors would touch the vegetables and reconnect to memories of their childhood.

Albert held Community Garden days and loved when preschoolers asked him: "Where did the squash and potatoes come from?" He told them squash grew on vines from a seed planted in the ground and that potatoes came out of the ground, from the eye of another small potato. All this brought Albert joy.

In his last moments on earth, a next door neighbor and another neighbor who'd been a fireman worked frantically with paramedics to try to revive Albert. He pulled out his phone and called 911. My neighbors were both in tears praying with me, Alden and Kimiya. I was so anxious to get in my car and follow the ambulance to the hospital. I didn't know yet what those gentlemen knew: Albert had already left us.

Albert and I struggled as most couples do, but we loved hard and were faithful to each other. At age 19 and 23, we formed an inseparable partnership, and Albert still lives on in my head and my heart.

Two weeks before he died, I asked Albert: "Do you regret marrying me?" He seemed shocked and replied: "Why would you ask me that question?"

I reminded him that when we met he was a big-time baseball player with an athlete's body and a big social life. I said, "Your life changed big-time after you met me."

He said "Sophia, hear me. Marrying you gave me a life far beyond what I could have ever imagined. I would have been dead long ago if I had continued on the fast lane I was on when we met. I am proud of you and our children and the things I've been able to accomplish." Remembering that conversation has brought me a lot of peace since Albert's passing in 2008.

For a long time I felt guilty about keeping from him the doctor's desire to amputate his leg until the tech who took him through dialysis passed along what Albert had told her: "Melinda, they want to take my leg, but I'm not going to let them." So, he had known.

At a service for Albert, my colleagues Alex Burger and Evan Milligan paid tribute to him. Alex said Albert was a proud man who was fiercely loyal to his family and worked a solid, steady job for years to support us. Alex recalled Albert's wicked sense of humor, the precise way my husband watched the world around him, never missed a beat, and always saw the humor in everyday life.

Evan paid tribute to Albert as the master gardener who worked the earth with a passion to see things grow. He said Albert was a man who knew there was a time to prepare, to plant, to harvest, and a time to let the ground lie fallow. He saw Albert as a lover of his fellow man; and a man of strength and humor who loved the earth and tried to follow its natural rhythms. Alex closed by saying, "May he find peace and know that the seeds he planted have borne fruit."

In 1970, Albert had sent me a love letter, promising to love me always, both in life and "beyond the grave." I can't vouch for beyond the grave, but Albert certainly kept his promise while here on this side.

# 42

## TRYING TIMES IN AMERICA

*"We must never give in to bullies; never give in to violence and we must never, ever give our children away."*

Other people have written better than I can about the political miracle and strategic genius with which Barack Obama, a first-term African-American U.S. Senator from Illinois, made himself the Democratic Party nominee in 2008, and got elected President. But I have to share how this election affected me, and those I knew. Like most black people, I was euphoric on Election Day. I cried tears of happiness. I saw black elders weeping and saying: "I never thought I would live to see this day!"

But as Senator Obama prepared to take office, I felt some of that same unease I'd felt as a child. I worried that he would be assassinated, that his wife or daughters would be attacked. When I saw the angry defiant protests of the Tea Party, I felt that old fear of the dominant power rising, and using violence to wreak its revenge on what these people saw as a perversion of the natural order.

Let me share with you the parable of The Elephant and the Blind Men. There were once six blind men who learned that an elephant was in their village that day. They had no idea what an elephant was and went to feel it. Afterward, each man described the elephant. The first man touched the elephant's leg and said, "The elephant is a pillar." The second man grabbed the elephant's tail and said he was a rope; the blind man who had the elephant by the ear said he was wide and flat like a hand fan; a fourth blind man held the elephant's trunk and said he was a thick tree branch; still another who touched the elephant's midsection said he was a huge wall. "The elephant is a solid pipe," said the sixth man who'd touched the elephant's tusk. They quarreled until a wise man said: "All of you are right. Each tells it differently because each has touched a different part of the elephant."

When we look at issues of race in America, we are all "blind men," generalizing from our own narrow experience. The best way to acquire a broader vision is to meet and talk to others, and to read history. I spoke with my 30-year-old unemployed cousin after the 2016 election. I was appalled to hear him say he had voted for Donald Trump. He said: "If he's smart enough to make himself a billionaire, then I believe he could do something for me." I probed: What about Mr. Trump's beliefs and policies on immigrants and Muslims, and his sympathy for white supremacists who want to take our country back to the dark days of segregation? My heart cried when he said, "It's not like that anymore; things are different now. You all who grew up back then need to move on. It's a new day." He had touched that part of the elephant: the tolerant modern attitudes of many Americans.

Each generation thinks it's a new day and that they are the center of the universe. Not their parents or caregivers but them and their peers, and what they see right now. They read in school about the history of this country, but many young people see no relevance in that history.

African-American youth have a further problem because very little of our real history is ever told in the history books, in Hollywood movies or on television. We have to process the history we get with a filter, consult with trusted teachers and parents, and try to make sense of the warped and woefully thin history passed down to us by our national culture.

What a strange national ethos we have, which adores and idolizes aggressive, grasping figures like military generals, Indian fighters, cowboys, and astronauts, but at the same time teaches that Americans are kind and modest. Many Americans have no idea of the atrocities committed in our names against African Americans, Native Americans, Latinos, Chinese and various "others." The victims of these atrocities and their children are left with scars and trauma. For hundreds of years my African-American ancestors were brought as chained captives, sold, enslaved, and told they were less than human. This history left us poor, and planted seeds of self-hate. Abe Lincoln's Emancipation Proclamation could not change that.

Try to imagine a life spent in captivity, treated like an animal, unable to decide whom to marry, and how to rear your children. What would you do to preserve your sanity? That brutal system remained in force for more than 250 years. Racist systems, laws and attitudes remain 150 years after the Emancipation Proclamation. As the South's economic systems became dependent upon slavery, its defenders argued that science and religion "proved" that white people were harder-working, and more intellectually and morally evolved, while black people were dumb, lazy, child-like, and in need of guidance.

Survival techniques of enslaved peoples formed and passed on to loved ones to help them survive captivity are still present in attitudes and behavior, often feeding the notion of white supremacy. Deference in thinking about what's in one's best interest; being sold something that you don't need because the salesperson's nice; voting for someone who doesn't support your best interest because your employer says, "He's a good man;" hesitant to protest mistreatment or ask for a raise because you shouldn't "make trouble." Lacking vision of one's future, and lacking an action plan for achieving, leads to defeatist thinking and despair.

In 2008, with the election of our first black president Barack Obama, I heard the cries of wounded whites: "We must take our country back!" When I heard these exclamations of rage, my thoughts were, "Back to where? When was there a time when whites did not dominate this country?" I watched angry white faces and thought: "These people are willing to blow their country up rather than accept a black person as its leader."

Then came government shutdowns, name-calling and bogus questions about whether President Obama was an American. There were mass killings in churches and elementary schools. African-American males being gunned down by rogue police gave rise to the Black Lives Matter movement, and even this mild statement that the lives of a group of American citizens matter was taken by many whites as a radical and dangerous motto. These were ominous signs, and I prayed daily even harder that our African-American President would not be assassinated or his family hurt. I could feel the dominant white power rising.

If America is the world's greatest model of freedom and democracy, how do we reconcile these differences in what we say and what we do? These contradictions expose a festering cancer of racism, and a sense of white entitlement. Some people would rather destroy the planet than submit to the idea that they are not its dominant rulers. Thoughts came to mind of my freshman year at the two-year Christian college when a white professor quoted Scripture supporting the inferiority of blacks to whites.

In his book, The Third Reconstruction, Bishop William Barber explains the scheme for turning the clock back for the country's "deconstruction" called "The Southern Strategy." This strategy shows patterns of the old deconstruction, using new tools to attack voting rights, public education, fair tax structures, labor rights, women, immigrants, and minorities.

Twice in our history, there have been challenges to unjust systems that forced human beings to live as livestock and be denied all sense of human dignity and decency to provide for themselves and raise their families. We are now experiencing a push to return to the era of domination by the white powers that be.

Had we known our history, we would have learned that the gains made soon after the Civil War allowed African-Americans to be elected to statehouses and the U.S. Congress and for some to even become well-educated, business owning middle class citizens. But push back against the rise of former slaves brought on Jim Crow laws.

It was the makeup of the Supreme Court which allowed for the passage of the *Plessy v. Ferguson* decision which declared "Separate but Equal" to be legal under the Constitution. This ushered in Jim Crow laws that allowed states to re-segregate African Americans across the South and allowed lynch mobs to terrorize black people while the federal government turned a blind eye. We would have understood better why the presidential election in 2000, with its "hanging chads" in the Florida vote, was so crucial; the winning candidate would appoint Supreme Court Justices who could change the face of America for 50 years.

*Brown v. Board of Education* in 1954 threw out Separate but Equal practices in public education and signaled the start of a second Reconstruction. It was a law that gave hope to my family, and to thousands of others, that we could go to schools that would help us build a better life. Had we understood our history better we would have seen the warning signs 15 years after the passage of the Civil Rights Act of 1964 and the Voting Rights Act of 1965. The election of Ronald Reagan in 1980 confirmed the resurgence of a deconstruction movement.

Many in the struggle for justice were not asleep, or blind to the coded language being used: the "welfare queens" taking taxpayer money were clearly people of color, as were those taking advantage of affirmative action programs, and the predatory drug dealers and their thuggish customers. Let's lock them up and throw away the key.

These deconstructionists were telling white people that "others" were taking away what was rightfully theirs. Those who knew better were protecting their wealth and trying to acquire more. All the while, black and poor neighborhoods were flooded with drugs and guns, and the masses believed things could never go back to the way they were. The "war on drugs" has been jailing young black males by the hundreds of thousands.

Reading The Third Reconstruction helped me understand what we weren't teaching our children yet. We must be clear about why we don't want America "great" again and what we do want.

I was burdened with the weight of "What should I do?" It appeared we were in a tsunami of change, and people were paralyzed. On the one hand there was this euphoria. This historic election of our first African-American president: I recall televised tears of joy by millions. The other hand held a fist of discontent, led primarily by the Tea Party, connecting themselves to the start of the American Revolution (Boston in the 1700s). Elders wept, saying "I never thought I would live to see this day!"

Folks without medical insurance proved ready to wade into the waters and get medical treatment under the President's Affordable Health Care plan. I for one was laboring with a $500 monthly payment for health coverage after my son was laid off from his job. Hopes were dashed when opposition to Obamacare, along with the help of the Supreme Court, gave states the choice to opt out of expanding Medicaid. In Alabama an estimated 300,000 uninsured people would have had health coverage if the Governor had agreed to this plan which would have come at no cost to the state for the first three years and only 10% of its cost thereafter.

In the midst of the Obamacare fight, I developed an illness that could have resulted in instant blindness or a stroke, because my body was producing high levels of inflammation. In January 2014, Alabama's governor, Robert Bentley, called Medicaid Expansion another federal handout to folks too lazy to work, and I was furious. I knew that more than half of the 300,000 uninsured held paying jobs. I knew how hard my own case would have been without health insurance. My friend and colleague Callie Greer had just lost her daughter Venus to breast cancer.

Venus, a young organizer, had no health insurance and was in and out of emergency rooms with pain in her breast area. She was given pain pills and sent home. When she was finally diagnosed with cancer, you could smell her deteriorating flesh. A young woman's life was shortened because of the lack of health insurance. The face of Venus and many others were on my mind as I told my friend, State Senator Hank Sanders, "We must help the Governor to understand, having health insurance is not a handout."

My son Alden and four of his friends lost their state government jobs and their health coverage when their division was shut down. He was disheartened to see that a white coworker who was laid off with him, and who had no more skills than Alden had, was brought back as a contractor several months later. It's an old story in state government.

The hard-earned gains we'd made were rapidly being taken away, and those of us who were justice workers were stymied when asked how we could respond. I was so unsettled that I made an appointment with my therapist, Fafar. After listening to my agony at my own impotence and that of others struggling for justice, she advised me: "Sophia, your sphere of concern is much greater than your ability to influence. If you spend your energy worrying about things you cannot change, you will have nothing left for the things you can change… You are not God. You can only do what you can, and trust that God is in charge of you and the universe."

These words tempered my thoughts, but I still heard Bernice Johnson Reagon singing the old freedom song "We Who Believe in Freedom Cannot Rest." I knew that I could, and should, call out the political tsunami that was upon us. Everywhere we looked — at the bank, the doctor's office, car rental agencies, and restaurants —television sets were on Fox News or Christian broadcasting stations. For rural people with limited broadband access, conservative news outlets were often the only source of news.

At FOCAL, years ago, we set out to create "community ambassadors" to set up community meetings, part of our Civic Engagement Project. In 2008, we joined the national campaign Equal Voice For America's Families sponsored by a FOCAL funder, the Marguerite Casey Foundation. We asked people to spend a weekend of training to learn about key issues being debated in Congress and at the state level.

For the Equal Voice for America's Families campaign, I was a leader on the national, regional and state planning committees. We held focus meetings across the country involving over 20,000 people. I'd been taking care of children for 36 years but this was the first time I'd really accepted that I was smart and valuable.

The campaign was designed to culminate with simultaneous conventions in four regions of the U.S. Our convention would be held in Birmingham. Five days before the convention opened, Hurricane Ike ravaged the Gulf Coast. Galveston, Texas had 110-mile-an-hour winds, and a 22-foot storm surge. In Texas, 100,000 homes were flooded. Many of our 5,000 participants, including a number of immigrant families, found themselves displaced and homeless. In the midst of a family Labor Day gathering, I received a call from the President of the Foundation, distressed, thinking we should cancel these events.

After an intense, consoling half-hour, she agreed we should go ahead.

We began to make arrangements to help people with transportation and shelter. When the call ended, I sat in my bedroom thinking, "Sophia, do you realize you have impacted the lives of over 20,000 people in just 30 minutes?" I thought about Albert, gone just three months before; and I thought: "Yes, Sophia, you were speaking boldly and confidently with the leader of a large foundation, a FOCAL funder, and head of a national campaign. You spoke your truth and offered guidance with no hesitation or second guessing yourself. Yes, you did!"

There wasn't much time to savor this new awakening. The 2008 election of Barack Obama created a new wave of hysteria. There were lies about the "incompetence" of the President, and of a federal government "out of control." Congress couldn't agree on a budget, services were being slashed and I worried about the future of child care, Head Start, and elderly care services.

After Alabama passed the nation's most mean-spirited immigration law, FOCAL forged alliances with our immigrant friends through the pushback coalition Saving Our Selves. At one of these community meetings, my hope returned for a political awakening at the grassroots. I'd been invited to Catherine, Alabama, a little town in the Black Belt, 30 miles from Selma. I was to talk about health care, social security, early education and the immigrant bill. When I arrived, the group was upset that a local family had chosen to close access to a road used by the public for many years. One person told a local Commissioner: "You can't take my road. I've been traveling on it all my life, and I will die first."

After a two-hour wait, I stood before the group and described the changes taking place in Montgomery and in Washington, D.C. that paralleled what they'd seen with their local road. I shared the loss of voting rights because of tighter voter ID requirements. When I asked folks to raise their hands if they had health insurance, fewer than half raised their hand. I told them Alabama was turning down millions of dollars while far too many people had no access to health care or health insurance. I finished my remarks, and 20 minutes later people were still standing in line with their contact information, hoping to help us fight back.

Many re-segregated schools, some called "charter schools," furnish more inmates for prisons than freshmen for college. Our children are bullied and suicide rates have soared. On average in 2012, every eight hours a child or teen took their own life. Every three minutes a child was arrested on a drug charge.

But we can change this. Justice seekers must go where the people are and help them make sense out of the coded and confused messages being spread across the airways. That night in Catherine, Alabama, the energy of the people I met gave me clarity and the will to fight harder.

Baby boomers and older justice seekers are dying off and retiring, and younger minds must carry the torch. Technology rules the day. Facebook, tweets, blogs, and cell phones have become our Bible. We have 24-hour news and hundreds of TV stations to watch.

Recently, I tried to visit my childhood home place, Redland, where the firebombing occurred in 1966. It was hard finding the old road that connected the main highway to the acreage where my family farmed and lived. When I grew up there, about ten families lived in a three to four mile radius that now held several hundred homes. Now I found houses jammed together in subdivisions laid out in cul-de- sacs that made it difficult to drive through the neighborhood. Searching for what used to be my Aunt Sophia's property, I spotted a narrow gravel road and a posted sign, "Road privately maintained." As I neared the old turn-off to our home, I saw posted: "NO TRESPASSING. Video cameras in place."

I felt my body tighten. Was this the place where I'd once picked plums and blackberries, chopped firewood, fed chickens and pigs, and watered our mules? I'd never felt completely safe or welcome here as a girl but it was beautiful farmland. Now I saw enclaves of homes on dead-end streets, and the occasional Confederate flag pasted to a mailbox or fixed to a pickup's bumper.

On this Sunday afternoon in January 2017, driving through an unfriendly enclave of cul-de-sacs and dead end roads, I felt some degree of ease that my companion was an elderly white woman. With luck, the two of us would appear harmless. My heart understood the issue was more about hate than harm.

When I returned home from my Sunday afternoon outing, I heard news accounts of detainees being held at international airports, caught in the middle of the President's new executive order restricting the travel of people into our country. At airports across the country, crowds of people were protesting this apparent violation of the U.S. Constitution.

Having traveled outside the country several times, I can imagine how frightening it must be for refugees, coming from lands of war and strife, often injured physically or spiritually, unable to speak English or read gestures and customs. Excited to be finally reaching a place of safety, they're instead pulled off a plane like criminals, detained and interrogated for hours. Some of them have risked their lives serving as interpreters for our military. What will Judgment Day look like for the United States?

I can't shake the feeling that in our present racial tension and polarization, America has reverted to her old self: overt discrimination against minorities. There's a risk of a growing tribalism.

But I'm hopeful seeing throngs of marchers protesting the travel ban and the need-less deaths of unarmed black men. The power of crowds can work for us as well as against us. It's heartwarming to see millions taking part in women's marches, in this country and around the world. Maybe the tide of hate, division, and intolerance has crested in America and will begin to recede, but only if we work to make it so.

Bryan Stevenson is doing some of that sacred work. Bryan is a lawyer who has com-mitted his life to helping people wrongly imprisoned on death row. I am blessed to have Bryan as a friend, and he and I have shared staff, discussed the state of the world and shared our burdens, large and small.

Stevenson explains in his book Just Mercy that we have the world's highest incar-ceration rate. Our total of 300,000 prisoners in the early 1970s has ballooned to 2.3 million inmates today. About 6 million more are on probation or parole. One in three black male babies can expect to be incarcerated. Cash-strapped state gov-ernments have had to shift funds from education, health, and welfare to pay for incarceration. Private prisons and a range of services for them have made mass incarceration a financial windfall for a few, and a costly nightmare for the rest of us.

Many of Stevenson's clients were victims of our racist criminal justice system, get-ting life sentences before they were old enough to drive a car. From my life at FO-CAL, my church and family, I see young people feeling discounted and overlooked by busy families, often headed by a struggling single parent. Mental health issues are rampant as people both young and old face joblessness, isolation, and drug use, with fewer and fewer places to turn.

The managers of humans ("corrections officers") of our jails are often black single moms, managing men who should be home and part of a family, helping children with homework, and issues of the street and life. My daughter Kimiya was one of these single mothers. Her 12-hour shift required seeing her daughter Timiya a couple of hours in the evening after work and bringing her to me before bedtime. I took her to school in the morning and picked her up after school. Timiya got to be with Mom on her days off.

Support for social programs has been slashed including child care and mental health. Without treatment and support, these people often end up living on the street. I heard from Kimiya and four other family members who worked in Corrections, that jail became the place to house many people who need mental health care.

My grandchildren, Timiya and Alden Jr., have grown up surrounded by social media. Why can a 5-year-old access telephone icons and game sites better than his 67-year-old grandmother? How do we instill the values we want in our children, and reinforce the social mores and boundaries they need to become healthy adults? How do we nurture compassionate, sensitive children who love human connection, when so many forces threaten to coarsen and distract them?

A society is judged by how it protects its most vulnerable: children, the elderly, the sick, the incarcerated and strangers. What judgment will be rendered on us 50 years from now? I am hopeful because I believe in God, the Creator of the universe. But God can't do it alone. Each of us has a duty to try to make this world a little bit better, by confronting injustice and by showing love.

Justice never arrives without a struggle. We will always face challenges and threats from those who believe that the world and everything in it belong to the strong. Many came before us and risked their lives to stand up for justice. We must never give in to bullies; never give in to violence; and we must never, ever give our children away.

The sickness I found in my hometown of Wetumpka, the dream of white supremacy, is still alive. It is being cultivated today at the highest levels of government in these United States, and that makes my heart hurt. Too many brown and black people are being held down in the chicken yard and denied their chance to soar as eagles. And to see Christians condoning white supremacy gives me special pain, since this belief totally disregards the teaching in Mark 12:31: "Thou shalt love thy neighbor as thyself."

It's been 400 years now since the first slaves were herded over to this country and forced to work. But like Dr. King, I believe that justice will prevail over tyrants, and that it is always the right time to do the right thing. We must be vigilant in watching for the signs of need and of injustice, and we must find wholeness by always working for justice. We must not allow our antagonists to pit people against each other.

We seek not some utopia but for all people to live in dignity, able to give and do for our families, ourselves and others. Our purpose is not riches nor domination, but dignity, peace, and the freedom to achieve our purposes.

The slogan "Make America Great Again" reminds me of the hollow claim from my childhood "Wetumpka Has Everything." We must know our history and call out people whose arguments are coded and wrapped in falsehoods. I was encouraged by a Proclamation from Elmore County Probate Judge John E. Enslen, presented to my parents posthumously in January 2018, honoring "your courageous contributions to the betterment of Elmore County, Alabama." The Proclamation came 52 years after our home was firebombed, but it's never too late to do the right thing.

Every generation fights a new for freedom, in a changing world. If we elders share our stories and offer support and love, there can be greater camaraderie as we work together to make the changes needed to make America truly the greatest democracy in the world, and my hometown slogan of 1966, "Wetumpka Has Everything", can become a citadel of fairness and justice for all its people who inhabit this historic Creek land.

America is getting the message 400 years late, but late is better than never. I missed a whole year of school as a child but I came back strong. So can this country.

# 43

## THE POWER OF LOVE

*"To me, living well means living honestly, full of faith, love and gratitude, defending liberty and justice and helping this fragile earth to sustain itself."*

Near the start of this memoir, I told the story of my English teacher at Wetumpka High School in 1965 who asked our class, on the first day of racial integration, to write a composition on Utopia. I talked about the ridicule that followed when I had to say I didn't understand the assignment. That incident set in motion insecurities about my writing that lasted for most of my life.

In writing my memoir, I have tried to rid myself of this feeling of inadequacy once and for all. What I have learned about my Utopia in my life's journey may be uncommon, but it fits. Having reached the age of 70, I see clearly how I once let other people value or devalue my worth on this planet. I also see ways in which I have soared far beyond what most people would have expected to be "my lot" in life. I want to encourage young people to seek their own personal utopia and do all they can to live the changes they want to see in the world.

My utopia is no blissful tropical island. It's not a geographical place at all. I have found my utopia in open-hearted relationships. To me, living well means living honestly, full of faith, love and gratitude, defending liberty and justice, and helping this fragile earth to sustain itself.

One of my life's deepest, most fulfilling friendships has been with the person who became my writing coach. Knowing Marty Makower has helped me to move beyond feelings of inadequacy I had never been able to shake.

In July 2009, I met Marty at the former Maya Miller Ranch where I was retreating with an Alton Bannerman Fellowship. When Marty met me at the airport in Reno, Nevada, I was confused for a moment because of her physical and spiritual resemblance to Maya. Marty's voice, the way she took charge of my bags and her mothering qualities were just like those of my old friend who had passed away three years before.

The community room of the Maya home, Orchard House, was full of activists and friends who had gathered to support each other and reminisce about their relationship to Maya and her husband, the environmentalist Dick Miller.

For 25 days, Marty and I spent the early morning hours sitting in this large kitchen/dining area, encased with picture windows revealing Washoe Pines Lake to the east and the mighty Sierra Mountains to the west.

Mountains have always inspired me. There is something about mountains that reminds me of the vastness and majesty of God and how infinitely small my life span is in comparison to His creation. Deuteronomy tells us that Moses never reached the Promised Land; it was Joshua who led his people there. But God let Moses go up on the mountaintop, and look out, and take in that glorious view of the Promised Land.

In Dr. King's last speech, he spoke of having been to the mountaintop, and God allowing him to look over, and see the Promised Land; that speech has inspired me all of my life. In the months following Dr. King's death, I was touched by the Green Mountains in New England during the summer I lived and worked in Brandon, Vermont, after graduation from Wetumpka High. The shack where we lived following the bombing sat on a mountain that's now called Emerald Mountain; and, let's not forget, it was only on the mountaintop that the eagle finally flew off to fulfill his greatness, as God intended.

Now I was looking at the Sierras and Marty, a writer with a legal background, gently prodded me with questions about my life, and I shared with her like an overflowing fountain.

Here were all these stories about the Deep South, and growing up in a large black farming family that was deeply Christian. My parents were poorly educated. And here is Marty, an only child raised in a Jewish family in a big city on the West Coast.

Her parents were educators. She and her husband were both lawyers. She and I were totally opposite in our backgrounds, but we connected.

Each day near 10:00 a.m., a family of eight quail, mom, dad and six chicks, crossed the lawn 20 feet from where we sat. No matter how quietly Marty tried to fetch her camera, the parents guided their babies to safety. Each day this act repeated itself, and brought me to tears, reminding me of my own broken family. It was eleven months since I'd lost Albert.

Finally, one day Marty turned to me and said, "Sophia, it's obvious you have many stories you want to share. Why don't you list all of them?"

When I had 27 stories listed, I felt I had finally emptied my reservoir of tears and had none left. Marty offered to read whatever I wrote about my 27 stories. Our amazing friendship had begun.

Marty and I could not have been more different in our cultures and backgrounds but what we had in common was a quest for justice and against poverty, and a belief that knowing each other is the best way to bridge our divides.

Marty knows how to confront me in a purely loving way, and that has been a rare gift to our friendship. I've tried to do the same for her. She has confronted her own white privilege and has decided to use white privilege to serve others, rather than herself. I also came to know and cherish her witty, rugged husband Joe Keffer, who looked on as Marty and I enjoyed and fussed over each other, and at times went at each other like sisters.

Marty had retired in the late 1990s due to Parkinson Disease and had lost her confidence in public speaking, but not in writing. I hadn't yet found my confidence in writing but was comfortable speaking in public. We were a perfect fit in that respect. Marty's Parkinson's often gave her a visceral feeling of inadequacy which helped her to understand what many people of color deal with for a lifetime.

While my focus here has to be the impact that my friend Marty Makower has had on my life during this past decade of illness, loss and change, I cannot overlook Joe, who grew up in a fairly conservative part of Pennsylvania, and often sported a working-class jacket and jeans. With his medium height, broad shoulders and graying bread, he looks like a regular southern "Bubba." His direct, matter-of-fact manner suggests his accountant-lawyer background, but nothing hints at his 37 years of labor negotiations in which he earned the title "The Hammer." When he first met my folks at a family gathering in Wetumpka, there were definitely some questioning looks. Who is this fellow Sophia has brought into our mix?

For the decade I have known Joe, he has not strayed from his altar boy upbringing, with acts of kindness from picking up my grandchildren from school, to taking me on trips to Birmingham for my doctor visits. I can't begin to count the many ways Joe has supported Marty as she's supported me in writing my story.

On several occasions, Joe came into a room where Marty and I were huddled, deep in struggle over whether this latest writing piece addressed the "point" of the story. Joe would look at Marty and then me, and leave without uttering a word. When he returned, the size of the bag of M&M candy depended upon how red and puffy our eyes had been from our push and pull: big scrap, big bag; small scrap, smaller bag. One particular Sunday afternoon he took longer than usual and returned with a five-pound bag.

Before Joe retired as a Union Organizer in 2013, Marty had practically moved to Montgomery. In 2014, at my request, Joe brought his organizing skills to Alabama in our fight to Expand Medicaid under the Affordable Health Care Act and better wages. Although we were unsuccessful with the Campaign to Expand Medicaid, Joe brought his community labor organizing skills to the Fight for Fifteen and the Poor People's Campaign activities, from Birmingham to Tuscaloosa, from Montgomery to Mobile.

As fate would have it, I was diagnosed with a rare disease called Temporal Arteritis, an inflammation of the giant cells of the head, which impaired my immune system and required high doses of steroids. There is not enough space to recount what Marty has meant to my well-being these past ten years, but I will share two instances.

In 2012, I was able to travel to South Africa on a tour with Shared Interest. I didn't know what was happening to my "buzzing" head. But after three attempts to travel to South Africa, sick or not, I was determined to go. At the same time, there was nagging fear that I might not make it back alive, therefore creating a large expense for my family.

I shared with Marty this embarrassing fear I had of dying overseas. Two months before the travel date, Marty had fallen, broken her hip and was on a walker. When we arrived at JFK Airport in New York, Marty handed me an envelope. To my surprise, it was an insurance policy she'd bought that would cover all the expenses for the return of my body if I should die overseas. Her kind gesture allowed me to enjoy my trip as best my health would allow.

"Sophia, how are you feeling this morning?"
"What do you mean?" I responded.
"Are you feeling better or worse than you were last night?"

My response did not satisfy Marty. She hung up and called both my sister Katherine and Alden to tell them "Sophia is not sounding right and needs to be checked on right away."

It was Christmas Eve and I had seen my doctor the day before, fearing that I had come down with influenza, which my granddaughter had caught a few days before. All my vital signs were normal and I was told to check back if I detected fever or chills.

It turned out to be a day that I have no memory of and would end up in the hospital later that day. Marty hopped a plane and 12 hours later, arrived in Montgomery where she stayed for 13 days. I recall a teary phone call to Joe, who spent Christmas and the New Year's holidays without his wife, saying how grateful I was that he supported Marty becoming my nurse for this period. He reminded me that I had done the same for her when I came to her bedside following her hip surgery.

It was Marty who held my feet to the fire on retirement from FOCAL. She knew that my work intensity was taking a toll on me. She also understood my fear of losing the two major pillars in my life; I lost Albert who had been my partner since I was 19, and FOCAL, which I'd nurtured since I was 23.

When I was unsure that I would make it through my health ordeal in 2013, she insisted: "I have been to your church, Sophia. Now I want you to come to California and allow me to show you my church."

I cried in my doctor's office, sharing again my fear of dying on an airplane. Dr. Jones answered, "Ms. Harris, I'm not a religious leader, but you have got to have faith and stay in the game with us. Go, get yourself a mask, order a wheelchair and go. You need to change your scenery."

Marty took me to every beach from San Francisco to Monterey. I saw boulders with huge waves, whales, bird sanctuaries, beautiful sunrises and sunsets. I saw the wonders of God's creation like never before. I wanted to see more, to experience more of nature. I wanted to live!

I believe that God sent Marty to me. He knew I had given all I had, but had not yet told my story, and needed help to do so. He knew I needed a friend. For a decade, Marty and I have been sewn at the hip. We share, confront, care-take and call each other our accountability partners for quality of life, a compact we made early on after reading Gail Caldwell's book, Let's Take The Long Way Home: A Memoir of Friendship.

My life has not been easy and I've been in grave peril a number of times but, with God's help, I've come through it all intact. Despite external hardships and internal blocks, I'm still here practicing and growing. I'm thankful for all the many wonderful friendships I've had with women and men, of many different backgrounds, reflecting all types of diversity, but I think especially of Marty. Our friendship gives concrete meaning to my story of a life well lived, and wraps neatly around my definition of utopia.

# AFTERWORD

Someone asked me why I am so low-keyed about the awards and recognitions I have achieved over my lifetime. It was certainly not from a lack of gratitude; that is something Mom instilled into each of her children. It was my feelings of a duty and obligation to do even more because someone had acknowledged me, and what I know better now was more so about feeling undeserving. During my 45 years in leadership, I received 15 awards; three were monetary. I have always viewed the many other acknowledgments and encouragements that I've received through published interviews, presentations and keynote speeches as opportunities for my work through FOCAL to be elevated.

In the late 1970s, someone asked how I came to be known by a member of one of America's preeminent families, John D Rockefeller, III. I didn't have an answer. In 1977, I was the recipient of the Rockefeller Public Service Award, along with my mentor the late Frieda Mitchell, a well-known child advocate from Beaufort, South Carolina.

During a reception at the Mayflower Hotel in D.C. prior to the presentation of the award, I was asked by Mr. Rockefeller my age. When I replied, "Twenty-seven," he remarked, "I cannot imagine one of my children having achieved half as much as you at your age." Some years later while serving on the Ms. Foundation Board with his daughter Alida, I shared my conversation with her dad. She responded that her father was adamant about his children giving back. "His saying to us was, to whom much is given, much is required."

I was honored to be named Woman of the Year by the Alpha Rho Zeta Chapter of Zeta Phi Beta Sorority in 1978 and given the Montgomery Emancipation Proclamation Celebration Committee "Community Service Award" the same year. These early acknowledgments were confidence builders for the "shy little girl." It demonstrated to me that others felt I had the leadership ability to take on the huge task of supporting and protecting African American and poor Alabama children.

During the 1980s and 90s I was propelled into the spotlight through my board service with national and local groups such as the Southern Regional Council, Women's Technical Project, Leadership Montgomery, New World Foundation and the

Calvert Fund. Being honored as one of Mother Jones Heroes for Hard Times was a tremendous boost to the childcare base and our work at the state Legislature. After being recommended by former Family and Children Services Director Louise Pittman and her former assistant Paul Vincent, I was named the National Association of Social Workers' National Public Citizen of the Year in 1997.

It was heartwarming to be acknowledged by my mentors, Drs. Elridge McMillan and John Griffin, with the Southern Education Foundation's John A. Griffin Award for Advancing Equity in Education. Dr. McMillan, the first African American on the Georgia Board of Regents, helped me find wings into the foundation world and this honor was bestowed 27 years after I was awarded the internship that led to the development of FOCAL. He would tell this story at our 30th anniversary where he was honored: "Sophia's shyness almost prevented her from being awarded an internship in 1972, but her determination was definitely underrated. I still don't know how she acquired my home phone number and called me on a Saturday morning, after I hadn't responded to her call at my office the day before."

In 1990, I received the Gleitsman Foundation's People Who Make A Difference Award. Two friends, Eileen Paul and Colin Greer, recommended me for the award without my knowledge, nor were they aware the other was making a recommendation. I learned later that both had done so out of concern about my health and felt I was nearing a breakdown from exhaustion. They were correct. Several months after receiving the award I had to take an eight-month medical leave from my work due to illness. I was honored to have my family accompany me to the presentation, especially since they were so often left behind.

In 1990, I, along with six other women, were recognized by the Montgomery Advertiser with the "Woman of Achievement Award" in the area of social advocacy. This honor brought home the national recognitions and clearly added strength and legitimacy to our voice at the Alabama State Legislature. We were also becoming known for our internalized racial oppression work and our bi-racial efforts through Leadership Montgomery. Dr. Laurie J. Weil developed a modified curriculum from FOCAL's "More Is Caught Than Taught" model called Interchange and we co-presented it as a model to the City of Montgomery for its strategic planning process, called Envision 2020.

My long-standing desire was to go back to school and finish work on my master's degree, but there was never enough time. When I was notified in 1993 that I'd been awarded the Honorary Doctorate of Humane Letters from Dartmouth College, I was in awe. I was moved to tears when I received a standing ovation from the entire graduating class following my remarks after being awarded the degree. Receiving this honor alongside acclaimed journalist Bill Moyers with my family, including my sister Katherine, and FOCAL Board Chair Clara Card present for the event, I felt my Elmore County community of Redland and the communities of FOCAL were being honored, too. Dartmouth's Endowment Committee Chair John Rosenwald became a regular donor of FOCAL from that point on.

When the call came announcing that I'd received the MacArthur Foundation "Genius" Award — a prize of $260,000 awarded over five years — Elizabeth McCormick, the foundation's board chair asked if I was OK when I was unable to respond. To say I was in disbelief was definitely an understatement. Several days after the call, traveling back through the Montgomery Airport, when I inquired about my baggage, the gate representative said, "You are the lady in the paper that has received that Genius Award!" I had not seen the paper and was stunned.

People from all over the country congratulated me; some that I knew, former roommates, funders, teachers, family, friends and others I did not know. I wasn't prepared for the spotlight nor to be seen as "rich." It didn't take long for the requests to come for emergency financial help. I was encouraged by friends and family to not make a hasty decision about the use of funds and not to feel obligated to give them away. A positive aspect of the award was it was paid in annual installments over the five-year period. This took away some of the pressure and later it was a great way to think in terms of annual projects.

After some soul-searching and speaking with a couple of confidants including my legal advisor, I decided that FOCAL would receive a year's endowment of the award and I would use a portion to give back to those closest to me who'd made sacrifices to support me both professionally and personally.

The downside of the award were the comments I received about being undeserving. I was not a scientist, researcher, inventor, nor had I published an important piece of work. Some felt community organizers and social activists were not deserving of such an honor. In some instances, funding for FOCAL dropped. After all, I'd received all that money and what had I done with it anyway?

For a while I felt hurt and defensive. The entire five-year grant did not total half of the organization's annual budget, but I soon learned that I did not need to provide an explanation of how I used the funds or justify being a recipient. This thought was validated when I received a letter from a childcare provider from across country that I did not know who said, "Your receiving this award, Ms. Harris, has provided validation for our entire profession. Thank you for the confirmation that what we do is important for the country."

The MacArthur Award significantly challenged my thinking — I deserved to experience simple things that others took for granted: a comfortable home, a family vacation, to rest and yes, to be a helping hand, too. I recalled asking Jack's assistance in purchasing a laptop computer and took a fourteen-day trip to Maya Miller's ranch to reflect on writing my life's story. I also spent a long weekend in the home a former MacArthur Fellow and friend Billie Jean Young. We spent the weekend recording my thoughts from childhood to the present, and what I needed to feel whole. I came away with the sense (although I wasn't there yet) that writing and sharing my story could unlock awareness for me and others.

A year later, I received an invitation to participate in an oral history interview with Duke University's Southern Rural Poverty Collection. Robert Korstad and I spent eight hours across the hall from my office at Beulah Baptist Church in 1992 sharing my experiences growing up and life as an adult that had brought the recognitions and attention I had received. After the interview was completed, I was provided a transcript which I tucked away in my archives. Fifteen years later while being introduced to speak at a presentation in Seattle, I heard descriptions of my life that I hadn't shared nor were they included in my bio.

"Cynthia," I asked, "Where did you get the information you shared about me." She responded, "Wikipedia."

I was stunned and felt foolish. Whatever shyness I had about being in the spotlight was history. My life and work was now accessible to anyone around the world. As the young people say, I could officially say "Google me".

My granddaughter reported that a few of her 8th grade friends told her things about me that she didn't know and wanted me to be a presenter at her school's Black History Program the following year. Whether the honor was large or small, monetary or not, each recognition provided a pillar towards my self-acceptance and worth and validated my life's work.

# ACKNOWLEDGEMENTS

I want to thank Marty Makower who spent 10 years supporting me in writing my story. I also thank Joe Keffer for his support to me directly and his assistance to his wife Marty in her working with me this past decade; and to their daughter Cody Keffer and their friends who sacrificed their proximity for the four years they spent in Alabama. Carson "Kit" Miller, daughter of Maya Miller representing Orchard House; Kit's daughters Anika and Shaya Christensen, and the entire Washoe Pines Ranch families including the Gilberts, McClary and Carlon, Boeger, Nash, Raven and Michon Eben: thank you for the love and support during the many writing retreats held in Washoe Valley, NV.

Thanks also to Andrew Szanton, my memoir collaborator who has helped me share my story in a more personal way as opposed to my report writing style that I was so accustomed to these past 40 plus years at FOCAL, and thank you Phyllida Burlingame for your insights and identifying Andrew to me.

Thanks to the Southern Courier staff whose news reporting documented the firebombing of the Bracy home. Without this account much of our history would have been lost. A special thanks to reporters Viola Bradford and the late Barbara Howard, and to photographer Jim Peppler whose photos of the Bracy family are on file at Alabama Department of Archives and History.

A heartfelt gratitude to the late Constance Curry, Addie Ringfield and the late Winifred Green, three of the Guardian Angels of the Bracy Family, along with the NAACP Legal Defense and Educational Fund Staff, including the late Jean Fairfax.

A special thanks to FOCAL's Board of Directors, especially the 2010 Directors who gave me permission to include the work and people of FOCAL in my memoir. I thank the individuals who served as staff, and added greatly to my growth and leadership.

Thanks to Marian Wright Edelman and to Gloria Steinem. These women share center stage in the struggle to insure a just and compassionate world. They are a major part of my journey.

To Bryan Stevenson who provided a visible teaching tool to carry forth the teachings that are so necessary to create a just world; and to Billie Jean Young who brought me to her home in Jackson, MS in the early 1990s for a weekend to capture on a VCR tape, early stories that needed to come out of my head. Thanks to Jon Christensen, who did a first read of my sketchy thoughts of what I would like to share with the world about my journey and to Colin Greer, whose affirmation of my gifts as a leader were encouraged through leadership opportunities.

Alta Starr, I didn't forget your tutelage in the late 1990s on capturing my thoughts in print. Thanks to author Laura Fraser, who gave me early pointers on memoir writing, and also publishers David and Mary Lee Cole.

Thank you Mary Lassen for your strategic questions and encouragement, the Center for Community Change (CCC), for providing a year's fellowship to exit FOCAL; and a special thanks to Marisol Bello for her edits of the first product Marty Makower and I created. I'd also like to thank Minnette Coleman for her self-publishing advice.

Memoir Readers: I thank those individuals who read my memoir and provided feedback on areas where I left storytelling and strayed into reporting. They are: Alex Burger, Fafar Guillebeaux, Jack Guillebeaux, Jack Keffer, Jeanne Keffer, Joe Keffer, Sandra "Makeda" Mayfield, Kit Miller, Georgette Norman, Billie Jean Young, Katherine Bracy Moore and Aretha Bracy, Christine McGuiness and Phyllida Burlingame, Gina James and Jack Anderson.

I want to thank my children Alden Harris and Kimiya Harris and my grandchildren Timiya and Alden Jr. whose love and support gave me the determination to see this book become a reality.

To my family who strongly supported this memoir project with their love, guidance and input.

Siblings and Family:
Harvey and Helen Fleming
Debra Bracy
Edwin and Gloria Bracy

Georgia and David Robinson
John and Juanita Bracy
Charles and the late Yolonda Bracy
Katherine and Rev. Lorenzo Moore
Aretha Bracy
Delores Harris Mayes and the late Walter Mayes
Nieces and nephews of my late sister, Dorothy J. Young
Nephews and nieces of my late brother, Charles Mitchell
All of my nieces and nephews, great nieces and nephews who make up my village; a special thanks to two beloved nieces: Lequita Mayes, my barber and Dr. Kim Marie Evans who carries the banner of public education advocacy in her role as Superintendent of Schools in VA. I'd also like to recognize my nephew Desmond Knight, who became Assistant Coach at Wetumpka High. A special thanks to three cousins, the late Robert Bracy, James Grace and Bartholomew Prince, Kourtney Oliver Miles and family, nephew Adair Stallworth for tech support and the Bernard Frye and Larry Oliver families.

My neighbors who have been watchful eyes, especially during my illness: Johny and Bernice Moses, Connie Jackson and Eddie Hart, Randy and Sheila McFarland, Lee and Lynn Gray, and Amy and Allen Sanford.

Book Endorsers:
Bryan Stevenson, Martha Hawkins, Gloria Steinem, Billie Jean Young, Marian Wright Edelman, Rebecca Adamson, Richard Bailey, Leymah Gbowee, George Littleton, Kit Miller, Michael Seltzer and Dorian Warren

Church Community Friends:
The Community Congregational United Church of Christ Family:
Pastor Ray and Minister Krystle Speller and members
Moderator and Montgomery, Alabama Mayor Steven Reed
Deacons Mollie Reed, Kenneth Scott, Joseph Thornton and Ronald Scott
Deacon Ellis Hooper and Ann Oldham, Co-Chairs of the Albert L. Harris
Food Pantry
Willie and Stephanie McCladdie and Dorian Ross
Larry and Cynthia Stinson

Pastor Dorinda Broadnax, First Congregational United Church of Christ, Birmingham

Pastor and Mrs. Bennie Liggins, Unity Worship United Church of Christ

Pastor E. Baxter Morris, First Baptist Church

Pastor Walter E. Ellis, Pilgrim Rest Missionary Baptist Church

Pastor Andre Morgan, Cathmagby Baptist Church

Trustee Sylvia Buckhannon, Cathmagby Baptist Church

Pastor Porter Olsby, Jr and Deacon Kenneth Strong, Trustee Chair, Beulah Baptist Church

Pastor Claude A. Shuford, Mount Zion AME Zion Church

Legal Advisors:
The Honorable Delores R. Boyd, the Honorable Vanzetta McPherson, Attorney Terry Davis, Attorney Barbara Wells and Barry R. Holt, CPA

Doctors:
William Jones, MD, Michael Vaphiades, MD, Thomas Wool, MD, Teresa Allen, MD, Prameela Goli, MD, Kelvin Leon, MD and Pricilla Fowler, MD; Art Steineker and Darren Dillon, MDs: your expertise guided me through a difficult seven years of health challenges.

Child Advocate Cohorts:
Teumbay Barnes, Melanie Bridgeforth, Comm. Nancy Buckner, Fran Clampitt, Abby Cohen, Mary Davis, Senators Vivian and the late Michael Figures, Esq. Ron Gilbert, Rep. Laura Hall, former Rep. John Knight, Wendy McEarchern, Earline Mitchell, Mary Lynn Porter, former Sen. Hank Sanders, Deborah Thomas, Linda Tilly and Paul Vincent.

FOCAL Stalwarts:
Clara Card, the late Thelma Craig, Mary Jones and Nancy Spears.

Social Justice Collaborators:
Ellen Abel, Ph.D., the late Ella Bell, Fred and Patricia Bennett, Lynn and Robert Beshear, MD, Carol Blackmon, LaTosha Brown, Kimberly Dees, Scott Douglas, Fannie Etheridge, Oleta Fitzgerald, Kimble Forrister, Alicia Foster, Ron Gilbert, Callie Greer, Presdelyne Harris, Albert Holloway, MD, Shakita Jones, Tim King,

Eileen Knott, Wanda Lewis, Sheryl Threadgill Matthews, Evan and Jennifer-Taylor Milligan, Mary Moncrease, Alice and George Paris, The late Gwendolyn Patton, Eileen Paul, Dr. Joe L. Reed, Cynthia Renfro, Isabel Rubio, Faya Rose Toure, Esq, Kathy Sawyer, Shirley Sherrod, Earl Tarver, Ethel White, Randall Williams, Sarah Bobrow-Williams, Tari Williams, John and Carol Zippert, Ph.D.

Friends and Financial Supporters:
Joan Abrahamson, Richard Bailey Ph.D., Cynthia Brown, Dave Borden, Alex and Tania Burger, Peter Edelman, Ph.D., Colin Greer, Ph.D., New World Foundation, Dr. Freeman Hrabowski, III, Erica Hunt, Mary Reynolds Babcock Foundation, Marguerite Casey Foundation, The Orchard House Foundation, Gina James, Barbara Kamara, Starry Kruger, Mary Lassen, Marty Liebowitz, Wekesa and Afiya Madzimoyo, Penny McClary, Dr. Elridge McMillan, Barbara Meyer, the late Dr. Gwendolyn Patton, Cydney Pullman, Kim and Julian McQueen, Andrea and the late Alan Rabinowitz, Nancy Raven, Rebecca and the late, Jerry Roden Ph.D., E. John Rosenwald, Dana Salisbury, Jane and the late Hubert Sapp Ph.D., Michael Seltzer, Jeanne Keffer and Bill Sneeder, Nancy Spears, Steve Suitts, Frazine Taylor, Judge Myron Thompson, Gladys Washington, Penny Weaver, Dr. Laurie Weil and Loutricia Wilson.

Special thanks and photo credits:
Alexander Lee, Wekesa Madzimoyo, Marty Makower and Joe Keffer, the Alabama Department of Archives and History, and Bracy Family Collection.

My journey for 45 years would not have been possible without the 60 visionaries that gathered at Tabernacle Baptist Church in 1972 and the courageous board members, those willing to sign on FOCAL members and the attendees at our trainings and State House visits, being watched and at times targeted. Your courage and diligence helped me to pursue my vision for change. Thank you!

Production, Marketing and Editorial Support: Mona Taylor-Davis of Noir Notes Creative Services and book designer of *50 Years Plus One: Sophia Bracy Harris A Photo Story of a Journey For Justice*, your non-intrusive advice, support, professionalism and skill were amazing and beyond words. Your support made my words on paper assessable to the public. Thank you. George Littleton, as copy editor, your contribution was an important part of completing my memoir, especially with an eye towards details that only a fellow Southerner would catch. Thank you for elevating my reconnection over the past several years with the Auburn University family.

# ABOUT SOPHIA BRACY HARRIS

Described as a warrior for children by Equal Voice News, Sophia Bracy Harris has given more than 40 years of distinguished service to the fight to improve the accessibility of childcare for children of color, and further leadership and economic development in marginalized communities by equipping and organizing them to advocate for themselves.

Harris' passion for equipping others to transform their lives has been recognized with numerous prestigious awards including the Rockefeller Public Service Award and the John D. and Catherine T. MacArthur Foundation's Genius Award.

She and her work have been featured in numerous publications and on national platforms including National Public Radio's StoryCorps, Auburn University Magazine's "125 Years of Women", Huffington Post, and Duke University's Sanford School of Public Policy's Rutherfurd Institute's Living History Southern Rural Poverty Collection.

Harris currently lives in Montgomery, Alabama and has two children and two grandchildren.

---

## CONNECT WITH SOPHIA BRACY HARRIS

 @FindingMyOwnWay2020

 findingmyownway2020@gmail.com

 findingmyownway.godaddysites.com